Larry
LEGEND

Mark Shaw

MASTERS PRESS

NTC/Contemporary Publishing Group

Library of Congress Cataloging-in-Publication Data

Shaw, Mark, 1945–
        Larry Legend / Mark Shaw.
            p.   cm.
        ISBN 1-57028-235-8
            1. Bird, Larry, 1956–   .   2. Basketball players—United States—Biography.
        3. Boston Celtics (Basketball team).   4. Basketball coaches—United States—
        Biography.   5. Indiana Pacers (Basketball team).   I. Title.
        GV884.B57S53   1998
        796.323′092—dc21   98-27767
        [B]   CIP

Photograph credits: Page 1: Indiana Basketball Hall of Fame; page 47: AP/Wide World Photos; pages 119, 203, 263 copyright © Steve Lipofsky

Interior design by Nick Panos

Published by Masters Press
A division of NTC/Contemporary Publishing Group, Inc.
4255 West Touhy Avenue, Lincolnwood (Chicago), Illinois 60646-1975 U.S.A.
Copyright © 1998 by Mark Shaw
Printed in the United States of America
International Standard Book Number: 1-57028-235-8
18   17   16   15   14   13   12   11   10   9   8   7   6   5   4

"Larry Bird would kill to win at a game of jacks."
BILL FITCH
Former coach, Boston Celtics

"Larry Bird is half athlete, half legend."
BOB RYAN
Author, *The Four Seasons*

"I don't mind admitting being a little awestruck by Larry Bird. Truth is, I can't believe I'm playing for him. We've got three godfathers of basketball. Magic was the godfather of the West. Larry was godfather of the East. And Michael rules all points in between. We're playing for one of the heads of the families. I feel like a kid again."
REGGIE MILLER
Indiana Pacers

"I've never considered myself a super athlete. I admit I'm not the quickest guy in the world. In fact, I'm slow. But I've always tried to make up for that in other ways. I block out and I follow up shots for rebounds. And if there's a loose ball on the floor, I'll be down there bumping heads."
LARRY BIRD

This book is dedicated to Roger Brown, Mel Daniels, Bob Netolicky, Freddie Lewis, Billy Keller and the rest of the ABA *Indiana Pacers championship teams who gave their hearts to the game of professional basketball, and to Coach Larry Bird and the 1997–98 Indiana Pacers who continued that tradition,*

and to

Indiana Pacers' president Donnie Walsh and owners Mel and Herb Simon, true believers who made it all possible.

CONTENTS

ACKNOWLEDGMENTS . . . . *xi*
INTRODUCTION . . . . *xiii*
PROLOGUE . . . . *xxi*

PART I *1*

① IN THE BEGINNING *3*
② BULLS VERSUS THE WORLD . . . *13*
③ THE HICK FROM FRENCH LICK . . *19*
④ LARRY RULES *29*

PART II *47*

⑤ BAPTISM BY FIRE *49*
⑥ BOBBY'S LAMENT *61*
⑦ OFF AND RUNNING *73*
⑧ THE BIRD IN FLIGHT *91*
⑨ REGGIE AND THE BOYS *107*

PART III *119*

⑩ CELTIC GREEN *121*
⑪ BIRD TALK *143*
⑫ CELTICS CHAMPIONSHIPS . . *161*
⑬ LARRY'S ALL-STARS *175*
⑭ TEN DEEP *193*

PART IV *203*

⑮ THE STRETCH DRIVE *205*
⑯ LARRY: PAST AND PRESENT . . *213*
⑰ COACH LARRY *237*

PART V. *263*

⑱   CAVS AND KNICKS. *265*
⑲   TALE OF TWO LEGENDS *289*
⑳   MICHAEL'S MAGIC. *305*

POSTSCRIPT. *325*
BIBLIOGRAPHY. *329*

ACKNOWLEDGMENTS

Writing *Larry Legend* has been a labor of love, for covering the 1997–98 Indiana Pacers season permitted me to reacquaint myself with cherished friends and colleagues from as far back as the early 1970s.

For their cooperation with the book, I thank longtime Pacers loyalists Jerry Baker, Reb Porter, Paul Furimsky, Mike Furimsky, Bill York, Bob Shorter, Don Wright, David Craig, and Nancy and Bob "Slick" Leonard. These people have Pacers blue and gold in their veins, and their friendship is a true blessing.

During the course of the season, respected journalists such as Mark Montieth, Conrad Brunner, David Halberstam, Bill Benner, Phil Richards, Robin Miller, Roscoe Nance, Lynn Houser, Skip Bayless, Ron Rappaport, Bill Brooks, and Steve Fields, among others, were most kind. All are true professionals who brought the magical Pacers season to life for fans across the nation.

Sportscasters Mark Patrick, Ed Sorensen, Don Hein, Tim Bragg, Darrell Francis, Sage Steel, Larry Bryant, Dick Rea, Eric Richie, Mark Boyle, Quinn Buckner, Clark Kellogg, Tanya Billips, Vince Welch, Kerry Fowler, Kevin Madden, Dave Johnson, Dave Calabro, Joe Smith, and Christy Lee treated me like one of their own. Don Hein, Lynn Houser, and Darrell Francis were kind enough to review drafts of the manuscript, and their comments were appreciated. ESPN producers Eric Lundsten and Bill Fairweather offered helpful suggestions for the book.

The Pacers media staff, led by David Benner (who seemed to be in 50 places at once, scurrying around Market Square Arena, ever the gentleman to both friend and foe), MaryKay Hruskocy, John Bolin, and Kelli Towles, were most helpful. They are among the unsung heroes of the team, people who work countless hours attempting to keep the media from revolting.

The Pacers media room staff, including Kay Tottle, Julie Cordes,

Lela Perry, Debbie Hughes, Melinda Kesterson, Bob Bernath, and Charles Eversole were gracious hosts who welcomed me into their fold. Pacers people are good people, and I was most thankful for their courtesy.

Thanks also go to Christine Albritton, John Nolan, and Tom Doherty for their belief in the book; Julia Anderson, Rob Taylor, Maureen Musker, Nick Panos, Terry Stone, Deborah White, Beth Broadrup Lieberman, and Jacqueline Blakley for their literary assistance; and to Tom Bast, whose creative thought and editing skills were appreciated. I also value the friendship of Rick Wolff, whose professionalism echoes that of his father, Bob; and I thank Dick Cardwell, the legal beagle who stood by me when I needed his support and advice.

Most of all, I thank my wife Chris, a superb editor whose love and support keeps me going, and our children Kimberly, Kevin, Kyle, and Kent for putting up with an eccentric. Canine pals Bach, Snickers, Peanut Butter, Shadow, White Sox, and (believe it or not) Reggie Miller, named during the Pacers' drive toward a championship in 1995, also lent their support.

Above all, I thank the Almighty for the wonderful blessings in my life. I tell people I am the luckiest man on the face of the earth, and it is the Good Lord who has guided me along.

INTRODUCTION

"Wait a f...... minute!" the sloe-eyed gent with dyed hair the color of puke barked while thrusting his trigger finger in the air for emphasis. "What you guys sayin'? Larry Bird ain't no better than Larry Brown. Hell, give the *players* the credit, not the coach."

Dennis Rodman, the most dangerous man in professional basketball, sat hunched over in a tiny cubicle in the far corner of the visitors locker room at Market Square Arena in Indianapolis. One ring-sized gold earring dangled from his nostril; two more decorated his left ear. Oversized black headphones draped the proverbial bad boy's head, and his tattooed torso swayed with the music. Huge hands kept adjusting the bulky icepacks taped to both knees, and sleepy eyes flicked up and down as the mischievous man-child surveyed the probing faces surrounding him.

Those faces belonged to a zealous bevy of reporters clutching tape recorders and notebooks. They scribbled furiously as Rodman, always the court jester, held court. He'd seen these faces countless times and knew each reporter was poised to record an outlandish quote from the NBA's version of a freak show.

Since the five-time World Champion Chicago Bulls had just been soundly defeated by the Indiana Pacers in late November of 1997, questions centered around Rodman's perspective of new coach Larry Bird. Comparisons with Bird's predecessor, Larry Brown, had been discussed, as well as a wide range of other topics.

For twenty minutes, Rodman, a.k.a. "The Worm," having substituted a gold baseball cap for his headphones, chattered on about whether Scottie Pippen would rejoin the team when his injured foot was healed ("He will, what the hell else has he got to do?"); whether he would play another season ("f..., no, I'm too old for this damn game"); his new motto ("Have fun, regardless of whether we win or lose"); and when his new book would be released ("It's full of dirty pictures"). Convinced they had captured the best of Dennis, the press ambled over to where Michael Jordan, who had been outplayed by the Pacers' Reggie Miller, would appear once he'd showered and pulled on his expensive designer suit.

Suddenly alone with the man who possessed four NBA Championship rings (two with Detroit, where he battled Bird: "In the early days, he kicked my ass, but later on I whipped his," Rodman said), I stammered out a few words, attempting to strike up a conversation. I did so assuming Dennis the Menace wouldn't dare attack me in front of all the reporters. Or would he? I could see the headline: "Rodman Strangles Stupid Author Asking Dumb Questions."

Disregarding that thought, I queried Rodman about his uniform number—91. "I wanted 10, but somebody else had it, and so 9 and 1 make 10," he explained with exquisite and unarguable logic, his gruff voice barely above a whisper. A Pacers ballboy was beginning to clear the locker room floor of used tape, wet towels, buckets of ice, and black Nike shower shoes when I asked about the state of sports in general. "It's all about money, no loyalty, just money," Rodman said.

Feeling that Dennis and I had achieved a bond of sorts, I asked if he thought the Bulls would repeat. "Hell, yes, we'll win it," he predicted. "Nobody gave us a chance last year and look what happened. We need a few players, a good shooting guard, somebody off the bench, but we'll be all right."

When Michael Jordan appeared, the Bulls bad boy scooped up his headphones and prepared to leave. As I was scribbling down his comments, Dennis leaned over and muttered, "You want to know what I *really* think? Bird's gonna be a hell of a coach. Just don't tell anyone I said so."

"I can't do that," I replied, my feisty side emerging despite being intimidated by the man. "All right, then go ahead," my new best buddy bellowed while rising to tower over me with his 6′7″, 220-pound frame.

Dennis Rodman's prediction 13 games into the season portended great things for both Larry Bird and the Indiana Pacers.

Before the season began, I had been asked to collaborate on a book with Coach Bird documenting his rookie coaching season. Dubious publishers in New York, aware that most superstar-players-turned-coaches had been flops, wouldn't come up with the necessary dollars to satisfy The Legend, and the deal fell through.

Having just completed *Diamonds in the Rough*, chronicling the legends of golf on the Senior PGA Tour, and *Testament to Courage*, which featured the poignant diary of a courageous Holocaust victim, I was seeking a new challenge and was reluctant to give up on a book about Larry Bird, the Pacers, and the NBA season. I was unsure if the Birdman could coach, but based on my preseason observations, I felt he could—especially with a veteran team like the Pacers, who might surprise everyone and contend for an NBA Championship.

That quest would occur during a season that was sure to be filled with dazzling displays of basketball by many of the finest athletes in the world, one that might very well mark the last hurrah for such heralded players as Rodman, Charles Barkley, Patrick Ewing, John Stockton, Karl Malone, Clyde Drexler, and Michael Jordan.

Using the notes I'd made in preparing the book proposal for the Bird collaboration, I decided to weave portions of his life story (these chapters are denoted with the symbol ○ in the table of contents) together with the Indiana Pacers' season performance against the best of the best in the NBA (these chapters are denoted with the symbol ● in the table of contents). If I was right, by June of 1998 the team might well own a world championship. If I was wrong, I'd still have documented the life of the ultimate over-achiever, Larry Bird, by recording for posterity his first attempt at coaching instead of being coached.

What compelled me to research Bird's life, and to attend NBA games, was the enormous respect I had for this one-of-a-kind athlete. From the first moment I watched him walk on the court for a Pacers preseason game in Fort Wayne in October to the kind of standing ovation reserved for few in *any* walk of life, my heart told me this was a story I had to tell.

In addition, my research of Bird had uncovered several characteristics we had in common. We both were from small towns in Indiana and had endured painful seasons as diehard Chicago Cubs fans. We shared a disdain for the telephone, we carefully guarded our privacy, we hated to dress up (Larry's main objection to becoming an NBA coach was being forced to wear a sportcoat and tie instead of basketball gear), and best of all, we were both animal lovers.

During the exhibition season, as Coach Bird dipped his toes in unfamiliar waters, I became more excited about bringing the legend's story to life. It had been eight years since he and revered *Boston Globe* sportswriter Bob Ryan had written *Drive*, a bestselling autobiography. A new generation deserved to learn about one of the great role models in sports history.

Modern professional basketball was unfamiliar territory for me. Free agency and multimillion-dollar contracts had produced trash-talking prima donnas who appeared to play all-out only in the final few minutes of the fourth quarter. Dennis Rodman was correct that the game had lost some of its luster despite the emergence of such budding superstars as Grant Hill, Kevin Garnett, Kobe Bryant, Keith Van Horn, Antoine Walker, and Allen Iverson. That development made me curious: How would Larry Bird handle certain players whose primary loyalty was to money and their own celebrity status?

I'd seen that question addressed by another legend, Bobby Knight, the controversial Indiana University basketball coach who nearly became Bird's college mentor. In late 1997, Knight was asked if he thought Bird could coach. "I think he has the imagination and determination to succeed," Knight said. "Whether he has the fortitude to accept all the bull that he's going to have to accept, I don't know, because he's going to have guys making $2 million a year who can't play. That's what would bother me about the pros. I'm in a huddle looking at this guy making $2 million and he can't crush a grape."

My roots in the game Knight chastised ran deep. During my law school days in the early 1970s, my roommate and close friend was bouncing Billy Keller, the 5'10" bolt of lightning who lit up the sky for the Pacers with Bird-like, never-give-up tenacity and three-pointers that seemed to be launched from the cheap seats. Like Bird in his later years, Keller was a true inspiration to every kid who thought he had a chance to play, to follow the yellow brick road and win it all like the players at Milan, Indiana, the model for the Hickory High Huskers who captivated moviegoers in the film *Hoosiers*.

During the early 1970s, Indiana Pacers games were played in the State Fairgrounds Coliseum, where Roger Brown, Mel Daniels, Freddie Lewis, Keller, and others dominated the American Basketball Association Championship Series. Use of the three-point shot and the red, white, and blue basketball were ridiculed, but they became the catalyst for the introduction of the entertainment aspect of the game. That led to the modern Hollywood-style atmosphere that elevated professional basketball to its lofty stature.

At the Coliseum, I sat in seats surrounded by sawdust, watching Keller, his Pacers teammates, and superstars such as Julius Erving, Dan Issel, Artis Gilmore, Louis Dampier, David Thompson, and George McGinnis strut their stuff. Fans who loved basketball cheered them on, and I fondly recall those days cherishing every moment spent in the company of Keller and his Pacers teammates who flocked to our apartment.

My interest in the Pacers was rekindled in 1994 when they beat Atlanta in the Eastern Conference semifinals. After Indiana's victory in Game Six, my family and I paraded through downtown Indianapolis waving rally flags out the windows of our van. That year I also witnessed New York Knicks basketball fan frenzy. While in the Big Apple, I scalped a ticket to see the Pacers battle Patrick Ewing and company. Little did I realize that it would be me and 23,000 boisterous Knicks supporters. Needless to say, I sat silent through much of the game, unable to clap for my favorites.

When Larry Bird entered the NBA in the early 1980s, he reminded me of the ABA players who gave their heart and soul to the game. Big money was never a factor. It was the competition and the will to win, to be the best, to persevere despite any obstacle, that kept them striving for perfection.

Like fans around the world, I watched as Bird, a study in contradictions, exploded onto the scene and became one of the five greatest players to ever don an NBA uniform. His success in leading the Boston Celtics to three NBA titles was due to one outstanding ability: Larry made everyone who ever played with him play better, especially at crunch time when championships were won or lost.

Through the 1992 season, Larry Bird epitomized what the NBA, first conceived as the Basketball Association of America in 1946, was all about. No wonder Matt Goukas, player-turned-coach-turned-broadcaster, said, "Bird, like Magic, saw the game as if it was happening in slow motion." Isiah Thomas had another perspective, saying, "Johnson was the smartest, Jordan was the best, and Bird was the toughest, the type of guy who could meet you in the back alley and beat the shit out of you." Magic Johnson had a different mind-set: "Larry was the only player in the league that I feared, and he was the smartest player I ever played against. . . . Even when we weren't going head to head, I would follow his game because I always used his play as a measuring stick against mine."

Despite his burning desire for the game, injuries forced Bird, the uncharismatic, shy one, to retire in 1992. For four-plus years, the athlete many thought an oddball spent time trying to make three-foot putts on the golf course instead of kissing jump shots off the glass, all the while laboring unhappily as an overpaid consultant to his beloved Celtics.

When Pacers coach Larry Brown called it quits after the team's disappointing season in 1996–97, Larry Bird took dead aim at the position. For $4.5 million a year, a small percentage ownership in the team, and various perks including a country club membership, the Pacers found themselves a living legend not only to inspire their veteran players and boost attendance, but to put the finishing touches on efforts to build a new stadium in downtown Indianapolis.

Bird's challenge began in the summer of 1997 when he began one-on-one chats with Reggie Miller and the boys. His journey through a wondrous rookie coaching experience, filled with joy and heartache, would end nearly a year later.

While the season progressed, I realized that watching Coach Bird and his players from my perch at the media table had rekindled a kinship for me with the highs and lows of professional basketball. With the Pacers, I witnessed both. I watched them sink the Bulls in a midseason "statement" game when they were operating on all cylinders; hit rock bottom when they set a record for fewest points in a game (since broken by Utah in the 1998 NBA Finals) by scoring only 55 against San Antonio; and then achieve a milestone when they set their NBA franchise record with a hard-earned 53rd victory. After that win, I stood in the Pacers locker room amidst a band of happy warriors truly proud of their accomplishment.

Five more victories came to the Pacers, and they finished with 58 wins and just 24 losses. After the final home game, a rout of Toronto in April, my favorite image of Bird, in a season filled with many memorable images, occurred. Larry Legend stood in the middle of the court at Market Square Arena on Fan Appreciation Night, holding his beloved five-year-old daughter Mariah as fans cheered him from the stands. Mariah kept kissing her father on the cheek and holding him tight around the neck with her tiny hands as Larry loped toward the locker room, his face aglow with that mischievous grin of his.

Six days later, the playoffs began. I took advantage of the break in the schedule to visit French Lick, Indiana, where Bird had grown up in a clapboard house set on a hillside near the railroad tracks, and Terre Haute, where his Boston Connection Hotel and Restaurant features enough memorabilia for any Birdwatcher. Then I returned for the first playoff game for Larry Legend, a 106–77 thrashing of the Cleveland Cavaliers.

I also attended the news conference on May 12 when Larry, dressed casually in tan khaki shorts and a blue Pacers golf shirt, sat uncomfortably behind a table and received the NBA Coach of the Year award. His arms folded, the Red Auerbach Trophy planted beside his huge left hand, Bird, scratching his neck or tugging at the collar on his shirt, entertained reporters with his "Awshucks, I'm not a great coach" spiel that mesmerized the audience. Talk about humility. To hear Larry Legend tell it, the ushers at Market Square Arena had more to do with the team's success than he did. That didn't jive with other coaches around the world, all of whom would be studying the "Bird method" in their sleep trying to figure out how he had taken a bunch of underachievers and molded them into a championship contender.

During the ensuing playoffs, Indiana stepped over Cleveland and the New York Knicks before matching up with the revered Chicago Bulls. I watched them fall short in Games One and Two, and rebound in Games Three and Four when Reggie Miller played like Larry Bird during the final seconds. After Game Four, I sparked irritation in Michael Jordan, resplendent in a peach-colored suit, by asking him whether the Bulls had become whiners regarding the officiating. Michael looked at me as if to say, "How dare you ask such a question?"

In Game Five, I watched from the nosebleed media seats high atop the United Center as M.J. and his buddies demolished Indiana, and in Game Six, cheered silently as Indiana nipped the Bulls to stretch the series to seven games. On the final day of May, 180 days after it all began, I saw the Pacers season end with a heartbreaking five-point loss to the world champions, even though Bird and his charges fought like world champions themselves.

In late June 1998, Larry Legend enjoyed yet another honor when he was elected to the Naismith Memorial Basketball Hall of Fame. While accolades poured in regarding his amazing skill (Tom Heinsohn said, "He played chess; everybody else played checkers. Larry was five moves ahead."), Bird downplayed the feat, telling reporters, "I was always told at a young age that I wasn't big enough, wasn't strong enough, and wasn't quick enough. I fooled them, didn't I?"

More than anything, chronicling the NBA season and writing this book provided me with a sense of history, for there would never be another rookie coaching season, one filled with firsts, for Bird. Thus follows the chronicle of the life and times of Larry Legend, and his quest to bring an NBA championship to a franchise already steeped in basketball tradition.

PROLOGUE

With five seconds left in the game, Pacers forward Chris Mullin—who wore number 17 in tribute to Celtics great John "Hondo" Havlicek—spotted up to take an open 20-footer from the right baseline. If he hit it, Indiana would tie the Nets and force overtime.

A second chance to win their season opener was all rookie coach Larry Bird could hope for. His veteran squad had blown a 13-point lead, playing offense like a bunch of disorganized schoolkids in a pickup game. Only Reggie Miller had provided any spark, scoring 35 points. Mullin, acquired from Golden State to bolster Miller's efforts, had suffered a shooter's nightmare, missing seven of eight left-handed jumpers.

Bird himself had also contributed to the disaster-in-the-making. In the fourth quarter, with the lowly Nets fighting for every loose ball and errant rebound, the coach had left his offensive weapons (Miller and Mullin) on the bench too long. His substitution pattern had forced 7'4" center Rik Smits to play too many minutes, and his lope-along gait indicated a fatigued warrior. Bird had also not ordered that the ball be passed to Smits in the low post, where he towered over the opposition.

To make matters worse, at a critical point in the game, Bird had shown inexperience by playing erratic point guard Travis Best instead of 1996–97 NBA assist leader Mark Jackson. The rookie coach seemed bewildered at times, unable to counteract playcalling or defensive schemes employed by Nets coach John Calipari.

Nonetheless, the Pacers still had a chance to win if only "Mully" could connect at crunch time. The burr-haired former All-Star seemed in perfect form as he launched the shot—but the ball careened around the rim, bounced off the backboard, and touched the rim again before catapulting into the air, where eight hands attempted to retrieve it. Fortunately for the Pacers, Smits cradled the ball, fell back, threw up a quick toss, and was fouled as he tumbled to the floor of the Continental Airlines Arena in East Rutherford, New Jersey.

Larry Legend, standing nonchalantly at center court with hands in pockets, turned and marched back to the Pacers bench. His face widened in amazement that Mullin had missed the critical shot. *He* had always made those, and he expected no less from his players.

Within seconds, Smits, the Pacers Dunking Dutchman, was at the foul line for two shots. His face was flushed, his long blonde hair wet and stringy. After two bounces of the ball, his shot clamored against the front of the rim and fell to the floor. At the Pacers bench, Bird—3-time MVP and 12-time All-Star during his playing days in the NBA—lowered his head in disgust, and signaled for a timeout as he called his balky minions to the bench. Smits was instructed to purposely miss his second shot in the hope that one of his mates might rebound and score within the 4.5 seconds remaining on the game clock.

Obeying his coach's instructions, the tall center intentionally missed the free throw, but the ball fell unceremoniously to the floor as the gun sounded. The Nets had beaten the Pacers 97–95, leaving a haunting memory for the game appropriately played on Halloween night.

Larry Bird, his face grimacing as if someone had just punched him in the stomach, slowly made his way toward the locker room. The first game of his coaching career had been a major disappointment, and he must have wondered whether he'd made the right decision to give up retirement for the wars of NBA basketball. Eighty-one more regular season games loomed ahead for the man born 41 years earlier in a small town in southern Indiana.

PART
1

(1)

IN THE BEGINNING

"Once [Coach Jones] would show me something, it would just seem to click in my mind. It didn't matter what it was: a reverse pivot, boxing out, getting rebounds, whatever."
LARRY BIRD

As his brother Mark stood nearby, the young boy held the potato in his right hand and took careful aim at the wicker basket across the room. "Let it fly, Larry!" Mark exclaimed. "Let it fly!" An instant later, the brown tennis-ball-sized potato flew through the air. The brothers stood transfixed until it landed squarely in the middle of the basket. "All right!" the shooter yelled. *"All right!"*

The voice of future NBA legend Larry Bird was shrill in his early years, but the accuracy he possessed with the potato was a sign of things to come. Whether it was a basketball or a rubber ball tossed into a cut-out coffee can rigged to the back of the kitchen door, Larry was destined for stardom. He just didn't know it yet.

Larry Joe Bird was born at the Bedford (Indiana) Medical Center on December 7, 1956, the 15th anniversary of the Japanese bombing of Pearl Harbor. His size was evidence of things to come. He was big (11 pounds and 12 ounces) and very long (23 inches), with Scottish, Irish, and Indian blood flowing through his veins.

The fourth child born to Georgia Kerns and Claude Joseph (Joey) Bird Jr., a veteran of the United States Army, Larry followed brothers Michael and Mark and sister Linda and preceded brothers Jeff and Eddie in the Bird household. For the first 12 years of his life, home was West Baden, Indiana, which along with kiss-close French Lick, made up what locals called "The Valley." Confuse one rival town with the other and the words meant war. "When I was a child, the line between French Lick and West Baden might have been an imaginary one," a former resident recalled. "But to me it was a brick wall. Especially when the Red Devils [French Lick] were playing the Strudels [West Baden]. That was all-out war."

West Baden neighbor Menta Elliot, who helped raise young Bird, believed the tiny tot was destined for greatness. "He had such big hands and feet," she told a neighbor, "and his body was really strong." No wonder—Georgia Bird, a thickly built woman, stood an even 6 feet tall.

By the time he was three months old, legend had it that the infant was doing push-ups, egged on by his older brother. At seven months, he stood alone on the living room floor and looked up at his parents with a big grin. Two months later he was walking around the Bird house, his arms flapping.

Shortly thereafter, the youngster astounded family and friends in an escapade dubbed "The Great Escape." After putting Larry in his bed, which featured a high bar intended to prevent him from escaping during the night, the Bird clan retired to the living room for a bit of television. Moments later, Mike looked up to see tiny Larry grinning at him beneath curly blonde hair. "Mom," Mike called out. "Look who's here." Larry was returned to bed, but less than five minutes later he was back. Determined to discover how Larry was escaping, the family hid in the corner of the bedroom. They watched as he clutched the front bar on the crib, pulled himself up, and then squeezed the catch together so that the bar disappeared from view. Larry then turned over, slid down to the floor, and scampered for the door. His father intercepted him, and used some twine to tie the catch and keep Larry in bed. Later he broke the crib, triggering a move to his brothers' room, where he shared a bed.

The Bird family moved often, living in 17 different homes in 18 years. They were close-knit, but a demon lurked within. Joey, who found work in construction, at a shoe factory in Paoli, and at the nearby Kimball Piano and Organ company, was a heavy drinker. Worse, when he drank, he became abusive; on several occasions friends and neighbors noticed bruises around Georgia's eyes. After one incident, a cut above her eye required several stitches.

Larry's father was a troubled man, a product of war. Born in 1926 to Claude, an alcoholic for all but the last few years of his life, and Autumn Bird ("the meanest woman I ever met," Georgia Bird told friends), Joey, a willowy man with sandy red hair who was a chain smoker, joined the U.S. Navy in 1944. He served honorably for two years, returned home for three, then joined the Army in 1949, intent on a military career. Months later, Joey's Twenty-Fifth Infantry Recon unit was ordered to Korea.

Combat changed Joey forever. When he returned, he couldn't put the horrors of war behind him. Despite warnings that the marriage was ill-fated, Joey and the former Georgia Kerns, who had met while working in a shoe factory, became man and wife on September 20, 1951, the day before Joey's 25th birthday.

Living with Joey was difficult, for he often awoke with nightmares, visions of Korea. Guilt-ridden over being forced to remove frail, old Koreans from their homes and then torch them so the enemy couldn't hide, Joey cried out for help to suppress his demons. He also couldn't forget a frightful night in Korea that changed his life forever. After searching for enemy stragglers during the day, the weather worsened, and during the night the men nearly froze. In the morning, Joey and his best friend stalked the enemy until they heard the pitter-patter of gunfire. They leaped into a foxhole bunker only to find a young Korean soldier already positioned there. Instantly, Joey saw a flash and watched his comrade fall to the ground mortally wounded. Without hesitation, Joey raised his rifle toward the eyes of the youngster who had killed his buddy, and squeezed the trigger. He fell to the ground, but from that moment on, Joey Bird was never the same. "Those haunting eyes," he explained to a friend. "I can't ever forget them. *I* should have died, not *him*."

Georgia often warned family and friends never to shake Joey awake, fearing he would lash out at them. Family friend Virginia

Smith found out what she meant. "I was sent into the bedroom to wake Joey to tell him that Georgia had gone into labor with Linda, but in the excitement I forgot the warnings," she remembered. "I grabbed Joey around the ankle and shook him. I ducked just in time as Joey sat up and aimed a hard right hook at me."

Returning to his unit, Joey continued to struggle. He would wander off, then be arrested for being AWOL. He was promoted to corporal, but then was demoted for being absent. MPs rounded him up, and he served many of his remaining days in uniform in the stockade.

After his discharge, Joey Bird worked hard, but he was drunk on weekends. He refused treatment for his alcoholism and drowned himself in sorrow. "Joey drank because he had to," Georgia Bird once said. "Not because he wanted to."

Some time later, when the abuse worsened, Georgia, whose stubborn nature and feistiness contributed to the marital discord, filed for divorce. Joey ask for a reprieve and his wife agreed, but he was unable to cope with life. On February 3, 1975, he took his own life with a shotgun. "We all knew what he was going to do because he came right out and told us," Larry Bird said later. "Not that he wanted sympathy or anything. He simply said, 'I am not going to be around much longer. No use me living this way. You kids would be better off if I was gone.'"

According to Bird's recollection, his father called his mother on that fateful day and told her what was going to happen. Joey was delinquent paying support to Georgia, and the heavy drinking had continued. Police had come to arrest Joey, but he asked if he could have the afternoon to straighten things out.

After the authorities left, Joey visited his brother-in-law's gas station and said his good-byes. After a drink at a local tavern, he returned to Larry's grandfather's house and called Georgia. When the police returned, Joey laid down the phone and shot himself with the shotgun. "I was over at my Granny Kerns's house," Larry Bird recalled. "My sister Linda came by and she was crying. I wasn't surprised, but I was still shocked that it really happened. I was upset, but I understood. I felt as if I should cry, but I remembered how tough he was, and how tough he said I should be."

Larry's reaction to his father's death was true to form for a person who had never let others know his inner feelings. Tough to the core, the result of upbringing by Georgia and grandmother Lizzie Kerns, Larry kept his emotions to himself. After turning professional, one of the first things he did was buy a headstone for his father's grave. "I remember so many good times with my dad," Bird said in 1989. "He was a great father to all us kids, always trying to push us to be better. I missed him as soon as he was gone and I still miss him today." Bird was proud of his father, frequently recalling his generosity. "People always talk about how my father was generous. He would give anyone the shirt off his back." A relative put it another way, saying, "Joey had a heart as big as the world, but his drinking problem was even bigger." Larry's high school teammate Tony Clark said, "Larry learned a lot from his father. He really loved him."

From Joey, Larry inherited two vital characteristics—a clever wit and athletic ability. "Dad was a great kidder," Larry told reporters, "and friends told me he would have been a very good basketball player if he'd worked at it." Later on, the son wouldn't make the same mistake his father had.

Despite Joey's problems, Virginia Smith remembered good times for the Bird family. "Especially around Christmas," she recalled. "[My husband] Marty and I gave Mike, Mark, and Larry cowboy hats, bandannas, sheriff badges, guns, and holsters. Larry was particularly proud of his guns and holsters. . . . Little did anyone know that years later Larry would become a well-known sharpshooter, only using a basketball instead of a gun."

An earlier Christmas present was Bird's first ball. He was only four years old at the time. "It was one of those cheap rubber balls," he explained. "I was so proud of it that I stayed up for hours bouncing it." Another Christmas provided Larry's first basketball. "When I unwrapped it, I thought it was the greatest thing I had ever seen in my life," Bird recalled, signaling the start of a love affair with the roundball. Though it was cold outside and snow covered the ground, the young boy took the ball and played all day. When the ball deflated, Bird brought it in beside a pot-bellied stove until it inflated, and then ran outside to play some more. "One night I left the ball by the stove by accident," Bird said. "I got up in the morning and discovered a basketball with bumps all over it. I kept that ball for two years because I couldn't afford a new one, and when I would dribble the ball it would go this way or that."

During Larry Bird's heyday with the Celtics, he often ran down the court with his mouth open. Childhood allergies and sinus problems caused him to breathe through his mouth. That was a minor problem compared to the propensity the young Bird had for getting hurt. During a visit to his great-grandmother's home, he leaned over a railing, fell, and hit his head on a large rock. Five stitches were required, but that was mild. Over the years, Bird endured a broken nose, a fractured cheekbone, a shattered knuckle on his right index finger, a broken clavicle, torn ligaments in his right pinkie, right elbow lacerations, Achilles tendon discomfort, bone spurs in both heels (requiring surgery), and two back operations—all before he reached his 40th birthday.

Bird the youngster was interested in all sports. Depending on the storyteller, either brother Mark or Mike would drag him everywhere, or Larry was tagging along. "Sometimes I would have to pitch for both teams," Larry said later of his boyhood baseball games. "Or just chase balls after they hit them." Brother Mark explained, "Larry was a smart little butt. If we told him he couldn't play, he'd go home and tell Dad."

Bird played basketball and baseball, but he loved football. That career ended when he broke his clavicle in grade school. At age 14, his schoolyard sports days were interrupted when he was struck by a tricycle while visiting relatives in Hobart, Indiana. The metal fender gashed his leg, and a trip to the doctor for stitches was required. Told to stay off the leg, Bird instead did as he pleased, climbing on a bicycle and speeding off. The laceration broke open, the doctor refused to restitch it, and Bird was forced to elevate the leg for the remainder of the day.

Larry Bird discovered basketball while visiting those same relatives. In his autobiography, *Drive*, Bird recalled, "When I was out walking around, some kids stopped me and asked me to join their basketball game . . . I took my first shot in the game and it went in. I took my second shot and that went in, too . . . The kids on my team started slapping me on the back and telling me what a great player I was . . . and I just loved it." Bird continued to play well all afternoon. "They asked me what team I played on and when I told them I didn't play on any team, they couldn't believe it," Bird remembered. "One of the boys said, 'You must be the best player down there. . . . Would you be able to come up next week and play with us again?' " Bird's love affair with basketball had reached another level. "That was it. I was hooked on basketball," he said. "I went back home and started practicing every morning. I found that the more I did something, the better I got at it."

When he was healthy, he played against his older and taller brothers, and the competition was rough. "Those brothers were so competitive, and they just pounded on him," Jim Jones, a coach of Bird's since his early days, remarked. "Boy [Larry] would fight them tooth and nail, and then he'd stay around after they'd leave. Even at the age of eight, . . . he was someone who played hard and never backed down."

Fundamentals were stressed to Bird from day one in organized basketball. "Coach Jones is the man I have to thank for drumming basketball fundamentals into my head," Larry recalled. "He taught me every basic maneuver there is." Realizing he couldn't compete with his older brothers Mike or Mark, or other kids who outsized him physically, the youngster began to find other methods of attack. "I think," brother Mike observed, "that Larry just reached the point where he didn't want to get beat anymore. So he began finding ways to beat you. He was always thinking about the game, figuring strategy."

Later, Michael Jordan pointed to Bird's ability to play the mental game as the reason he found success. "My respect for Larry comes from the fact that he didn't have the quickness lots of other guys had," Michael said. "But he had a knowledge of the game that made his ability better. He'd outthink the defense, and that made it seem like he could jump higher and run faster. It was amazing to see."

Bird's bent for practicing his shooting came at an early age. Whether it was tossing the potato into the basket, or the rubber ball through a tin can (many times the Bird boys put two cans up on facing archways and played "full court" in their home), Larry was always practicing. Most times, alone. "When I'm out there by myself, what I'm doing is practicing my rhythm," Bird said, recalling his youth. "You can play three-on-three for an hour and a half and you'll take maybe 100 shots. I can go out myself in the same time and take 1,000—maybe more—anywhere I want."

Bird's experience with practicing in solitude was cited by several NBA experts later when they were queried as to why Larry was such a great shooter in the clutch. "When that little picture machine of his goes off," Celtics coach Bill Fitch observed, "he's in a world of his own. That little voice starts talking to him and he's in the backyard again." Kevin McHale, Bird's teammate with the Celtics and current general manager of the Minnesota Timberwolves, pointed out: "The game can be on the line, and for [Larry] it's just like playing H-O-R-S-E in his backyard."

Bird admitted he thought about basketball nearly all the time when he was young. "I'd sit in school and listen to the teacher for about 10 minutes," he recalled. "Then I'd be thinking about basketball. When was I going to play next? How many kids could I play with? How long could we play? I'd go into these trances. Then I'd start to worry about myself. I actually thought I should go see a doctor, get checked out."

Gary Holland, Bird's coach during his senior year of high school, said, "I never saw a kid who played basketball so much. He didn't have a car or any money, so he just played and played." Teammate Tony Clark recalled seeing Bird "up at the basketball court on the hill playing in the rain. He just stood there and kept shooting, all by himself."

Holland's comment was an understatement—the Bird family was dirt poor. From time to time, they were evicted for nonpayment of rent, and the electricity was sometimes turned off, even in the dead of winter. Joey Bird made minimum wage and Georgia added little even though she worked two jobs, mainly as a waitress. Orange County, home of French Lick, was the poorest county in Indiana. That despite the presence of the French Lick Hotel and Spa, which became famous for its "Pluto water" that was guaranteed to cure every illness known to mankind. The slogan, "If nature won't, Pluto will," combined with the action of the casino inside the hotel, lured such luminaries as Jack Dempsey, Howard Hughes, Al Capone, and even President Franklin Roosevelt to the premises in the earlier decades of the 20th century.

Hobnobbing with that part of the Valley society wasn't in the cards for the Bird family. "Mom and Dad always worked so hard, but our family was too big for our means," Larry said. "Dad was lucky if he made $120 a week and Mom $100. We were always in the hole for money. All of us kids helped with our paper routes and odd jobs, but it still wasn't enough." Georgia Bird, whom one West Baden resident said did "a hell of a job raising those six kids," said Larry never asked for much, not even a high school ring or letter jacket. He knew those things were beyond his reach.

Being poor didn't keep Larry from practicing his favorite sport. Janitors at Larry's school scolded him about banging on the gym door, trying to gain entrance well after the facility had closed for the day. "When I was younger," Bird remembered, "I played for the fun of it, like any other kid. I just don't know what kept me going and going and going."

Those who remember Bird shooting hoops by himself until the sun went down believe the youngster from the troubled home was escaping reality. "He had it tough," a neighbor recalled. "Larry hated that his father drank, and there were many unpleasant times. Going off by himself and shooting baskets provided a way to forget all that. Larry just seemed to be in his own world. What I remember is what great instincts he had with the game. He always seemed to know where the ball was going."

That certainly was an asset for Bird, but another side of his personality threatened to hold him back. The future star played what French Lick residents called "Biddy Ball" for Agan's Market during the summer months. Fundamentals were stressed; Bird learned how to dribble left-handed for the first time. The youngster's shot was an unruly one that found little success until brother Mark helped him fine-tune it, but Bird was known more for his quick temper than his basketball prowess.

While he was quiet and unemotional off the court, on it he was a wild man. He'd yell and scream at other players, taunt officials, use profanity, and slam the ball down, resulting in technical fouls. Twice in the eighth grade, Bird, so much of a neatness freak that his mother called him "Mr. Clean," was benched for his irrational behavior. When he reacted to coach Butch Emmons's punishment by missing practice, Bird was thrown off the team. If Larry lost, or his team lost, he'd stalk off crying. "He couldn't handle defeat," Emmons said. "Couldn't believe that someone could beat him. He hated to lose."

When Bird, who chose number 33 (the same number that his brother Mark had before him), entered his freshman year in high school, coach Gary Holland realized that his temper was Larry's Achilles heel. Several times he told Georgia that Larry had incredible potential if only he could control his tongue and just play basketball.

That observation coincided with a miracle that suddenly occurred in Larry Bird's young life. It happened without warning, he recalled later. "I don't know why, but one day I just started making all my shots. Every one. I can remember that day exactly. And after that, all the older guys started choosing me first."

The year was 1971. As Larry Bird was headed toward his 15th birthday, the NBA's Boston Celtics missed the playoffs for the second consecutive year. Little did the team realize that in a small town in southern Indiana, a gangly kid with wavy blonde hair and a love for the game of basketball had begun the sojourn that would result in his wearing Celtic green by the end of the decade, taking his teams and the storied franchise to new heights of glory.

BULLS VERSUS THE WORLD

*"I feel I've got some level-headed [players], some great ones.
I'm going to get the best out of them. . . . We've got a
nice little team here."*
LARRY BIRD

When the NBA tipped off its 1997–98 season on the final day of October, it shared a week filled with headline-making news events around the world. First, the stock market jolted the financial world when the Dow Jones index fell a record 564 points, the result of the collapse of the Asian market halfway around the world. Closer to home, the premier of China visited the White House and dined with Bill Clinton and wife Hillary, who had celebrated her 50th birthday in grand style at festive events across the country.

When the first basketball was tossed in the air on Halloween night, 29 teams had their sights set on one goal: an NBA championship. Some knew they were dreaming great dreams, and that a more realistic goal was winning 30 or 40 games.

For Phil Jackson's Chicago Bulls, seeking their third consecutive championship (sixth in the 1990s), there were question marks galore. Could Michael Jordan, at age 34, continue to play at a level like none before him in his 13th season? No one doubted the possibility, but Jordan would be targeted from game one because his scoring buddy Scottie Pippen was sidelined with continuing foot injuries that required surgery before the season. Without Pippen's scoring potential and deft ability to feed Jordan at crunch time, the Bulls were severely limited.

And what about Dennis Rodman? The tattooed, rainbow-haired freak with the irascible personality and "f... you" attitude toyed with retirement when the Bulls wouldn't cough up enough cash. In the end, the Trenton, New Jersey, native came to his senses and signed an incentive-filled contract that by season's end would earn him nearly $10 million.

With former Bull Brian Williams in the fold, and Lindsey Hunter and ageless Joe Dumars gunning from the perimeter to complement the gifted Grant Hill, Doug Collins's Detroit Pistons squad believed they could challenge the Bulls. They were joined in that quest by the Atlanta Hawks, a talented group of high-flyers spearheaded by center Dikembe Mutombo, and coached by the all-time winningest coach in the NBA, Lenny Wilkens.

Cleveland, sporting superstar Shawn Kemp, and Milwaukee, bolstered by the additions of Tyrone Hill and Terrell Brandon to support former Purdue forward Glenn Robinson, thought they might contend, as did Toronto, a feisty team led by Damon Stoudamire. Larry Bird's Indiana Pacers (the nickname was chosen by investors in the franchise since Indiana had a rich heritage with horse racing "pacers," and a "pace car" was used to start the Indianapolis 500) and the Charlotte Hornets, led by pure shooter Glen Rice, rounded out the pretenders to the Bulls dynasty in the Central Division of the Eastern Conference, all hoping to wipe the smile off Michael Jordan's face once and for all.

In the Atlantic Division of the Eastern Conference, the New York Knicks were determined to provide Patrick Ewing with a championship ring—but the Miami Heat, with dapper Pat Riley at the helm, was the team to beat. Washington (armed with a new nickname, the Wizards), Orlando, Philadelphia, New Jersey, and Boston all sought to find respectability.

In the Midwest Division of the Western Conference, San Antonio, featuring David Robinson and rookie Tim Duncan, was ready to challenge the Utah Jazz and last year's MVP Karl Malone. Houston's Rockets, Minnesota's Timberwolves, Dallas's Mavericks, Vancouver's Grizzlies, and Denver's Nuggets hoped for a playoff berth.

The Pacific Division of the Western Conference was loaded with contenders. The Lakers of Los Angeles boasted Shaquille O'Neal and Kobe Bryant, the latest "next Michael Jordan." They would battle Seattle, where "Vin Baker, the Basket Maker" took over for the departed Shawn Kemp, and Phoenix, where Larry Bird's ex-teammate Danny Ainge was in charge. Portland, a tough opponent on any night, the Clippers, the Kings, and the Warriors rounded out the field.

Regardless of the challengers and the pretenders, the 1997–98 NBA season promised to be scintillating, filled with the wondrous play of such veterans as Jordan, Barkley, Ewing, Reggie Miller, Hakeem, Scottie Pippen, Karl Malone, and Shaq. They would be joined by the new kids, Kevin Garnett, Keith Van Horn, Allen Iverson, and Tim Duncan, all of whom aspired to assume Jordan's lofty position and bring home a championship for their teams.

While the rest of the league prepared for the new season, Larry Bird readied his Pacers for the challenge ahead, confident that his squad could compete with anyone. From the moment he'd agreed to coach Indiana, the self-proclaimed "Hick from French Lick" had poured himself into his new job, ready and willing to instill in his team the same fire for the game that had made him a three-time NBA Most Valuable Player.

Bird inherited a veteran team that had come within a basket or two of reaching the NBA Finals in 1995. Expected to contend during the 1996–97 season under another Larry (Brown), the Pacers had been dubbed underachievers, losing more games than they won and missing the playoffs for the first time in nine seasons. Team members thought the label unfair, pointing to Rik Smits's injury as the critical factor in the disappointing season.

The most talented returnee to Bird's nest was the redoubtable Reginald (Reggie) Miller. At age 32, Reggie—who had been born with pronated hips that caused his legs to be so severely splayed that he slept in steel braces until he was four years old—might have lost a step or two. But his shooting touch, tenacious defense, admirable work ethic, and will to win were as keen as ever. Snubbed in the All-Star balloting the previous year, Reggie had something to prove, and Bird hoped the brother of WNBA coach and TNT commentator Cheryl Miller could lead the Pacers to the promised land.

Though Reggie's play was crucial, the key to the new season was Rik Smits. The brittle 7'4" Dutchman with the shoulder-length blonde hair was a menace to opposing teams when healthy, but his play had been limited by foot injuries that had made him little more than a bystander during the previous season. Bird had signed NBA journeyman Mark West as insurance, but prayed that Smits would stay healthy so he could be the team's force in the middle.

The third ingredient in the Pacers offense, former Warriors star Chris Mullin, had been acquired in the off-season. The left-handed gunslinger could still shoot like a championship marksman, and his play-hard mentality was a welcome addition to a team that had been chastised for simply going through the motions on occasion. Mullin would be spelled by Jalen Rose, the ex-Michigan Wolverine swingman whose defensive liabilities had landed him in Larry Brown's doghouse. Derrick McKey, another veteran who had undergone surgery to repair a stress fracture in his left foot during the off-season, and Fred Hoiberg, the shooter from Iowa State with a delicate touch, were also available.

Point guard required a player with ballhandling expertise to distribute the ball to Miller, Smits, and Mullin. Larry Bird had two candidates to fill that role, with a third possible if he recovered from injury. The returning veteran was Mark Jackson, who had been rudely traded by the Pacers to the Nuggets during the previous season. Despite Jackson's having snagged the assist leader championship from Utah's John Stockton, Larry Brown thought he was too slow and couldn't defend. Once the Pacers powers-that-be realized they desperately needed Jackson, they traded to get him back. A true professional, Jackson responded well to the flip-flop and was the team's most consistent player down the stretch.

Jackson's competition came from Travis Best, a third-year veteran from Georgia Tech, and from Haywoode Workman, a hard worker who was rehabilitating a potential career-ending injury to a left knee ligament. Best, a left-hander like Mullin, was a will-o'-the-wisp player with a passion for the game. He had potential, but only time would tell if his talent could measure up to those quality point guards who controlled the game.

For help with rebounds, the Pacers had the famous Davises: "Double D" Dale, a Clemson Tiger, and Antonio, the board battler from Texas-El Paso. Along with Smits, they were expected to scrape the boards and send the ball zinging to the point guard for the uptempo pace Larry Bird had in mind. Both Davises were improving—especially Dale, who had developed a decent jumper from the paint. Points from either Dale or Antonio would be a welcome bonus, but Bird's main expectation of them was ferocious rebounding and intimidating defense.

Bird's assessment of his squad was predictable and in line with the thinking of other experts in the game. "I like what I see," the rookie coach commented. "We're a bit slow of foot, so we'll have to work our tails off on defense. The offense—well, I'm one who believes it will take care of itself."

With that, Larry Legend—the nickname first pinned on Bird by reporter Peter Vecsey—bounded into the new season, ready to take on all comers. Though Bird had never coached a basketball game in his life, he believed he had the ingredients for a professional championship team. That confident, keep-the-faith attitude had been a Bird trademark ever since high school, when the French Lick, Indiana, native had been marked for greatness.

③

THE HICK FROM FRENCH LICK

"When a man is open, he should get the ball,
whether it's 30 feet out or underneath."
LARRY BIRD

When 6′1″, 131-pounds-dripping-wet Larry Bird fell to the floor, he knew his ankle was broken. A teammate had fallen on him during a Springs Valley junior varsity game, and Bird's sophomore season in high school came to a sudden and unceremonious stop. This was a huge disappointment, as the previous year the lanky youngster had improved his play considerably while winning the trophy for most free throws made. Simply earning a spot on the team had earned him a $20 reward from his dad.

Bird had also been bit by the celebrity bug after watching his brother Mark lead the Springs Valley team in scoring. "Everybody was cheering for him," Bird recalled. "I wanted to be *that* guy. I wanted the people cheering for me."

Bird's love for the game and his passion for playing made him refuse to attend games and watch from the sidelines while he was injured. "It just made me too nervous to sit and watch," he said later. "If I couldn't play, I didn't want to be there."

But that didn't stop Bird from practicing. Using a friend to retrieve the ball after misses or makes, Larry stood day after day, hour after hour, shooting until either the sun went down or the lights were turned off in the gymnasium. Propped up on his crutches, he'd fire away, not willing to lose time improving his shot. In his early school years, that shot was a one-handed set released from his waist. As the years went by, he began to release the ball a bit higher, but the form was never altered.

All the while, Larry Bird was growing like a wild weed. He wore his hair in early-60s fashion, longish on the sides with a carefully groomed wave that curled up in a V as it spilled down over his forehead. Flips flowed over his shirt collar, and he had a tendency to "comb" his hair with his hand.

It was during that time that young Bird began amazing the hometown folks with his jumping ability. "The first time I dunked was on the court at the old school yard," Bird remembered. "My life really changed then." Onlookers were shocked. "We'd never seen anyone who could dunk like that," a friend commented. "Nobody around here could jump like Larry."

Bird showed a flashy side at an early age by not only practicing traditional dunks, but ones where he threw the ball against the backboard, caught it in midair, and then dunked the ball from behind his head. "It was as if the ball was molded into Larry's hands," coach Jim Jones said. "Like it was made to fit."

Bird the playmaker was born at an early age. "By my freshman year, I started to sense that I could do more things out there," he said. "Once I realized I could pass the ball, my game changed completely." So much so that when coach Gary Holland asked all the kids in his class to write down what they wanted to be when they grew up, Bird wrote, "professional basketball player." "I just sort of laughed," said Holland.

Larry didn't. "I never wanted to leave the court until I got everything just right," he recalled. "I would practice different kinds of moves for hours on end and work hard to make my left hand as strong as my right. By then my dream was to become a pro. . . . You dream about it, but you never think you're going to make it, because there are too many roadblocks."

After sustaining the ankle injury in his sophomore year, Larry fought back. He had hoped to play in the final few junior varsity games, but pain continued to plague him. Nevertheless, he drove coach Gary Holland nuts, begging for more playing time. "I hated to put him on the floor," Holland recalled, "because I knew he was hurting."

Finally, to convince his coach he could play, Bird bet him that he could handle the dreaded "death valley suicide" drill. It forced the player to run from the baseline to the free-throw line and back, then to midcourt and back, then to the opposite free-throw line and back, and finally to the opposite baseline and back. Time permitted: 35 seconds. "Larry tried and tried, but he couldn't make it," Holland said. "He was nearly in tears a few times, but then finally made it."

Six games' worth of play told Holland and varsity coach Jim Jones that Bird was ready to compete with the big boys as tournament time came around. Larry figured he wouldn't get to play. "Suddenly I heard someone holler, 'Bird,'" he recalled. "I assumed it was a fan I knew from home, so I was busy scanning the stands when I heard someone call my name again. 'Larry, *get in there!*' . . . My heart was pounding and I threw my warm-up jacket off and was at the scorer's table before I even knew it."

The spindly youngster with the bird legs made an impact immediately. "The first time I got the ball, I launched it from about 20 feet and it went in," Bird recalled. "The crowd went absolutely crazy while I'm passing everywhere, rebounding, sinking all my shots."

With time running out, Bird was fouled. The team was down by one point, and suddenly Larry was the man. "I go to the free-throw line and I try to pretend it's 6 A.M. in the gym [Coach Jones required the boys to shoot free throws every morning] back home," Bird recalled. "And these are just two of the 500 free throws that I shoot every morning. *Swish!* Both shots are good and we win the game by one point. Pandemonium."

Thus began Larry Bird's high school varsity career. "The next day's newspaper headlines read 'Bird Steals the Show,'" Larry said. "That day my life was made. I couldn't believe that it was *my* name in all the stories, and that something that I loved to do—and could do well—could make so many people happy. It was a new and exhilarating experience for me and I decided that day to dedicate myself to being the best basketball player I could possibly be."

Larry Bird's forte during his junior year at Springs Valley, when he sprouted up to 6'3" and sported a frame without an ounce of fat, was passing the ball. He played guard (Magic Johnson said later, "Larry was always a point guard at heart"), and the experience permitted him a whole new perspective on the game. "The big man handled the scoring," he remembered, ". . . I'd pass the ball off a wall, off the fence, didn't make any difference. If other guys score, you see the gleam in their eyes. Besides, passing is more of an art than scoring. . . ."

An indication of Bird's yearning to be a team player came when close friend Steve Land, a fellow Springs Valley Blackhawk, was trying to gain the attention of college coaches. Against North Knox, Land was within six points of breaking the school record, set by Marvin Pruett, who later played at Evansville.

In the final few minutes of the game, Land was frustrated and unable to get the ball, let alone shoot it. Coach Jones heard a plea from Bird, sitting beside him on the bench. "Put me in, Coach," he barked. "I'll get the ball to him." And he did, enabling Land to break the record. Larry told his mother, "Since I'm not planning on college, I'm glad I could help Steve get to go."

Though he had averaged 16 points a game, and nearly 10 assists, no one who saw Bird play in 1973 imagined the greatness in store for him. Most expected he would become a small-college player like his brother Mark, who attended Oakland City College. "Larry was a good player, but not a great one," Coach Holland recalled. "I never thought he could be that good."

Springs Valley went 19 and 3 that year, but when it came time for Bird to attend the awards banquet, he was a no-show. Coach Jones found him shooting baskets at the playground. After some insistence from the coach, Bird followed him to the school.

Four inches were added to Bird's frame by the time he began his senior year in high school. Gary Holland was the new coach, but he had more than just a 6'7" player to deal with. Over the summer, Bird had bulked up, working seriously with weights for the first time in his career. Armed with new strength and the added height, Bird moved from guard to center.

Seeing the new version of Bird, Holland reassessed his prized player. "He had grown to nearly 6'7", put on some weight and strength, and best of all, not lost any of his ballhandling skills. I told everyone who would listen, 'I think we've got an All-Star on our hands.' "

The season was barely under way when scouts from around the state (and a few nationally) began hearing about the shy kid who resisted the limelight but scored points like a machine and rebounded with a vengeance. Every game meant more requests from college recruiters looking for a prospect, and from sportswriters yearning to cover the story of the local boy who made good.

Despite the publicity that came Larry's way, his off-court activities were like those of most other 17-year-olds. He hung out at the local Shell Station and played pool at Shorty's with friends. If Larry and his buddies were bored with French Lick or West Baden, they'd go over to Jasper and cruise around the courthouse square. Or pile in Shorty's Volkswagen and drive over to nearby Northwood, where they could listen to Harry Caray's broadcast of the Chicago Cubs games. "I loved those times," Bird remembered. "And I'm still a Cubs fan."

As the legend of the enigmatic kid from a small, out-of-the-way school continued to grow, Bird began playing at a level unseen in basketball-crazy Indiana for many years. Hoosiers recalled the superb high school days of such formidable competitors as Oscar Robertson, Rick Mount, George McGinnis, and others. "Bird-watching" became the favorite pastime of coaches and players around the state. Who was this kid and how had he suddenly become a star after being only the number-two scorer on his team during his junior year? Teammate Tony Clark couldn't figure it out.

"I never saw him play like that before. It was like a magic wand had touched him."

Bird's ability to put the ball in the basket like few in the sport was apparent in a Springs Valley home game against the Orleans Bulldogs. For four quarters, Larry, wearing a black uniform emblazoned with gold letters (Valley) and numbers (33), pounded inside against 6'7" Curt Gilstrap, but the duel was clearly won by Bird. At game's end, he had totaled a school-record 43 points. Gilstrap finished with 31.

The game that woke up pundits and fans alike occurred in Jasper, another small town rich in Indiana basketball history. The Cats, who had won the state championship in 1949 with a win over the Auburn Red Devils, sought revenge for an upset loss the previous year. Larry laid 30 points on them, and the Blackhawks cruised to a 14-point victory. Word spread that Springs Valley had a big kid who shot like a guard, one who was a definite threat to win the state scoring title.

By the time Bird turned 17 on December 7, 1973, college scouts were frequenting the Springs Valley gymnasium. Attention increased when he scorched the nets for 97 points in one weekend. Larry victimized West Washington for 42 on Friday, then blasted Corydon High School for 55 while hauling down 24 rebounds the next day. Truly, the volcano inside Bird was rumbling, and the outside world took notice.

In the Corydon game, Bird was remembered more for an assist than for the 55 points he scored. Headed down the left side of the court on a fast break, he had been surprised to receive a pass from a teammate who was on the opposite side. The toss was behind Bird and destined to go out of bounds if he didn't slow down to catch it. What the future star did next became the talk of the town—and of players on the opposite team, their coaches, and scouts, who wondered if they had really seen what they thought they saw. When the film of the play was run the next day, Coach Holland, his staff, and all the players—including Bird—simply laughed.

What Larry had done was to instinctively reach behind his back with his left hand and, without breaking stride, change the flight pattern of the ball so that it popped up and flowed directly into the hands of another Blackhawk who was streaking toward the basket. With the ball nestled snugly in his hands, Bird's teammate easily converted the layup.

By the time the team played archrival Loogootee, there were representatives from six colleges in the stands, including Indiana University coach Bob Knight. Nearly 4,000 fans packed a Springs Valley gym that was supposed to hold 2,700. In that game, the overexcited Bird made a crucial error. After a jump ball at the Loogootee end of the court, he grabbed the ball and laid it in the wrong basket. The team lost by two points, but the lanky youngster had impressed all who watched him.

Though Springs Valley won their sectional championship, Larry and the team were sent to the sidelines in the regionals by Bedford, a larger school to the north. In his final appearance in a high school uniform, Bird totaled 15 points. Later, Bird showed his mother bruises on his upper thighs. "The guy guarding me pinched me during the game," Larry explained to the dismay of Georgia.

Bird's small-town roots, and the inability of Springs Valley to advance in the state tournament, restricted state honors. Larry was named to several all-state teams, but was left behind in the vote for Mr. Basketball, a coveted award shared by Roy Taylor and Steve Collier.

Several times during the season, crowds at Springs Valley had been treated to a visit by a celebrity. Fifty-five miles to the north, the General, Bobby Knight, held court as coach of the Hurrying Hoosiers. When he started appearing at Bird's games, the gawkers were in awe. So, in fact, was Knight—in awe of Bird. "He's a good scorer, has the required offensive skills, and as good a pair of hands as I've seen all year," Knight told reporters.

Though Bird was excited about attending IU and playing for Knight, he was reluctant to do so. The small-town kid wasn't intimidated about competing in the Big Ten conference, but in reality he didn't want to go to college at all. His mother told others Larry felt he should get a job so she wouldn't have to work so hard.

Larry's father wanted him to attend Indiana State University in Terre Haute, but Georgia favored Indiana. Coach Denny Crum at Louisville coveted Bird, but lost out after making the most regrettable bet of his life. "We'll play H-O-R-S-E," Crum challenged Larry. "If I win, you come to Louisville for a visit. If you win, I'll leave you alone." Five shots later, Crum headed back to Louisville, alone.

Many coaches coveted Bird, but some thought he had little talent. Kentucky's Joe B. Hall said, "He's too slow." Bob Knight didn't agree with that assessment. He told Quinn Buckner, "Bird is a special player, one of the best." The coach even sent Steve Green, Kent Benson, and John Laskowski, three of his best players, to French Lick to see Bird. Knight wanted Bird badly, though there were those who said that if he'd gotten another recruit (Steve Collier) he wanted more, Larry would have been left by the wayside.

That didn't mesh with the facts, especially since Knight was impressed with more than Bird's basketball ability. Later he said he admired the way Bird dealt with a phone call from Purdue athletic director Fred Schaus. "Boy, he was tough the way he handled it," said Coach Knight, who happened to be in Bird's living room at the time. After much deliberation, Bird chose to play for Knight, who compared Bird's hand-eye coordination skills to those of Cincinnati Reds Hall-of-Fame catcher Johnny Bench. As he readied himself for the battle with Kentucky as a member of the Indiana All-Stars, fan support for Larry around French Lick was never greater. A bus emblazoned with "The Bird Flies Again" and "French Lick's Super Bird" banners traveled to Louisville's Freedom Hall, where his fans cheered on their hero, much to his embarrassment.

Late in the game, Bird's immaturity showed through. He had played early, scoring six points before Indiana coach Kirby Overman yanked him from the game. Larry steamed while riding the bench during the third and fourth quarters. With time running out, Overman motioned for Bird to re-enter the game, but Larry would have no part of it. He ignored Overman's request, telling his mother later, "If the coach didn't want to play me during the rest of the game, then why should I play when it's almost over?"

Later, Bird reflected on his decision to defy Coach Overman. "I know I reacted wrong," he said. "But I was young. However, if I had to do it all over again, I would probably do the same thing because I know how embarrassed I felt that night . . . I can remember how I felt . . . , just sitting there, totally forgotten."

But Larry never forgot people who crossed him, especially Overman. Years later in Dallas, Kirby stopped by the Celtics' hotel looking for tickets to an evening game. Urged on by a Boston teammate of Bird's, Overman sauntered up to Larry's room. "I said, 'Nice seeing you, and have a good life,'" Bird said, refusing the coach's request.

That episode with Overman brought closure to a high school career for Larry Bird that had appeared almost as if by magic. Somehow he was catapulted from being a decent player in his junior year to one of the finest high school seniors in Indiana basketball history—one who had truly become not only a great scorer and passer, but what his high school mentor Gary Holland called "my coach on the floor."

LARRY RULES

"Coaches need to let the players use their instincts. Individuals are less important than the team, and I intend to let the players play. I'm not going to try to substitute my judgment for theirs."
LARRY BIRD

"I'm going to give it everything I've got," the tall, lanky former NBA superstar promised as he sat beside Indiana Pacers president Donnie Walsh. "Just the way I did when I was playing." On that monumental day—May 8, 1997—Larry Joe Bird became the 11th head coach of a team rich in professional basketball history. But it was a team that departing coach Larry Brown, who had led them to within one game of the NBA championship series in 1995, believed was filled with a group of players who had lost their zest for the game.

Regardless of Brown's assessment, there was no doubt Bird wanted to be, as Donnie Walsh proclaimed, "back home in Indiana." "Indiana is the only team I wanted to coach, and I'm excited about the new challenge and new career," Bird explained. So were Pacers fans. The day that Bird was announced as the new head coach, telephone lines were lighting up at the team's headquarters in Indianapolis. Ticket sales soared.

The sojourn that led Bird to take the Indiana coaching job began five years earlier, when he hung up his sneakers after a grueling 13 years in the league as a Boston Celtic. The Beantown Bandit was sent to the sidelines with chronic back problems so severe that he had to lie on his stomach in front of the bench during times when he wasn't playing. For Bird, there were days when he barely could stand up, let alone compete physically in a game reserved for musclemen whose arms resembled iron girders. Two subsequent operations quelled much of the pain, but Bird's body was ready for the golf course instead of the hardcourt.

Displaying their loyalty to Bird, the Celtics "promoted" their beloved superstar to the front office. That meant Larry was now a vice-president in charge of something, though no one knew exactly what. He'd labor in that position for years while watching as his Celtics became the doormat of the NBA, their team and their coaches in disarray, much to the dismay of their fans and longtime general manager Red Auerbach. "I had to wait until the surgeries to see what was possible for me to do," Bird said. "There was no way to know. I kept working with the Celtics, but I missed the competition of the game. After awhile, playing golf every day and enjoying the sunshine of Florida wasn't enough."

Bird also was having trouble answering a question from his adopted son Conner. "Daddy, what's your job, anyway?" he asked innocently. Bird, who admitted he was a bit jealous when Conner insisted on buying Wheaties boxes with Michael Jordan's picture on the front, said he just shook his head, unable to come up with a definitive answer.

As Larry surveyed his options, he knew one thing for sure. "I was really leading, at least for me, a boring life. I knew full-time retirement wasn't for me."

Bird's duties with the Celtics were varied, but he was always on the outside looking in. Coach M. L. Carr, Larry's teammate during their playing days, felt intimidated by the living legend, and wasn't thrilled when Bird provided his two cents worth.

Throughout his days as an executive, Bird was fidgety and never comfortable in his role. He advised on player selection and potential trades, but playing was Larry's forte, not talking about it. More importantly, especially to Bird's ego, was that Boston officials disregarded his suggestions. Privately he ripped player trades, and questioned the direction the team was headed. Nobody—not even Auerbach, as savvy a basketball man as ever lived—seemed to care.

Rumors circulated that Bird might have financial troubles, but nothing could have been farther from the truth. With assistance from his agent Bob Woolf, a shrewd businessman who treated Larry like a son, the man who came from near poverty had accumulated a small fortune over the years. When 1997 dawned, had he never worked another day in his life, he and his wife Dinah would have been comfortable.

Since Bird couldn't play again, the only way to get back into the game he loved was to coach. Most colleges in America would have taken him in a heartbeat, but Bird was never comfortable in the collegiate setting. "The recruiting was something I could never do," he said. "Besides, big schools never were for me."

That didn't mean Bird wasn't paying attention to the game he loved. TNT sportscaster Craig Sager recalled, "I used to see Larry at clinics, college games, in Miami, all over. I could tell he was thinking about the game, watching this and that, soaking up things, thinking about what he liked and didn't. Looking back, I realize he was absorbing everything, focusing on what he might do if he coached. I tried to interview him, but he said, 'No, not now, maybe later.' "

The turning point came in 1996, when Bird's mother Georgia died of Lou Gehrig's disease. After laying his mom to rest, Larry's quest to find something to do besides charity golf intensified.

Wife Dinah knew Larry was unfulfilled. He was restless, and his displeasure with inactivity was apparent. Dinah encouraged Larry to coach. But where? The only answer was to secure a job in the NBA. The logical choice was to return to Boston, where the championship banners were a constant reminder of his glory days in Celtic green. Restore the magic at Boston Garden, the fans prayed. Bring back the Birdman.

When Boston approached him (despite their denials), Bird was lukewarm to the idea, fearing he might tarnish his great image as a player. Besides, his connection with the Celtics had waned, and his heart was now back in Indiana, and in Florida, where he spent much of his leisure time.

Bird also knew that Boston had its eyes on Rick Pitino, the successful Kentucky University coach who had just won the national collegiate championship. When Bird was nonchalant in his discussions with the Celtics, Boston decided Rick Pitino was the man for them.

While Boston courted Pitino, to the extent of offering substantial ownership in the team, the Pacers were dealing with the departure of Larry Brown, their mercurial coach who had come and gone from coaching positions so often he had trouble remembering the nickname of his current team.

Indiana players moaned that Brown had lost respect for them. "I like Larry, but he became so intense that my ears hurt when he yelled at me," Mark Jackson recalled. "Everything was wrong, even when we did something right. He lost control and the players didn't fight for him."

Larry Brown saw things differently. He felt the players, armed with their multimillion-dollar guaranteed salaries, hadn't given 100 percent—especially after Rik Smits, the key to the team, went down with various foot injuries. Ever the teacher, Brown felt closed off from the players, who had come to resent his constant barking and picayune habit of degrading them whether at practice or during a game.

No one questioned that the Larry Brown Show was headed straight out of town. At an emotional news conference in the spring, Brown sat alongside his friend Donnie Walsh, and explained that he was resigning as the Pacers coach.

Walsh had known of Brown's departure for some time. It was obvious that the sparkle in the former college coach's eyes had disappeared. He had lost the closeness with his team that had characterized the incredible run during the '94 and '95 seasons.

When the NCAA tournament was played in Indianapolis in March, Walsh and Bird discussed the Pacers coaching position after a mutual acquaintance called Walsh on Bird's behalf. "I gradually began to realize that he really did want to coach," Walsh said. "And of course we were interested."

Walsh knew that Pacers owners Mel and Herb Simon, the saviors of the Indiana franchise despite the loss of several million dollars a year, coveted Bird. "Herb tried to get Larry from the Celtics many times," attorney Phil Pecar said. "Either through trade or by buying his contract. But the Celtics always said no."

Before making his final decision, Bird discussed the matter with his wife and several close friends and basketball cronies. Larry's most pressing question was whether he might hurt his reputation as a player if coaching was a failure. "No one can ever take away what you earned on the basketball court," one coach told him.

"I talked to 25 or 30 people," Bird related. "After I ran everything by them, I asked them directly, 'Do you think I should get into this or should I stay away from it?' It was probably 50-50. I had good input, but I made the decision like I always do. By myself. . . . This is a dream of mine, so I jumped on it."

Discussions between Walsh and Bird intensified, and then Bird turned over the business end of the deal to agent Jill Leone, a former associate of Bob Woolf. The result was a whopper of a contract for $4.5 million a year—a far cry from the poverty that Bird's former Indiana State teammate Bob Heaton remembered. "We used to have card games at Larry's house on South 11th Street when Larry was a senior," Heaton said. "We played nickel-dime poker and blackjack. When Larry was a couple of bucks down, he left. He had no more money to lose."

The big three-year contract with an option for two more wasn't the main reason Bird took the offer. Jill Leone recalled his turning down $350,000 for an endorsement spot when he was with the Celtics. "If I miss my afternoon nap," Bird told his shocked agent, "I won't be rested enough to play my best for the fans."

He took that credo with him to the Pacers. "Money is only good if you really need something," he said; and prior to the regular season he turned down $200,000 to endorse Hanes Menswear, and another $300,000 to collaborate on a book chronicling his rookie year as head coach.

That didn't mean Larry Legend would go hungry. He had long-standing deals with such national sponsors as Converse, Viking Computer, McDonald's, and Miller Brewing Company. As his rookie season progressed, the Birdman joined forces with Marsh Supermarkets, Thomson Consumer Electronics, The Finish Line, and even Nordstroms, which provided new duds to wear on the sidelines at Market Square Arena.

Bird's asking price was pegged at $50,000 for a personal appearance, and 10 to 15 times that for a one-shot commercial deal. True to his work ethic, Bird never accepted an endorsement opportunity that took more than four hours, believing the whole business of shooting commercials to be a bore.

What Bird did crave more than anything was a challenge. He was a superb self-motivator in the mold of Jack Nicklaus, the greatest golfer who ever lived. Tom Weiskopf said of Nicklaus, "You knew he knew you knew he knew he was going to beat the shit out of you." Like Nicklaus, who never had the great natural talent, Bird fought hard to become the best in his sport and to continue to improve every day he played. He developed a cocky, you-can't-beat-me persona that said, "Give me your best and I'll better it." Present Larry Bird with a challenge, and stand back.

K. C. Jones, Bird's coach for the five years in the 1980s that produced two NBA championships, recalled an incident in Seattle. "The game was level with 13 seconds to play," he said. "In the huddle during a timeout, Larry said, 'Give me the ball and get out of the way.' So we called a play for Larry to shoot from the corner. Xavier McDaniel was guarding Larry, and I heard him say, 'Xavier, they're throwing me the ball. I'm taking two dribbles, then I'll step back and stick it.'" The X-Man replied, "Yeah, I know. I'll be waiting."

Seconds later, that precise scenario was played out, but with an added twist. "When the ball was in the air," Jones chuckled, "Larry turned and left the court. The ball went through the basket and he wasn't even watching. It was the damndest thing I ever saw." McDaniel turned away, shouting, "Damn!"

Quinn Buckner recalled an incident when he telephoned Bird the morning after the Celtics had won the 1985/86 championship. "I called his house and Dinah told me he was out running," Buckner said. "Later he tells me, 'Listen, if you're going to win another one, you'd better get started.'"

Frank Layden, the jovial former coach of the Utah Jazz, once tried to unnerve Bird by telling him he was going to pull his shorts down as he went up to loft a jump shot from the corner. Bird laughed, got the ball, headed to the corner, and then drained a three-pointer while gesturing at Layden.

When Bird and Donnie Walsh met to discuss the Pacers job, Bird sounded like a walking, talking basketball encyclopedia. He explained why the Pacers had failed during the previous season, the strengths and weaknesses of the player roster, who to bring in to supplement the squad, ideas about potential assistant coaches, appraisal of other teams in the league, and how the Pacers needed to become much more of an uptempo team to succeed.

Most importantly, he pointed out that Indiana wasn't tough enough mentally, comparing them to his 1984–85 Celtics who lost a rough-and-tumble championship series to the Lakers. "We tried to irritate them and get them to respond," Bird acknowledged. "But they didn't, they just played their game and beat us. They were tougher than we were."

By the end of the session at the Simon headquarters, Walsh was a Bird believer. "I walked in interested," the Pacers president recalled, "and walked out thinking this was our man. I told Herb there were two things I was convinced of. He was honest and he was smart."

Walsh's observations came despite his belief that Bird had no coaching experience. Actually, he did, although Larry probably didn't boast that he had been junior varsity coach and assistant to the varsity coach for the West Vigo High School *baseball* team during his student teaching days at ISU. Besides handling his coaching duties, Bird helped out by mowing the grass in the outfield.

The multimillion-dollar contract the Pacers offered didn't include yardwork, but Bird would have mowed Walsh's lawn if need be. Having been away from the game he loved for too long, Larry couldn't wait to get started, believing fate had played a hand in his selection to coach the Pacers. "The timing was perfect," Bird admitted. "I wanted to coach and the Pacers needed a coach. We both got what we wanted."

The first order of business for Bird was to find assistant coaches, and he didn't waste any time. A month after his appointment was announced, Dick Harter and Rick Carlisle were added to the staff.

Others had been considered—including former teammate Quinn Buckner, who had tried coaching and failed during an ill-fated stint with the Dallas Mavericks. "Larry asked me if I really wanted to coach," said Buckner, who finally accepted a position as the Pacers television analyst alongside gifted broadcaster Jerry Baker. "And when it got right down to it, I didn't."

Since Bird had never coached a basketball game at any level, Harter and Carlisle were much needed. Known as a defensive wizard, Harter, an ex-Marine Corps officer and former college coach, had been a Pacers assistant to Jack Ramsay for two seasons in the mid-1980s before accepting the job as the first coach of the expansion Charlotte Hornets. That experience he later called a "death wish," for the team had little chance. Besides Ramsay, Harter had also assisted Pat Riley in New York and Chuck Daly at Detroit, where the savvy Harter had initiated the "Jordan Rules" defense.

Harter, whose facial expressions at times reminded observers of a cuddly little chipmunk, had a plan to create a solid, conservative, make-no-mistakes defense that was fundamentally sound without gambling. Realizing the Pacers were slow afoot, he wanted to rely on a team defense reminiscent of Bird's playing days in Boston. In his superb book *The Big Three*, author Peter May described Bird's defense: "[He] was never a solid individual defender," he said, "but he could play outstanding 'help defense.' He cheated like a devious older brother playing monopoly."

True to that spirit, Harter, who admitted he "went to church a lot" [after looking at Indiana's slow-footed roster], devised a scheme to take advantage of the Pacers' strengths (quick hands, long arms, and veteran savvy), and downplay their weaknesses (lack of quickness and mobility). "My emphasis is on positioning, rotation, and recovery," Harter, whose voice rarely rose more than a few decibels above a whisper, explained. "We rarely will double-team, the players have to fight through picks, and they've got to think on their feet. Each guy has his own private battle to win or lose."

Boyish-looking Rick Carlisle, the second assistant, had been a teammate of Bird's in Boston. More than that, it could be argued that he owed Larry everything that had come his way in the NBA.

In the fall of 1984, Carlisle was a snot-nosed college guard from the University of Virginia with aspirations of making the Celtics squad. Bird had taken a shine to the rookie and wanted Carlisle on the team. To make sure that happened, Bird kept feeding his new friend the ball in a Celtics preseason game played at Worcester, Massachusetts. Rick cooperated by scoring 23 points. A few days later, Gerald Henderson, whose steal in the 1983/84 playoffs had been crucial for the Celtics, was traded to Seattle for a draft pick that turned out to be Len Bias. Carlisle became Bird's teammate, and thus began a relationship that culminated with Rick becoming a Pacers assistant 13 years later.

During his playing days, Carlisle loved to team up with Bird to play practical jokes. On one occasion, they tricked new acquisition Jerry Sichting. "They asked me if I had any plans for the evening," Sichting recalled. "I said no, and they told me to meet them at a bar called Ramrod. I went there after they set everything up with a phone call." When Sichting arrived, there was no name on the door. He went in and found only two guys there. "After awhile, I realized Rick and Larry had set the whole thing up," Sichting said. "The place was a gay bar. They never had any intention of coming."

The prank was reminiscent of one Bird had pulled in his youth. During a trip with an AAU team, Bird impersonated a hotel desk clerk and called guests, telling them they were in the wrong rooms. Soon after, the halls of the hotel were filled with sleepy-eyed people, bags in tow, meandering around trying to find their new rooms. Bird also became famous around Boston for tying together the laces on coach K. C. Jones's shoes while he was giving the Celts a pregame pep talk.

Fast friends with Bird, Carlisle had spent eight years as an assistant in the NBA with New Jersey and Portland. Considered for head coaching positions every year, Carlisle, who had advised Bird against taking the Pacers head coaching job, was a methodical man who could size up an opponent with the best of them. During Bird's sabbatical from the game, Carlisle often sent him scouting reports on NBA teams.

Bird joked that he hired Carlisle as a payback "for all those years he had to guard me in practice," but the Pacers coach had enormous respect for the sidekick with a nonstop work ethic that matched his. "Rick just goes and goes," Bird said. "You never have to tell him to do anything. By the time I've thought of it, it's already done."

Bird still liked to have fun with Carlisle. During the season, he told his assistant there would be no videotape viewing before practice, which was the norm. When Carlisle stepped onto the Market Square Arena court ready for the workout, there was nobody there but him. Realizing he'd been had, he walked into the viewing room, where Larry and the players were waiting for him.

After the assistant coaches were in place (Bird opted for just two instead of the standard three, at Carlisle's suggestion), the new coach began to examine the Pacers roster to get an idea of what lay ahead. Through the summer months, Bird met with every player, and then supervised practice sessions at the Indiana Basketball Academy in nearby Carmel, Indiana.

To gain experience on the sidelines, Bird coached in the Atlanta summer league. Pacers rookies and hopeful veterans learned firsthand the Bird method: practice hard, be prepared, and then go play. Lenny Wilkens, veteran coach of the Atlanta Hawks, liked what he saw. "Larry's got a knack for this," he told reporters. "A feel for the game. But that's not surprising, because he played the same way."

––––––––

When the Pacers opened training camp on October 3rd, they had already been off and running for several months. Besides the informal workouts at the Basketball Academy, Bird had them darting around the court or on the track at North Central High School in Indianapolis.

The effort by the players was the result of Bird's vow to provide "the best-conditioned basketball team in the NBA." He believed that most NBA competitors eased into the season, never "finding their legs" until late December or early January. His Pacers were going to be different, and his methods were different as well.

Where Jack Ramsey had tested his squad with a two-mile run in the mid-1980s, and Brown had used the mile, the new coach proposed less distance running and more sprints in keeping with the type of conditioning needed on the basketball court. "Players who have been in the league for 10 or 12 years, and have had two or three knee operations, they have a tough time," Bird explained. "Especially with long distances."

That didn't mean Bird discontinued his own regimen, which he had begun early during his days at Indiana State. While playing for the Celtics, his daily program included a long-distance run, practice games with teammates, multiple sit-ups, and short-distance runs, all sandwiched between lengthy shooting drills. No wonder he was such a superb fourth-quarter player—he was in better shape than anyone else.

More than 15 years later, Bird astounded many of the Pacers players by running a mile in 5:20. That achievement set the tone for the conditioning program the team endured over the summer as they approached training camp.

Veterans and rookies alike knew Bird had been obsessed with practice when he was with the Celtics, often showing up hours early so he could work on every facet of his game. Other NBA coaches had used Bird as an example of a superb work ethic. One brought his team to Boston Garden early to see number 33 in action. To his amazement, Larry wasn't on the court. Embarrassed, the coach headed for the sidelines before looking up to see Bird running on the track. He was working on conditioning that day.

As well as his shooting. While most NBA players waltzed into the locker room the required 90 minutes before game time, Bird had been on the floor by at least 6:00, more than two hours before tipoff. In the loneliness of Boston Garden, with only attendants and a few Celtics season ticket holders present, Bird shot more than 300 practice shots. He'd start with 6 to 10 free throws, move out on the court a bit, and then start firing away at a comfortable pace as comrade Joe Qatato hit him with perfect passes. Then the "Parquet Picasso," as he was dubbed, would speed up the routine, and by the end of the workout throw up rapid-fire shots, many featuring the Bird "drop back a step" maneuver that guaranteed him an opening from every angle. "I really don't count my shots," Bird said. "I just shoot until I feel good."

ESPN producer Bill Fairweather recalled Bird amazing even the great Mickey Mantle. "We had Mantle in the studio when I worked at WBZ in Boston, and the in-house camera feed showed Bird practicing at the Garden. It was like 4:00 and nobody was there but the maintenance people and a few ushers. Here's Bird out there shooting jumpers, one after another. Mantle watched for awhile, and then said, 'This guy hasn't missed a shot since I got here.' I could tell the Mick was in awe of Bird."

No wonder Bird told Boston reporters that every time he took a shot, he believed it was going to go in. Never one for false modesty, he said, "I just felt there was no one in the league who could stop me if I was playing hard. What makes me tough to guard is that once I'm near the three-point line, I can score from anywhere on the court. It's kind of hard to stop a guy with unlimited range."

The shooting practice was reflective of Bird's desire and his love for the game. "That's the number-one thing, the desire," he explained. "The ability to do the things you have to do to become a basketball player. I don't think you can teach desire. I don't know why I have it, but I do."

Inspiration for that work ethic came from one of Bird's idols, hard-nosed Hall-of-Fame Boston Bruins hockey player Bobby Orr. Before each Celtics game, cameramen captured Bird's head pointed skyward, his eyes focused on a pennant that read, "Robert G. Orr 1966–76—Number 4."

Pacers players had heard all about the Bird desire and his love for the game, but now they saw it firsthand. They learned their coach, the small-town boy who made good in the image of Horatio Alger, arose at 5:30 every morning and ran more than three miles before breakfast. Every morning. Without a miss. Three miles. Rain or shine. "When I heard that," veteran guard Mark Jackson said, "I knew we'd better get in shape."

Except for the times when Bird underwent the two back surgeries, he had never been out of shape. When he was a child, a friend challenged him, saying, "If you can outrun me to the post office, you can ride my bike for 10 minutes." Larry did, and he'd been running ever since.

In Boston, there were nearly as many stories about Bird the runner as there were about Bird the basketball player. Often, he would be named honorary starter for a race—only to fire the gun and then sprint down the street with the other competitors. On one occasion, he tried to compete in a 8.5-mile race with 14,000 other hopefuls. "It nearly killed me," he lamented. "Every bone in my body hurt after that race."

With Bird as their role model, the Pacers players sweated their way into condition. When they began training camp at Walt Disney World in Orlando, Florida, the team was raring to go. Instead of witnessing the brilliance of fall colors as the leaves turned in Indiana, players were exposed to Mickey Mouse and 60-degree temperatures under bright Florida sunshine. The Disney facility was a first-rate athletic facility. After practice, golf carts transported the Pacers to their luxurious accommodations.

Practices were rigorous, but not exhausting. "Basketball should be fun," Bird told reporters. "It's our job, but if you don't enjoy it, that makes it tough."

Reggie Miller was a believer. "You don't mind long practices when it shows in the results," the Pacers sharpshooter said. "Coach makes practices fun. You know what he wants, and he has a way of telling you with a smile."

Bird's emphasis on being "one of the guys" was evident from the first whistle. Instead of the Napoleonic stance the other Larry had taken, Bird's easygoing manner and willingness to encourage instead of berate put the players at ease. "It's going to be a refreshing preseason," Rik Smits predicted. "The enthusiasm is really back this year." Miller had a similar perspective. "There's been such a big change; it's almost day and night. It's so relaxed out here. And even though Coach is demanding, he says it to you in a very positive way. You can feel he's going to be one of those coaches you want to die for."

Taking charge was nothing new for Bird. At Boston during his playing days, he was a natural leader on and off the court. Kevin McHale even called him "Coach" a few times, something that

Bird dismissed immediately. But McHale was right, and many times the Celtics players paid more attention to what their star had to say than to coach Bill Fitch.

"Larry brought a quiet confidence to Boston," Quinn Buckner (a Pacer for 32 games during the 1985–86 season) stated. "Just like when he was a player. He knew what he was talking about, and you could always see the players respond to that."

Bird's practice drills at training camp were refreshing—even though it seemed strange, one of the players remarked, that during one drill the legend intentionally missed several shots in a row so the ball could be rebounded to start a fast break. "I like fast-paced basketball," Bird proclaimed. "Pressure defense and emphasis on team play. Get the ball off the board, up the court as quick as possible, get it to the people who can put it in the hole, and play good defense."

To emphasize his fast-break philosophy, Bird used an old high school drill. He divided the squad and challenged them to race up and down the court and make 82 layups in two minutes. "I could never do that, but these guys can," Bird admitted. And they could, recording 84 just as assistant coach Rick Carlisle blew his whistle.

"Larry always wanted to run," said Quinn Buckner. "For a guy who supposedly had no quickness and all that stuff, he always appreciated the value of getting out and running. I used to go down to French Lick and run with him on his trail. I'd be in shape but he'd just kill me. He'll bring that principle to the Pacers."

In training camp, Bird had the team run through regimented shooting drills, but he left ample time for them to practice on their own. Most had heard the heralded stories of Bird throwing up 200 shots, showing up at all hours to work on his shooting touch. Sometimes he shot three-pointers with this eyes closed to make sure he had his rhythm. Buckner recalled a time in French Lick when Bird refused to quit shooting until he made 10 consecutive free throws without touching the rim.

By the time training camp came to a close, the coach liked what he saw. "We're way ahead offensively," Bird explained. "I recognize that we lack foot speed [on defense], but that won't hurt us if we play together." Asked about the Pacers' offensive intentions,

Bird said, "We'll be an exciting team to watch. The ball's going to be moving, guys are going to be unselfish. They'll be kicking it out—finishing strong."

Most of all, Bird was impressed with the effort of his players. Dick Harter echoed his sentiments. "If we were going to rank this training camp on hard work," the assistant coach pointed out, "I think we'd be in the top four or five in the league." Bird had issued a vital challenge to the veteran club from the first day of training camp—a challenge concerned not just with achieving a winning record or simply making the playoffs. "I told them they had to win 55 games to get home-court advantage."

Despite the hard work, training camp had been fun. Pictures with Mickey and Goofy, good-natured teasing among the players and coaches, and even a chorus or two of selected songs by the rookies, a Pacers' tradition, kept things light. Tunes included Mark Pope's rendition of Marvin Gaye's "Let's Get It On," former Indiana University star Todd Lindeman with "The Devil Went Down to Georgia," and Austin Croshere's special arrangement of "Movin' on Up."

When the team packed up and traveled north for their first exhibition game against Cleveland, prospects looked bright. And best of all, Larry Bird was back in the game, where he should have been all along.

Eight exhibition games saw the Pacers compile a 6–2 record, matching the one achieved during the 1993–94 season when the Pacers battled the Knicks to the wire before succumbing in the Eastern Conference championship game. Bird saw that as a sign of good things to come, and Pacers fans hoped he was right.

The team began exhibition play with a loss at Dayton, Ohio, to the Cleveland Cavaliers. Bird admitted he had pregame jitters, but told reporters, "I always had them when I played, so why should this be any different? If I wasn't nervous, something was wrong." Austin Croshere had broken his wrist in the disappointing opening loss to Cleveland, and Antonio Davis sprained his ankle. They hobbled onto the court at the Fort Wayne (Indiana) Coliseum the following evening as the Pacers took on the Toronto Raptors, coached by Darrell Walker.

The Fort Wayne arena had seen play by the NBA Pistons in the 1950s, when George "The Bird" Yardley and Larry Foust were the stars of the day. It was now home to the Fort Wayne Fury of the Continental Basketball League, coached by former IU star Keith Smart (famous for "The Shot" that won the 1987 NCAA championship) and featuring homegrown hero Damon Bailey.

When Bird entered the Coliseum, the arena exploded with applause. Fans stood and cheered from the moment his tall frame emerged from the shadows of the tunnel until he crossed the court. Ever the shy one, Bird tilted his head downward before plopping down on a chair near the scorer's bench. The response five minutes later to the introduction of the players paled in comparison to the hefty hand for Bird. Fort Wayne fans had come to watch their Hoosier idol, to pay Larry Legend respect, and to wish him well for the season. "He's always been my favorite player," said a female fan wearing a "Birdwatcher" T-shirt. "Plus he's just so darn cute."

During the game, Bird showed two different sides of his personality. His team safely ahead, he walked by the end of the scorer's table, where media relations director David Benner was stationed. As his trademark grin lit up his face, Bird's left hand bumped over a cup filled with resin that was perched on the table. It toppled over, spilling the dusty substance all over Benner's papers. Later, Bird exposed his fondness for kids by teasing a ballboy. The youngster's eyes bulged with excitement and awe as he enjoyed this lighthearted moment with the living legend.

A win in Fort Wayne was followed by a home-court loss to Cleveland in which the rookie coach learned for certain that referees would treat him just like everybody else. After Chris Mullin was decked while slicing toward the basket (the bleeding wound required stitches), Bird objected loudly to the no-call. The official scampered down the court, completely ignoring him.

Two wins over Utah and victories in the final three preseason games brought the Pacers record to 6–2. Prior to the Charlotte game, Bird had made his customary appearance to watch his players warm up. Early arrivers at Market Square Arena caught a glimpse of the Birdman sitting at the west end of the court in the folding chairs section. With his hands wingspread on two adjoining seats, he relaxed and surveyed the court. From time to time, David Benner or Donnie Walsh would stop by to chat. Then Rick Carlisle and Dick Harter joined him. Eventually a fan or two gained the courage to approach Bird and ask for an autograph. Bird acquiesced, ever ready to be the public figure that he in reality disdained.

Truly Larry Bird was having fun at his new job, and loved being back in the game. "I can't believe how relaxed he is," Benner observed. "And he makes everyone around him that way. At our office he's become one of the guys. Knows most of the first names and always says hello or kids someone."

Donnie Walsh was amazed at Bird's work ethic. "He's always at the office before I am," he said. "Been there a long time. And with people, well, he's great. No falsity, just Larry. You get what you see."

Trainer David Craig believed Bird's work habits were part of his leadership qualities. "Larry leads by example," Craig said. "He's always early, 15 minutes at least. If he expects you to do something, he's probably already done it. Sometimes, he really doesn't have to say anything, you just know what he's up to. I knew there was something special about him, and there really is."

What team officials, Pacers players, and, most importantly, fans were seeing was a man more at peace with himself than he had been in years. "I love what I'm doing," Bird explained. "I knew this was the perfect job for me."

So did Donnie Walsh, especially when he saw the sensitivity that Bird exhibited with the younger players who dreamed of playing in the NBA. One was Todd Lindeman, who had labored under Bob Knight at Indiana University. The seven-footer hadn't been given much of a chance to play professionally, but Bird thought he had potential. He practiced hard against Rik Smits, and hustled his tail off working with the assistant coaches.

By the end of the preseason, Lindeman would be cut, but Bird made certain that the former Hoosier had a chance to play in Market Square Arena. With time winding down in a win against

Charlotte, the coach gestured to Lindeman, and with an encouraging word sent the big man into the game. Lindeman played the final minutes, taking a pass down the lane from Jalen Rose, pivoting to his right, and dunking the ball to put an exclamation point on a successful preseason for the Pacers. On the bench, Larry Bird smiled his special smile, rose from his seat, and headed off the court. He'd not only won the game, but had given a young aspiring player something he could always remember.

Bird also gave Travis Best and Dale Davis, who looked more like a tight end than a basketball player, a lesson they wouldn't soon forget. Bird's "be on time and play hard" credo was etched in stone, and Best and Davis found that out when they showed up two minutes late for a charter flight to Nashville. According to Larry's rules, that was a no-no. If a player was late for any scheduled event, Bird lifted $1,000 from his wallet. Three violations meant suspension for one game. When Dale and Travis were tardy, they stood on the tarmac watching the Pacers' charter plane as it lifted off. Realizing their error, they took another flight to Nashville, but delays made them miss the morning shootaround. Each lost $2,000, and Best's third violation caused him to miss a game.

More importantly, all the players knew Bird meant business. Slowly, the team was taking on a new personality, one molded by the personality of the coach himself.

PART

II

BAPTISM BY FIRE

*"As a coach you can't wear your heart on your sleeve. If the
players see me getting frustrated, upset, or out of control,
they're going to play out of control. . . . There's no use
ranting and raving at my players during a game."*
LARRY BIRD

When Bird agreed to become the
11th coach in Pacers history, he knew the odds were against him
to lead the team to an NBA championship. He realized what it
took to compete at that level; knew the ingredients for molding a
team into a cohesive unit; and understood how difficult it would
be for the Pacers to challenge upper-echelon teams like the Bulls,
the Lakers, the Jazz, and the Heat.

Nevertheless, he was ready to trade his seven-iron for a practice whistle and join such ex-players as George Mikan (9–30), Bill
Sharman (333–240), Bob Cousy (141–209), Bill Russell (341–290),
Wilt Chamberlain (37–47), K. C. Jones (522–252), Lenny Wilkens
(1,070–876), Magic Johnson (5–11), Wes Unseld (202–345), and
Phil Jackson (483–173), all of whom had taken a shot at coaching
in the NBA. As he flew back to Indiana after the disturbing last-
second loss at New Jersey in the season opener, he wondered if it
all had been a mistake. The next six games did nothing to alter
that feeling.

Despite the loss at New Jersey, the Pacers home opener was a
sellout and then some (16,729). It was an extravaganza not unlike

the opening ceremonies at the Olympic Games or the Hollywood premiere of the latest Steven Spielberg film.

At precisely 6:53 P.M. on November 1, 1997, Larry Joe Bird casually walked from the west entrance of Market Square Arena toward the basketball court. As he emerged, the applause began to swell. By the time he stepped onto the court, it had become deafening, with every fan in the packed arena standing and cheering.

The applause continued as Bird, stylishly dressed in a dark sportcoat, white shirt, and tie, sauntered toward the Pacers bench. An electrified version of "Back Home in Indiana" provided the backdrop as the lanky superstar plopped down on a metal chair embellished with Pacers blue and gold, chosen as colors by former general manager Mike Storen, a graduate of Notre Dame.

Appearing oblivious to the fuss, Bird refused to acknowledge the applause. Being center stage in a basketball uniform was one thing; having to sit in plain sight of 16,000-plus frantic fans gawking was quite another.

When Bird stretched his arms across two adjacent chairs, he looked a bit *like* a bird. The pointed nose, the bony cheeks, the newly cut hair that feathered down on his forehead, all were a familiar part of the Larry Bird persona. "When I was sitting on the bench," Bird later admitted, "It finally hit me. I'm coaching in the NBA."

After Boomer (the Pacers' energetic panther mascot) had descended on a rope from the ceiling amid the snap, crackle, and pop of firecrackers, flashing blue and yellow lights, and thick smoke, and the players had been introduced, Bird gathered his minions for a brief chat before tipoff. His advice centered around playing smart, something he'd done since high school.

Outfitted in their new pinstriped uniforms, the Pacers' opponents were the anemic Golden State Warriors—coached by P. J. Carlesimo, the bearded ex-Seton Hall coach who had curiously traded his tweed coat and serene life in New Jersey for the trials and tribulations of the NBA. His bombastic nature from the coaching box made Pacers officials keep a medic nearby since P.J., a screamer from the opening whistle, looked like a heart attack waiting to happen. He was a complete contrast to the reserved Bird, who rarely left his perch on the bench, and then only to encourage his players.

It took several Pacers possessions, but Smits finally hit a soft jumper for the first two points of the Bird era at Market Square Arena. Reggie Miller, who had christened the season with a three-pointer in New Jersey, followed with a basket, and the Pacers were off and running.

That didn't mean much. In the earlier game against the Nets, expected to be the cellar dwellers of the Eastern Conference, the Pacers had sped to a lead and then played like boneheads down the stretch. "I was real surprised by the way we finished that game," Bird admitted. "But from what I hear, that happened a lot last year."

The embarrassing loss didn't cause the rookie coach to pepper his players. "You've got to have a killer instinct in this league," Bird explained. "But these guys know that. I didn't see any need to get after them."

Instead, Bird, a self-proclaimed players' coach (which had several definitions, depending on who the players were), let his charges sort out the loss for themselves. "I didn't say much [after the New Jersey game]," Bird reported. "But we've got to hit the court believing we can win every time out. That's the only way you do."

Bird's coaching debut had been a loss, in contrast to another debut 18 years earlier when he'd played his first game as a Celtic against Houston. "I remember it vividly," the coach with the photographic memory stated. "In fact, I remember most all of them. Every play."

New Jersey coach John Calipari was pleased that Bird had not suited up against his Nets. "I've known Larry from when I was coaching at Massachusetts," he explained. "And I have great respect for him. I'm just happy he didn't play at the end of the game." Bird may have wanted to, but his postgame comments never included, "Well, if I'd been out there, we'd have. . . ." Even though the loss hurt inside, he calmly answered reporters' questions and then meandered off, his private feelings about the game remaining just that.

"I want to accomplish things people don't think I can," Bird said before the season. "That's the way it's always been. I'm trying to learn as I go in a game where there are many great coaches, but hey, I played this game and there are a lot of coaches who couldn't play. I want to win a championship. That's my ultimate goal."

The Bird style of coaching had been apparent during the New Jersey game. He sat placidly on his chair, his right hand nestled under his chin. He looked uncomfortable in the sportcoat and tie, but knew it was necessary. Several times he rose to his feet, sauntered down the sidelines, cupped his hands over his mouth, and hollered out a play or an encouraging word.

Bird's coaching philosophy most resembled that of Bill Fitch, current Los Angeles Clippers skipper and his mentor during four seasons with the Celtics beginning in 1979. Though he learned from observing many coaches, and watched game after game on television or tape, Bird always came back to the lessons he learned from Fitch. "He always sticks out in my mind," Bird explained. "Bill was a special coach, my first one in the NBA. He watched a lot of film and knew what was going on. Bill Fitch was by far the best I've ever seen. Still is."

Like Fitch, Bird wanted to mold his players into a cohesive unit and let them play. "I'm going to sit down and keep my mouth shut," he explained during the preseason. "A lot of coaches try to coach too much. Prepare the players, get them in good shape, tell them what you expect, and then stay back and let them play."

During the timeouts at New Jersey, the players gathered around him in awe as if in a classroom where the teacher was pointing out important lessons to be read in a book. "Sometimes I have to tell myself it's real," Miller had said in the preseason. "That Larry Bird is really my coach."

The coach's voice was never raised, except when the blasting sounds of dance music threatened to drown it out. During timeouts, Bird normally stood facing the Pacers bench, Rick Carlisle to his left, Dick Harter to his right. The two assistants jabbered back and forth, Carlisle making reference to his ever-present notebook. Bird listened intently, hands in his pockets, scratching his ear or tugging at his tie, until they were through. Then Bird made his way to the chair that trainer David Craig placed in front of the players, sat down, and listened while Carlisle diagrammed plays and Harter explained defensive assignments.

Moments later, Bird sent his charges back to the floor with words of wisdom that David Craig believed were most profound. "Larry usually had a different twist to what Dick and Rick said," Craig explained. "Something a little different, tips about the timing of a play, or where a player needed to be positioned. Sometimes he'd suggest which side to force a player to on defense or why it was important to hold the ball a bit longer to let a play develop."

During the game, Bird would call out the name of a replacement player while rubbing his nose or cracking his neck. From time to time, he'd glance upward toward the scoreboard above him, or simply watch the flow of the game. Many times it looked like he was simply a fan, though the Bird mind was hard at work

By relying so heavily on Carlisle and Harter, Bird had in effect introduced the concept of coaching specialization to the NBA. Like NFL coaches, Bird had Carlisle, his offensive coordinator, and Harter, his defensive one. Bird still had final say, but his delegation of responsibility, especially for a man who liked to be in control, emphasized his belief in his assistant coaches.

The laid-back nature of Bird's relationship with the Pacers was symbolic of his thoughts about the sport in general. "Basketball is basketball," Bird said. "It's a very simple game if you stick to the basics. Don't matter if you're from Kuwait or South America, it's all the same. It's just that the city guys play an uptempo, wild game, and if you're from the country, you play the way the coach tells you to play." Bird also explained, "Basketball is a simple game. Coaches make it difficult to play."

Against Golden State in the season's second game, the game *was* simple. Chris Mullin scored 12 points, Rik Smits 23, and Reggie 33. The Pacers waltzed to 96–83 win over the hapless Warriors, led by Latrell Sprewell, the best player on a bad team, who had 25.

Smits's performance was especially encouraging, for the big fellow was crucial to any potential Pacers success. He had followed an 18-point, 10-rebound night in New Jersey with 23 and 13 against Golden State. "Rik has played great," Reggie Miller said. "Teams expect to double-team Rik, and we have the shooters who can open things up for him."

The key to Smits's early success was his feet. The new model shoe Nike had sent him didn't feel right, so he reverted to wearing his old black ones in practice. "They feel much better," he proclaimed. "Much easier to get around." According to an archaic league rule, all players on a team had to wear the same shoe—which meant team officials had to scurry around, contact Nike, and try to find the old model in white, size 21, that Smits could wear. Fortunately, 20 pairs of the outdated white shoes were located, shipped to a shoemaker in Vincennes, Indiana, and customized for the big guy to wear.

The fact that Bird's first win as an NBA coach came against Golden State was ironic. On January 2, 1981, the Warriors defensive ace Larry Smith had guarded Bird and held him scoreless (0 of 9 attempted shots) for the only time in his career.

One and one for the season, the Pacers ventured to Cleveland to take on the new-look Cavaliers, who sported Shawn Kemp, the former wunderkind from the streets of Elkhart, Indiana. He had a new supporting cast as well, including Wesley Person and Zydrunas Ilgauskas, a towering 7'3", 260-pound behemoth from Lithuania.

Mike Fratello's squad nearly blew the game open, taking a 17-point lead, but mistakes in the final few minutes made the game close. The Pacers, led by Reggie's 21 points, closed to within one point—but Travis Best inexplicably failed to foul rookie Brevin Knight as he whizzed by to the basket. His jumper with 4.9 seconds to play meant Indiana needed a three-pointer to tie.

Miller was the designated gunner, but the Pacers moved the ball poorly from out of bounds, and all he could manage was a desperation, no-chance heave from midcourt. The miss meant an 80–77 loss, and Bird was not happy. "We should have gotten a much better shot than that," the coach explained, his disappointed face looking downward as he spoke.

Besides being displeased with Travis Best's mental lapse and the final shot selection, Bird knew that the real reason for the defeat was the poor play of Rik Smits. Ilgauskas clearly outplayed the veteran, something Bird hadn't counted on.

The big fellow was back on the beam in the Pacers' fourth game, played in Auburn Hills, Michigan, against Doug Collins's Detroit Pistons. The Dutchman scored 12 of his team-high 25 points in the fourth quarter, even though he was saddled with five fouls midway through the third. "With Rik's feet [problems], he really tightens up if he sits for more than a couple of minutes at a time," Bird said after the game. "Because of his injuries, you never know what you're going to get out of him, but he's a big guy who can shoot, and I decided to roll the dice."

Bird's hunch had proven correct, but Smits had plenty of support. Mullin scored 18, Reggie 14, and Detroit-area native Jalen Rose chipped in with 12 for the hometown fans in his finest performance in a Pacers uniform. The result was a 99–87 thank-you-very-much win on the road, despite Grant Hill's 29 points.

As pleased as Bird was with the win against Detroit, he was disappointed with yet another disastrous performance at crunch time in the next game against Seattle. Shawn Kemp was gone, but the Sonics had added Vin Baker, who meshed with Gary Payton, Detlef Schrempf, and Hersey Hawkins to create a formidable offense. The glaring error was an errant inbounds pass stolen by Gary Payton's quick hands with the score tied and only 23.4 seconds on the clock. Payton's game-cinching layup was the difference, though the final score was 99–93.

A trip to Charlotte resulted in their fourth loss of the young season, dropping the Pacers two games under .500. The Hornets, led by Vlade Divac and Glen Rice (voted by his peers to be the finest pure shooter in the league), nipped the Pacers 89–82 in a game that was close from the opening buzzer.

The loss clearly upset Bird, whose temper tantrum after the

game (his only one all season) exposed a side of the coach his players hadn't seen before. Falling to 2–4 could do that to a coach who was used to winning, especially close games. "We've got to play better in the last minute or so," he explained, realizing his team hadn't come ready to play. "Or it's going to be a long season."

Besides the losses, Larry Bird was upset about something else: the constant crybaby attitude employed by some of his players in dealing with NBA officials. The main culprit was Reggie Miller, known throughout the league as the number-one complainer to the men (and now, two women) who wielded the whistles. During the first six games, Miller's immature attitude had been accentuated. In the final minutes of the Seattle loss, he stomped his feet and jumped up and down several times like a spoiled brat. When he felt an official had missed a call, he glared at the referees, who ignored him.

Finally, Bird had had enough. Throughout his playing career, the Celtic great was known as a prolific trash-talker, but he never acted stupidly with the referees. After watching Reggie's annoying display through six games, the Pacers coach knew it was time for a heart-to-heart. "When you're reacting to officials' calls, you're not getting back on defense and going about your business," Bird explained. "If you look at the film, Reggie's arguing and not getting back, and that's costing us a number of points."

Bird knew of what he spoke. "It's the Kevin McHale syndrome. He always did that. What a player needs to do is wait until play has stopped, and then say what he wants to. Otherwise, if he hesitates and starts to call out, the other player is off and running toward the basket."

And how did Reggie react to the coach's orders to take it easy? Did he agree that his behavior was not only embarrassing to Bird and fellow players, but more importantly, caused officials to give the close calls to the opponent? "You don't want to show up the officials," Reggie commented. "Then you get no calls. If Larry wants to get on the officials, then fine, I'll just go out and score my 30 and help us win."

Bird was even more concerned about how Reggie's outbursts hurt his overall play. Twice in the final minutes of the Seattle loss,

Miller made ill-conceived passes to Rik Smits. "Anytime you're worrying about the officials, that takes away from your game," Bird said.

Miller's behavior was noticeably subdued against the high-flying Atlanta Hawks. He scored his 30 points, but it wasn't enough, and Lenny Wilkens's team made the Pacers their eighth straight victim of the 1997–98 season. The final deficit was three, a familiar story—once again, the Pacers folded in the final seconds of the game like a gambler on an unlucky streak. Permitting Atlanta an 8–0 run in the last three minutes was bad enough, but a crucial mental error involving loss of temper spelled doom. Atlanta led 83–82 when Travis Best committed the unpardonable sin. Upset with an official's call when Mookie Blaylock, who along with Dikembe Mutombo and Steve Smith totaled 64 points, deflected a pass off him out of bounds, Best used a certain no-no word that cost him a technical, and the game was history.

Bird couldn't believe his eyes. "I don't know what to say," he said, measuring his words carefully. "These guys have to get their emotions under control." The photo of Bird in the next day's newspapers said it all. It showed Larry looking downward, his hands covering his face, as if he was thinking, "Oh, no, not again."

A 2–5 record with losses coming by a total of 24 points meant Bird and the Pacers were gaining a reputation as chokers at clutch time. Keep the game close, and the Pacers will disintegrate, other teams realized. That reputation wasn't what the rookie coach had in mind for his team. Known for wanting the ball and doing something with it during the final few minutes of a game, the legendary player hoped some of his magic would rub off on his players. He had a three-year contract to coach Indiana, but Bird wasn't sure he'd make it through the first one unless his players started turning things around.

Hoping to end a three-game losing streak, the Pacers entertained Pat Riley and the Miami Heat, the overachievers of the previous season. Though Bird spoke fondly of Bill Fitch, Riley was the coach he most admired in the NBA. To that end, Bird had watched the former Los Angeles Lakers mentor closely during Bird's sabbatical from competition after retirement on August 18, 1992. "He adapts to any situation," Bird observed quite succinctly. "That's what impresses me."

Desperately needing a victory, the Pacers finally won when Mark Jackson returned to the form that had made him the league assist leader. He took control early, dividing his time between scoring, rebounding, and feeding his teammates while encouraging them at every turn. He also put the clamps on the Heat's Tim Hardaway, holding him to 12 points. Bird was ecstatic with Jackson's total effort. "He really came to play tonight," the coach said. "Mark's got to step up his game if we're going to find a way to win." Reggie Miller added 17 points to the victory and, better still, kept his mouth shut. Smits had 17, including 3 of 4 from the foul line after a shooting tip from you-know-who. "Coach Bird told me to quit practicing my shooting on the side goals," Smits admitted. "And that seems to have helped." Jalen Rose thought the Miami win was pivotal, telling reporters, "When you're starving, a cracker tastes like a steak."

To pull within one game of .500 for the season, the Pacers needed to beat Toronto on the Raptors home court. And they did, 105–77—playing good defense, rebounding, pushing the ball up the court, and shooting with accuracy. Chris Mullin's shooting touch produced 9 baskets in 11 attempts and 20 points, while Smits added 19 in just 24 minutes of play. Best of all, Jalen Rose (12 points), Fred Hoiberg (11), and Antonio Davis (10) came off the bench with stellar performances.

The coach was ecstatic. "It was beautiful basketball," he said. "Extra passes, good rebounding, good defense. That's the way the game should be played." Chris Mullin saw it another way. "Good rhythm," he told reporters. "That's what made the difference. . . . It's about learning with each other and getting in sync. We may be getting there." Rik Smits wanted to play in the big-as-all-outdoors Sky Dome every night. "I like these great big arenas," the tall Dutchman said. "I get claustrophobic in the little ones."

Four days after recording their fourth win, the Pacers made it three in a row with a 109–83 blowout in Milwaukee. Where did their 5–5 record place them in the Central Division? In the middle of the pack, five games behind the still undefeated Atlanta Hawks, whose 11–0 start had brought them within four games of the league mark shared by Washington (1948) and Houston (1993).

Atlanta's pursuit of perfection was matched by the Lakers, who rolled off nine consecutive victories. Shaquille O'Neal, named NBA Player of the Week, was terrifying defenses with strong inside play and receiving ample support from Robert Horry, Nick Van Exel, Eddie Jones, and Kobe Bryant.

Despite the play of the elite teams, Bird, calm and confident, seemed satisfied with his team's mark. "I still like our chances," he insisted. "We're a step slow, but we're working hard. Derrick McKey's return will help. I've got to settle on 9, 10 players who are going to get the minutes. Once we do that, we'll be all right."

Observers thought Bird's assessment was accurate, but wondered whether the Pacers were much more than a .500 ball club. "Bird seems to have them playing well together, but a veteran team like that makes too many mistakes," an opposing assistant coach said. "Reggie's still a hot dog, Mullin's slow as molasses, and Smits is Smits. Some night's he's a factor, others he disappears. Bird still hasn't shown me he can do any more with this team than Larry Brown did. Against the fast-paced teams like Atlanta, the Lakers, Charlotte, and Phoenix, they're going to get blitzed." Asked to assess Bird's coaching ability, the rival coach, who requested anonymity, said, "Larry seems to handle it well, though I'd question his substitution patterns a bit. And his inability to keep Reggie away from the officials is unpardonable. My question is whether Bird is tough enough to be a coach. He wants everybody to like him, but you don't win in the NBA by being a big brother."

Pacers players said they'd enjoyed the first few games under their new coach. "He's a lot more relaxed than coaches I've had in the past," Reggie Miller said. "Larry Brown was direct, a screamer, but Coach Bird is more subdued. You can tell when he's disappointed by his facial expressions. He doesn't have to say a whole lot."

Handling the losses, especially ones where the Pacers choked during the critical final minutes of the game, was difficult for Bird, but he was coping. "When I was a player, I'd watch tape and see where I broke down," Larry said. "See if I came off picks hard, was I trying to set up other people, all of that. Now I watch the players out there, and I pick up things I know we need to work on. I know exactly what's going on, so the players can't fool me."

True to that notion, Bird had been patient, tolerant, and willing to understand the faults of the Pacers—asking only that they be in shape, be on time, and come to play every night. And he was direct. "If guys can't give me 30 minutes a night, then they need to find another profession."

Donnie Walsh believed Bird was on the right track. "I'm even more convinced that he's going to be a great coach," Larry's boss said. "He's gone through some rough spots, but he's dealing with things. That's what's been impressive."

6

BOBBY'S LAMENT

*"A player can't believe in himself if he thinks his coach
doesn't believe in him. If you don't think a guy can play,
it's better to get rid of him than to bury him on the bench,
or scream at him in front of everybody."*
LARRY BIRD

Did Larry Bird leave Indiana University after only 24 days because he couldn't stand Bobby Knight? That question has lingered in the air since 1974, when the promising youth from French Lick called his uncle Amon Kerns from Bloomington and said, "Come get me. I want to come home."

Through the years, different versions of the story have been bandied about. In his autobiography *Drive*, written with veteran sportswriter Bob Ryan, Bird wrote, "I wasn't ready for a school the size of Indiana University. There were too many students. One classroom could have held half of West Baden—or so it seemed to me. Thirty-three thousand students was not my idea of a school— it was more like a whole country to me."

Besides feeling overwhelmed at IU, Bird had financial limitations. "I had no money," he wrote. "I mean *no* money. I arrived there with $75. Knight had me room with Jim Wisman, who was a very worldly 17-year-old kid—just the opposite of me." Larry Bird found himself a beggar. "I had virtually no clothes," he explained. "All I had was five or six pairs of jeans, a couple of slacks, a few shirts, some T-shirts, and my tennis shoes. I didn't even have a sportcoat or a pair of dress shoes."

The answer was to borrow from Wisman, who was the son of a postal carrier and certainly not well-to-do himself. But to Bird, he seemed like a millionaire. "I ended up wearing all of his clothes," Bird recalled. "He also gave me money when I needed it. I said to myself, 'How can I keep wearing Jim Wisman's clothes and accepting Jim Wisman's money?' "

The fact that Bird stayed even as long as three weeks on the Bloomington campus surprised his mother Georgia. "He called right after he got there," she told friends. "He was homesick. Wanted to come home. I tried to talk him out of it, but I finally couldn't."

Georgia recognized problems from the outset. "Larry was too young to go away to school," she said. ". . . the day Bobby Knight came to the house to get me to sign that paper [entrance forms], I had to bite my tongue to keep from telling him, 'Why don't you leave him alone. He doesn't want to go to school.' "

Larry's mother wasn't disappointed with her son's decision to leave Indiana University. "Bobby Knight doesn't recruit the boys for what they can do," she said. "He molds them into what he wants. I don't think that would have ever worked for Larry. I think he would have ruined him."

Bird says any mention that he and the bombastic Knight didn't get along is pure poppycock. "I just was never happy there," is his standard version. "Coach Knight had nothing to do with it. Everything was just so big. Even the halls where my classes were held. I couldn't even hear the teachers. I got lost in the shuffle. I like to be around small groups of people and there were so many times I didn't know where I was going." Later, he added: "I love Bobby Knight. I think he's the best coach in the nation. . . . He can be a little rough on his players. But if you can put up with that for four years, he'll make you a better player. . . . He'd have loved my game."

If feeling out of place, broke, socially inept, and confused weren't bad enough, the young freshman also knew he would have a rough season ahead under Knight, the fiery one. Long after Bird left IU, Knight refused to acknowledge that his leaving had anything to do with his tough discipline. One rumor circulated that

Bird left after Knight threw a trash can at him. Knight just laughed when he heard that. "He was a very promising player and I hated to see him leave," the coach recalled. "But he was from a small town, and he just couldn't handle it."

In 1997, Knight was quoted as saying, "I loved Larry Bird as a player. I recruited him over some guys who had much better reputations at the time, and one of my few coaching regrets is that for very personal reasons he didn't play his college years at Indiana. I can say this with all honesty; of all the guys we never put a uniform on, there's nobody I would have rather had than Larry Bird."

The truth of the matter was somewhere in between what Bird said and the General's proclamations, but no one contested the opinion that the young man was mesmerized by Knight. "He looked at the coach like he was a father figure," Springs Valley coach Jim Jones recalled. "When Bobby said, 'If you're deciding between Indiana and Indiana State, then you don't belong at Indiana.' That really made Larry want to go to IU."

Bird left school before practice began without informing Knight of his decision. While there, he witnessed two incidents involving the General that he would never forget. Apparently Bird and other team members were scrimmaging in a pickup game when suddenly they were aware Knight had entered the arena. "We're out there playing," Bird wrote in *Drive*, and I am moving without the ball—I'm moving, I'm cutting, I'm rebounding and doing everything. I make a nice backdoor cut and get open—and Jim Crews— he's now the coach at Evansville—misses me."

What happened next left a deep impression on Bird. "Suddenly you hear his voice," Bird explained. "*His* voice. . . . He stopped the game. He came down and started yelling at the top of his lungs. I can tell you it wasn't me he was yelling at." Bird used that example to indicate that Knight appreciated his true basketball skills, but it also emphasized what the 17-year-old believed he had in store for him when the season started. After playing for nice-guy coaches like Jones and Holland, Bird realized playing for Knight would be far different.

Janet Condra, Bird's girlfriend at the time, believed another incident was even more instrumental in his decision to leave IU.

While dining at a restaurant in Bloomington, the two were shocked to see Coach Knight walk in. "Larry spoke to the coach," Janet recalled, "but Knight just ignored him, and it just crushed him."

Years later, Knight reflected on the situation. "We were right in the midst of having a good basketball team, maybe the best ever. I wouldn't chase Buckner. I wouldn't chase Scott May. Well, I'd be damned if I was going to chase *this* kid. If it were to happen today, I would talk to him. I'd tell him what a mistake he was making, that Indiana was far and away the best place for him. . . . I'm older now. It was a mistake that I didn't do it then."

Bird said that leaving school was a big step for him. "That was the first extremely important decision I had ever made for myself," he said. "And I was sticking with it. I knew everybody would be angry with me when I made it . . . , but I didn't care."

If Bird was to be believed, Bob Knight wasn't the problem, but that didn't mean he felt the same way about fellow players on the IU basketball team. In his autobiography, Bird chastised one in particular. "Kent Benson can be a nice guy, but, point blank, he treated me terribly," he wrote. "He treated us freshmen as if we were idiots. . . . [He] came down one day while I was shooting and just took my ball and went to the other end to shoot. He'd say, 'You freshmen don't deserve a ball.' [He] would pull this stuff about every day." Bird also said Benson wouldn't let him play in pickup games. "When they chose sides, we'd never play," Bird wrote. "Wisman [Jim] and Radford [Wayne] were the ones who always sat out . . . Benson continued to treat me like a jerk, like I was nothing."

Kent Benson, the Most Valuable Player in the 1976 NCAA tournament—which the Hoosiers won, capping an undefeated 32–0 season—saw things differently. "I have no idea why he says that," Benson explained in 1998. "Why can't he be honest with himself? All that never happened. Why does he make up lies like that? The truth is that Scott May and Tom Abernathy [fellow members of the championship team] ate his lunch. He simply couldn't compete with them and he got discouraged and went home. He was only there three weeks."

Hearing Bird's accusations through the years left Benson with a sour taste in his mouth. "My character speaks for itself," he said. "And I helped Coach Knight recruit him, so why would I want to beat him up? I have no respect anymore for Larry as a person, but I do respect his ability as a player. I just don't understand why he keeps saying those things about me."

Backing up Benson's version was Brad Winters, a student manager for the Hoosiers at the time. "I was in the gym and watched Bird and Benson play against each other," Winters said. "I never saw anything of what Larry says happened. Shoot, Larry was only there a couple of weeks."

Bird's obsession with getting even with Benson continued in the NBA. Five years after they allegedly tangled in Bloomington, Bird said he relished seeing Benson get his comeuppance. In a game against Benson's Detroit Bucks (Benson was the first player chosen in the 1976 draft), Kevin McHale set the Celtics scoring record of 56 points. ". . . Benson was guarding him," Bird recalled. "[He] got so frustrated in the third period that he picked up two quick T's and then got ejected."

While Bird's friends swear Uncle Amon drove to Bloomington and took him to West Baden after Larry had spent just 24 days at IU, Bird remembered it differently. In *Drive*, he wrote, "I walked out to Highway 37 and hitchhiked. I figured I could catch a ride from someone heading back in my direction. A man picked me up in a truck and left me off in Mitchell and eventually I got home."

The mythical persona of Larry Bird began to grow shortly after he returned home to French Lick. His mother Georgia persuaded him to enroll at Northwood, a junior college located in West Baden. But when the family found out that if he played even one basketball game, he'd have to stay two years before returning to a major university, he withdrew. "Besides," the still confident dropout said, "I practiced with the team for a couple of days before realizing there wasn't enough competition and I didn't belong there either."

The legend was embellished when he became a worker for French Lick's Department of Sanitation. He drove a garbage truck, stenciled in "No Parking" signs in the appropriate spots, assisted with repairing potholes in the streets, and worked with the snow removal crew. Friend Beezer Carnes said he and Bird "painted benches, picked up trash, and unplugged sewers." He added, "Larry really enjoyed working on the garbage truck, claiming it was the best job he ever had." "I was making about $140 to $150 a week, and I was happy," Bird remembered. "I was able to save some money. I bought my first car, a 1964 Chevy. It was a piece of junk, but that was all right."

All the while, the boy wonder was playing basketball and scorching the nets. He totaled 39 points for an AAU team that beat the Indiana All-Stars. Headlines like "Larry Bird Still Flies High" appeared when his AAU team won several tournaments. Bird's Hancock Construction squad made it to the finals in Des Moines, Iowa; and although they lost to Detroit in the championship game, Bird scored 34 points and grabbed 35 rebounds. "Our offense," coach Chuck Akers explained, "was to give it to Larry and get everyone out of the way."

Despite putting up big numbers on the board, Bird was in turmoil. Passionate fans in French Lick thought he should be playing for Northwood College. Others believed he had failed Indiana University, letting everyone down, and should return there. Townspeople recalled residents crossing the street to avoid speaking to Bird. Small-town gossip criticized him, and he retreated from public view.

For a time Bird wanted to just forget college and keep working, but coaches from near and far weren't about to let that happen. Bird's play in AAU games only heightened their interest, and they were determined to convince him to re-enter school in the fall of 1975.

Indiana State assistant coach Bill Hodges was one of them. He became especially convinced after visiting French Lick to watch Bird play an evening exhibition game between the Indiana All-Stars and Larry's independent team. "[Hodges] came down to French Lick and found me putting up some hay," Bird said. "It took us all day to do it and it was a hot day—must have been 90 degrees. When I finished, I was heading right over to play a game." And quite a game it was. "He's a farmer himself," Bird remembered. "He knows how tough loading that hay is. . . . He thought I would be too tired to play. I scored 43 points and got 25 rebounds before fouling out, and we beat that All-Star team."

After that, Hodges continually made the trip from Terre Haute, 90 minutes by car northwest of Bloomington, to watch Bird play. When spring rolled around, he stood at the doorstep of Bird's home, only to be chastised by Momma Bird. "Why don't all of you college coaches leave Larry alone?" Georgia barked. "He doesn't want to see any of you."

Dismayed but not defeated, Hodges, at whom Georgia had once become so upset that she slammed a car door in his face, drove around French Lick looking for the gangly lad with blonde hair. He wasn't at any of the playgrounds, nor the school gym—and just when he was about to give up, he spotted Larry, not with a basketball, but a basket full of laundry. Making a U-turn, he drove up to a laundromat located on Highway 56, which ran through both French Lick and West Baden. Sensing the hand of fate, Hodges wheeled up beside Bird and introduced himself and fellow assistant coach Stan Evans. Larry gave the two a perfunctory hello, helped his mother into his car, and agreed to meet the coaches at his house to talk.

Once inside the car with his mother, however, he said, "When we get home, you get out and go on in. Then I'll leave and not come back until they leave." Her stern look told Larry immediately he'd said the wrong thing. "I didn't raise you this way," she said in no uncertain terms. "You told those men you'd meet with them, and a promise is a promise."

Bill Hodges had his chance, and he didn't waste it. He and Larry hit it off, and Bird agreed to meet with Indiana State head coach Bob King. When Hodges and Evans left, Georgia told Larry he had a God-given talent for playing and that he shouldn't waste it. She added something even more important to Larry. "Your dad thought ISU was the right school all along," Georgia said. "Right from the beginning."

Another visit to French Lick from Hodges led to Bird visiting the campus in Terre Haute. He had told Hodges that Kevin Carnes, a Springs Valley player, was right for the Indiana State team. "Come on up and we'll put you guys through a scrimmage with our players and see how he looks," Hodges said. "That's fair enough," Bird replied. "I'll come up."

Prior to the scrimmage, Hodges told the boys to suit up in shorts. "We're in jeans, T-shirts, and tennis shoes—our usual attire," Bird explained. "We get there and Hodges says, 'Come on back to the locker room and we'll get you some shorts.' We never played in shorts back home. We said, 'We're fine. We'll play with what we've got.'" Hodges was horrified. "This is crazy," he said.

The "game" was no contest. "They gave us Jimmy Smith and some itty-bitty guy, John-something, to go along with Mark [brother], Kevin, and myself. . . . We played three games and we beat them every time. We drilled them. No contest. Hodges couldn't believe it. . . ."

In addition to the pickup games that followed, Bird liked the small nature of the campus and the personality of head coach Bob King, a true players' coach. By the time summer rolled around, he had relocated to Terre Haute in readiness for a fall filled with basketball. "Bill Hodges won out," Bird said later, "because he was so persistent. I'd seen 50 to 60 recruiters by then, and heard all the b. s. But he'd go to one member of the family and be told to get lost, and then he'd go to another. I got tired of seein' the guy, and decided to go to ISU."

The 20th-century Huckleberry Finn sat out his first year at Indiana State as a redshirt. The Sycamore team was a good one, but the players and Coach King knew that their best player could only compete in practice. As the "star player" on the opposing team, Bird would lead his "white" team to victory over the regular "blue" team nearly every night. Concerned that his starting five were becoming demoralized because they couldn't win a game,

King finally sat Bird down. That nearly lost him his star-to-be player.

"That's it," Bird told King. "I quit." King followed him to the locker room, where Bird continued his tirade. "Hey, if you're not going to let me practice, what am I going to do? These practices are my *games*. All I want to do is play basketball." Coach King's explanation was simple. "Look, Larry, I can't get anything done with these other guys," he said. "They're scared to death of you. You make them look like idiots. Now how are they going to go out and play a game?"

"When Coach King put it that way," Bird recalled, "I realized it was a different matter." He stayed in school.

Though he never played a game during that first season, Bird left indelible memories with those who watched practice. "There were just a few seconds on the clock in a scrimmage when Larry picked up the ball with his left hand on the other team's baseline," assistant trainer Rick Shaw recalled. "He took a quick look at the clock, and heaved the ball the full length of the court, left-handed. Janis Ludek, a forward on the team, was standing down there, and the ball looked like it went right through his hands into the basket. Both teams ended up on the floor laughing. Larry just never gave up."

Bird was the dominant player in a drill King set up to see who was his toughest player. At the end of practice, a ball was rolled on the floor and two players raced for it. Whoever retrieved it tried to score. If he scored, he headed for the locker room. If not, it was back in line to repeat the drill. Rarely did Bird ever have to get back in line.

Larry Bird spent 90 percent of his time playing basketball during his first year at Indiana State, but he did have other things on his mind as well. On November 8, 1975, he married Janet Condra, but the relationship was doomed from the beginning. "I knew right away it wasn't going to work," Bird said. "I tried to make it work, but there was just no way."

The couple realized divorce was the only answer. Shortly after it was final, they tried to reconcile, but it didn't work. During that time, Janet, who was as introverted as Larry, became pregnant with Corrie Diane. Bird ignored his responsibility and began a new relationship with Dinah Mattingly, a longtime friend. "I noticed more and more how special she really was," Bird said. "We always had a blast together and laughed a lot."

The friendship quickly blossomed into a great deal more, and later Dinah became Larry's wife. "I began to fall in love with Dinah," Bird recalled. "I realized she was the one. She was perfect for me. She was beautiful, athletic, understanding, funny, and my friend." More importantly, Dinah loved basketball. "Dinah would rebound for me for hours in the gym," Larry said, "when I'm sure she would have rather been doing something else."

Through the years, though happy in his new relationship, Bird often chastised himself for not being around during the early years of Corrie's life. "To tell the truth, I've really never known how to handle the situation," Bird lamented in 1989. "But I love her and anytime Corrie needs anything, I will be there for her."

That didn't prove to be the case a few years later. Despite two letters from his daughter requesting permission to attend the retirement ceremony for his jersey in Boston, Bird ignored Corrie. "He invited the whole family," Tom Newlin, a Terre Haute attorney recalled. "But not Corrie. Many of Larry's friends didn't care much for that, but it was his business."

———————

Bird's first officially NCAA-sanctioned exhibition game was played against the Brazilian National Team. The Sycamores prevailed, with Larry ringing up 31 points for the victors. When the season officially opened against Chicago State, Bird duplicated his 31-point total, and also added 18 rebounds. Less than 3,000 fans filed into the Hulman Center that evening, but word quickly spread that Indiana State had a player worth the price of admission.

"Birdwatching" became fashionable as the Sycamores piled up victory after victory. With Bird driving the team, they finished the season with 25 wins and just 2 losses, to Purdue and Illinois State. Slogans such as "ISU is going to give you the Bird" began appearing, as did a song called, "Indiana Has a New State Bird."

The hometown Illinois State fans made their game memorable against archrival Indiana State. But Bird answered their cries of "Birdshit" with 40 big ones, even though the Sycamores fell flat in the final minutes and lost 70–64. A maturing Bird showed restraint with his temper. When he fell after being pushed out of bounds, an ignorant fan started screaming inches from his face. Bird slowly rose to his feet, walked away without a word, and calmly stroked two free throws. Quite a change from the freshman in high school with a temper that went from ignite to fully lit in seconds.

Against intrastate rival Purdue, Bird had a bout of insecurity. "I had about 28 points and 15 rebounds," he recalled. "But I felt a step slow against that level of competition. After that game, I said, 'Why am I backing off, when I should be going straight ahead?'"

Bird's first national exposure came when he and the Sycamores were extended an invitation to play in the National Invitational Tournament (NIT). Matched against future NBA star Otis Birdsong of the Houston Cougars in what the media dubbed "The Battle of the Birds," Larry kicked in 44 points (Birdsong had 30), but his last-second shot rimmed out and Houston won 83–82 to advance to the finals in New York.

All told, Larry's sophomore season at Indiana State was a success. His 32.4 points per game ranked third in the NCAA, and he was seventh in rebounds. Bob Knight ruefully told a friend, "Maybe I should have paid a little more attention to Bird. Made him feel more at home."

Rumors began to swirl about whether Larry would forgo his final two seasons at ISU and turn professional. Georgia, ever the pragmatic one, argued against it. "Money isn't everything," she told a reporter. ". . . [Larry] has two years in school and I'd like to see him stay."

Bird agreed. He was proud of his accomplishments, especially when a postseason honor came his way. "I called my uncle. Here

I had gone from being a high school player who had dropped out of college to a guy who made third-team All-American in his first year. That meant a lot to me."

Between his sophomore and junior years, Larry was asked to try out for the United States Basketball Team, scheduled to travel to Sofia, Bulgaria, for the World University games. The coach was Denny Crum, and anyone who could beat him at H-O-R-S-E, as Bird had done, could be on his team. Though much of the press in Europe dubbed him "Byrd," Larry played well. Exhibition games in Rome and Yugoslavia preceded matches against Belgium, Kuwait, Cuba, and Poland before the squad won the world title by beating the Soviet Union.

The trip marked Larry's first visit to foreign soil, and his impressions weren't favorable. He told his mother the places they stayed in were "dumps," and he didn't care for European women because they didn't shave their underarms or legs.

During the United States-Cuba matchup, several fights erupted. The Cuban players fought holding glass bottles in their hands. Asked by a reporter where he was at the time, Bird said, "I found the closest chair and crawled under it."

Returning home more of a celebrity than ever, Bird enjoyed seeing the "I'm a Bird Watcher" T-shirts, and hearing a tune entitled "Disco Bird" played for a time. His legend was growing as he began his junior year at Indiana State, especially after word got around that he had practiced against several Indiana Pacers veterans during the summer. "We brought a bunch of players, . . . Freddie Lewis, Roger Brown, and Bob Netolicky to Terre Haute to scrimmage against Bird," Sycamores assistant coach Mel Daniels recalled. "Larry dominated them all."

Coach Bob King knew greatness was ahead for his talented player. "He had the ability to turn a [college] program around all by himself," King recalled. "The key was his hands. He's naturally left-handed, even though he shoots with his right." Harry Morgan, a teammate of Bird's at the time, said, "He's got such a great all-around game. He makes things happen. If he sees you open, he'll get you the ball. And I've learned a lot from Larry as far as scoring goes. He takes his time and just puts it in the hole."

OFF AND RUNNING

"If you're going to play for me, you better be in shape.
The Pacers will all be in the best shape of their lives
or they won't be around."
LARRY BIRD

Beginning with opening night, when the Boston Celtics dumped the defending world champion Chicago Bulls, the NBA season had been an eventful one. Without injured Scottie Pippen, Phil Jackson's club appeared vulnerable.

That didn't mean Michael Jordan, one of the select few athletes to be known instantly by his first name, hadn't done his best to singlehandedly keep the Bulls above water. Despite being double-teamed nearly every time he bounced the ball, and struggling with a shooting touch that was less than stellar, Jordan—who wore his North Carolina shorts under his Bulls uniform for good luck—played at a level that few had ever known. "He's still the best ballplayer who ever lived," Charles Barkley expounded. "And nobody is a close second."

Of the wage-earners in the NBA, Michael was king. For his play during the 1997–98 season, he'd pull down a paltry $33 million in salary alone, plus endorsements. That was in contrast to teammate Scottie Pippen, who earned $3 million-plus and had to reconcile himself to waiting for the big money when he reached free-agent status following the season.

Though Pippen was a critical piece of the Bulls puzzle, a game against the lowly Clippers in late November symbolized what Jordan meant to Chicago on the court. His team down by two with just seconds to play, the great scorer had two free throws to tie the game. He uncharacteristically missed the first, then faced the prospect of making the second with no time to get the ball back and score again. Standing at the line, Jordan's face bore a sly cat-ate-the-canary-grin as he wiped the sweat off his brow. In a split-second decision shared with no one, he took careful aim, and then tilted the ball in his hands just slightly. The resulting shot careened off the left side of the rim and bounded toward the corner. The big guys on both teams jumped in vain, swiping for the ball, but it bounced toward Jordan, who had raced to the proper spot with split-second timing after his release. Clutching the rebound in his giant hands, he pivoted, surprised the would-be defenders by slicing through the lane, and scored an easy layup off the glass to tie the score. While the Bulls bench, including Scottie Pippen in street clothes, cheered the superhuman effort, the Clippers—on the brink of upsetting the world champions—walked back to their bench, their heads lowered in disappointment.

In the overtime, Michael dominated and the Bulls coasted to an 11-point win. He finished the evening a point shy of 50 and left Clippers fans in shock. Mr. Jordan had performed his magic once again, and the mere mortals of the game were left to lick their wounds.

Of the high-priced players positioned just behind Jordan, Patrick Ewing, at $20 million-plus, was the only one within shouting distance. Then came Orlando's Horace Grant, overpaid at $14 million; and Shaquille O'Neal, a.k.a. "The Diesel," and David Robinson, a.k.a. "The Admiral," who were paid $12 million–plus by the Lakers and Spurs respectively.

For the Indiana Pacers, Miller ($9,031,850), Dale Davis ($5,273,333), and Antonio Davis ($4,500,000) made as much as or more than Larry Bird earned to coach the team. Rik Smits checked in at $4 million, Derrick McKey $3.6, Mark Jackson $3.2, Chris Mullin just under $3, Jalen Rose $1.85, Haywoode Workman $1,260,000, and rookie Austin Croshere $1,165,000. Indiana's payroll was just shy of $40 million, only a few million more than Michael made by himself, and $20 million less than the entire Chicago Bulls team. The Pacers payout ranked sixth in the league, trailing the Bulls, Knicks, Magic, Spurs, and Wizards.

———————

Over the next 15 games, the Pacers strove to prove they were a viable team worthy of consideration with the best in the league. During a time when the Lakers, Heat, and Sonics were flexing their muscles; troubled Portland Trail Blazer Isaiah Rider was fined for spitting at an official; and the NBA's so-called "fashion patrol" fined members of the Timberwolves and Blazers for wearing shorts that hung more than an inch below the knee, a three-game winning streak propelled Indiana to a .500 record that had been marked not only by improved play down the stretch, but also by solid defense. Dubbed one the NBA's slow-footed teams, even by their own coach, Indiana had blunted that deficiency with what assistant coach Dick Harter called *help defense*. That meant the players covered for each other when someone was out of position or was a step slow in getting back on defense. Harter, a defensive specialist whose low-key personality meshed perfectly with Bird's, was an expert in defending the sophisticated offenses in the NBA. He was a no-nonsense technician who had earned a reputation for developing defensive plans filled with imagination. Realizing Indiana didn't have the quickness to compete in a horse race with other teams, Bird had Harter weave a plan that would put the stops on other clubs. Phil Jackson took one look and called it a "sink defense."

After 10 games, Harter made Bird look like a genius. The Pacers had allowed less than 87 points per game, fourth lowest in the league. The Milwaukee Bucks, the best-shooting team in the league when the Pacers met them in late November, came away with a loss on 34 percent shooting. "The key to what we do," Harter explained, "is trapping picks and rolls, attacking the ball when it gets to the low post, and trying to prevent the other team from penetrating down the lane." Benefiting from Harter's plan was Mark Jackson, who said, "You begin to get pride for stopping people. You're not an island out there, you know you're going to get help if you hang in there."

The Pacers continued to play good defense, but their next game had a familiar ring to it. When Jalen Rose and Mark Jackson each made critical mistakes in the final 30 seconds against Charlotte, the result was a 95–94 loss. First Vlade Divac stole Rose's risky inbound pass, and his free throw provided Charlotte a one-point edge. Then Rose's attempt to get the ball to Jackson for a last-second shot went through his hands as the buzzer sounded, handing Indiana its sixth loss against five wins.

"It was a tough loss, especially at home, where you want to go out and establish yourself," Bird lamented. "We took the lead and then blew it at the end." Bird wasn't pleased with his team's overall performance. "We had a couple of guys ready to play, but some others were just out there," he professed. "We were just reaching and made bad fouls." One of them, a questionable charging violation against rookie Mark Pope, resulted in another first for the first-year coach. Early in the second quarter, an official didn't agree with Bird's choice of words disputing the call, and T'd him up for the first technical foul of his professional coaching career.

Thanksgiving week was an eventful one in the basketball world. The Chicago Bulls discovered Scottie Pippen no longer wanted to play for them ("I ain't coming back," he told reporters), *Sports Illustrated* reported that two members of the Arizona State Sun Devils basketball team would be indicted in a point shaving scandal, and Houston's Hakeem Olajuwon became the latest superstar to be sidelined by injury. Meanwhile, the Pacers were playing the Vancouver Grizzlies, coached by former Orlando boss Brian Hill, followed by Chicago.

With Dee Kantner making her debut as the first female referee to officiate an NBA game at Market Square Arena, Chris Mullin, described by *Los Angeles Times* reporter Howard Cooper as one who "would just as soon surrender a kidney as go a day without hoops," made certain the Pacers regained the .500 plateau. He ran the court, true to his "gym rat" reputation, flying around, under, and through the Grizzlies—who underestimated the court savvy that made up for Mullin's lack of quickness. By game's end, Mullin totaled 27 points, and the Pacers had drowned the Grizzlies 106–85 on Thanksgiving evening before a packed house. "We got in a good rhythm," Mullin said simply.

The easy victory meant most of the Pacers regulars rested during the fourth quarter. Television announcer Clark Kellogg said the win was "low-stress." The only question left hanging was why Rik Smits, bad wheels and all, was still on the court with six minutes to go when the Pacers were up by 23.

When the Bulls, sans Pippen, skipped onto the court to play the Pacers on the 28th, electricity filled the air. Every time a team came to Market Square Arena, it seemed another milestone was set—and never was that more apparent than when Michael came to play. He and Bird had been rivals ever since Jordan had entered the league in 1984. Their head-to-head duels never quite matched Bird-Magic showtime, but comparisons nevertheless ran rampant.

When Jordan trotted onto the floor of Market Square Arena at precisely 6:23 P.M. the day after Thanksgiving, Bird was still encased in his Pacers office making final plans to test the Bulls. While other coaches had diabolical game plans to restrict Jordan, Bird had decided Miller could handle him by himself—and when he was on the bench, Jalen Rose, he of the long arms and enormous defensive potential that had never been realized, would take over the task.

During pregame warm-ups, Jordan moved about with the grace of a gazelle, gliding through layup drills. Most noticeable were his huge hands. The basketball seemed to cradle in his palm like it had been custom-fitted. When the Bulls dispersed to warm up their shooting touch, Jordan headed for the foul line, bouncing the ball once, twice, sometimes three times before flipping it in the air, catching it, and then raising his arms for a perfect launch. A jammed wrist had been a thorn recently, so he worked to find the right form that would yield consistency.

While Michael was burying a pregame turnaround jumper from the paint, Bird loped onto to the floor—and the Pacers crowd erupted. Jordan turned his head to find the source of the clamor. Realizing it was Bird, he smiled and resumed his regimen—a bounce or two with backspin, the catch, and then a pivot of the left foot that catapulted him into the air. At the top of his climb, he arched the shot, and then fell back. The ball barely ruffled the net.

For His Airness, the Pacers game marked the 863rd in regular-season competition. Throw in another 158 in the playoffs, and he had eclipsed the 1,000 mark. Few people realized that besides being the finest player in the game, Jordan was among the most durable. With the exception of the one season when he was injured, and another two when he traded his basketball togs for a baseball uniform, Jordan had played in at least 78 of 82 regular-season games each year. Seven seasons he had perfect attendance.

The last time the two giants of the game had been on the same court was in Spain as members of the 1992 original Olympic Dream Team. Now they would square off as coach versus player. A different venue, but bragging rights were still at stake.

———————

The Indiana Pacers still had 70 more games to go, but team officials, players, and especially Bird himself knew that the outcome of the game was critical. With Pippen and pure shooter Steve Kerr on the injured list, Chicago was shorthanded; and a victory for the Pacers would mean the first step over .500. A lengthy road trip loomed on the horizon, and wins over the Bulls and the 76ers, the next opponent, would bolster the team's spirits as they headed west.

From the opening tip, Michael Jordan displayed his athleticism. He sliced around defenders, faked them out of their jocks while twirling and laying the ball in the basket, and hit long-range jumpers that left the crowd oohing and aahing. But early in the second half, the *nine*-time NBA scoring champion fell and jammed his wrist. His touch disappeared, especially at the foul line, where he was an uncharacteristic 4 for 8.

The Miller versus Jordan defensive assignment was clearly won by the hometown favorite. Reggie harassed Michael at every step, keeping the Great One off-stride. When Reggie sat down, Rose did an admirable job on Jordan, and by game's end, Michael had hit just 11 of 26 shots. None of his 26 points could be labeled "all-world," though an underhanded reverse layup from behind the basket wowed the crowd. Twenty-nine more points against Washington the following night permitted Jordan to slide past Elvin Hayes into fourth place on the all-time NBA scoring list. His total of 27,361 was 77 points behind third-place Moses Malone.

Miller notched 24 points and received help from "Rosy," Rik Smits, Travis Best, and Antonio Davis. Pacers fans, worried that the team might fold down the stretch, were pleasantly surprised when they waltzed to a 94–83 win. Reggie's three-pointer with 2:31 left was a classic. Randy Brown was all over him, but Sir Reginald leaped in the air just inside the out-of-bounds line to the left of the basket, exhibiting perfect form on the follow-through as the ball scorched the net. When Jalen hit a high-arching jumper from the top of the key at the 2:07 mark, Slick Leonard began his radio version of The Fat Lady Sings. Fellow commentator Mark Boyle, the Pacers' excellent play-by-play man, cringed at the pitch of Slick's voice, but relished the win.

Bird's education as a coach was a work in progress. He showed savvy by leaving Rose in the game to defend Jordan, and his matchup of Dale Davis against Dennis Rodman was also successful. Though Bird was clearly pleased with the victory, he remained realistic, pointing to the Bulls' injuries. As always, he was a gracious winner, a characteristic he thought more important than how a player or coach dealt with a loss. Keeping an even keel, never getting too high or too low, Bird felt was a key to success—especially since there were nearly 70 games still to play.

Jordan paid tribute to the new coach after the game. "He's good for the game and it's good to have him back. We never got into the proper rhythm, but the Pacers were tough and that's a reflection of Bird's coaching." Phil Jackson, the pensive, professorial Bulls coach who had to endure inexplicable yearly battles with Chicago's management regarding his salary despite having led the team to *five* world championships, was impressed with Bird's style. "He's got them running," Jackson mused. "And playing good defense." As for his own team, the mustachioed coach added,

"The carburetor on our machine is damaged. We're moving like a Mack truck instead of a Ferrari."

Looking ahead, Bird was low-key. "Hey, we've got Philly coming in here on Sunday. If we lose then, this won't mean much."

The Birdman didn't have to worry. The night before, two of the NBA's aging superstars had reasserted themselves (Charles Barkley had 43 points and Karl Malone 42), and the Pacers then did a little asserting of their own, bolting to a 30–18 first-quarter lead and never looking back in a 101–89 victory over Philly.

Larry Brown came to town with 628 NBA victories to his credit to Bird's 7, but Brown's 76ers were outmanned from the opening tip. The Pacers defense continued to be their secret weapon as Philadelphia became the 14th consecutive team to score less than 100 points against the league's number-two defensive team. Whatever assistant coach Dick Harter was mixing in the locker room drinking water was working. Even Allen Iverson, the blue darter, quick-as-a-wink point guard destined for stardom, couldn't penetrate the Pacers "Help Me Rhonda" defense.

Rik Smits led the offense with 25 points, and Jalen Rose and Antonio Davis continued to contribute. Davis's play meant that Derrick McKey might be the odd man out when he was healthy—for Bird had settled into an easy-as-you please eight-, sometimes nine-man rotation that seemed comfortable for everyone. That meant Miller, Smits, Double D (Dale Davis), Jackson, and Mullin started each game. Near the end of the first period, Travis Best, A.D. (Antonio Davis), and Jalen Rose entered the game along with Fred Hoiberg, the Iowa State graduate and self-proclaimed pickle freak. The pattern was repeated near the end of the third quarter, but if they found a good rhythm, Rose and A.D. played with Smits, Miller, and Jackson or Best during the final minutes.

Of the reserves, Rose (who wore number 5 in tribute to his idol, Magic Johnson—3 and 2 make 5, proving that he was every bit the mathematician Dennis Rodman was) had by far benefited the most with the coaching switch from Brown to Bird. Teammates believed that Rose, a free spirit who grew up playing playground-type basketball, was less hyper under the new coach. "Larry knows that Jalen has a special gift," A.D. said. "He's going to get the ball a lot and he has to play smart basketball. When he makes a bad pass, Larry doesn't jump down his throat like Coach Brown did. He just praises his effort and tells him that he needs him to take control. And not to go off by himself." Bird's management of Rose was a far cry from that of Larry Brown's the prior season. Once, after Brown screamed at him during a game in Minnesota, Rose told him to shut up.

Jalen's good play early in the season signaled a strong bond building between him and his coach, one Bird had developed with all of the Pacers. "Larry brings a different aura to the game," trainer David Craig said. "He's a very positive person and has natural leadership qualities. He builds a player up, uses constructive criticism, and always challenges them to be better."

Another Bird trait Craig, whose career with the Pacers had spanned 28 years, noticed was the coach's concept of team play. "Larry always talks about *us* when he mentions the team. He even looks at himself and the assistants as a team. It's not 'I did this,' or 'I did that,' but *we*. When we win, he gives the players the credit. When we lose, he shares the blame. He really believes in the players, and the team responds to that."

The win against Philadelphia allowed Indiana to keep pace with Central Division leader Atlanta. "Our starters played very well," Bird explained. "We're playing better basketball. Now comes the ultimate challenge—going on the road for five games."

Every time Larry Bird visited an NBA city for the first time during the season, the atmosphere was supercharged. Even though he had only performed once in Minneapolis, that didn't keep fans from flocking downtown to see the icon. Curious to watch Bird on the sidelines, Bird's "first" appearance was a sellout.

The Pacers' game against the Timberwolves was somewhat overshadowed by other NBA headlines. The night before, the Washington Wizards had christened their new MCI Arena with President Clinton in attendance, and the Warriors had suspended Latrell Sprewell for 10 games and terminated his $32 million contract for trying to strangle coach P. J. Carlesimo. Oblivious to these distractions, the Pacers concentrated on the task at hand, but porous defense provided ample opportunities for the Wolves to score. The blue and gold gave up an uncharacteristic 56 points and found themselves down nine at halftime. In the third quarter, Harter's revised game plan produced better pressure on the ball, and the Timberwolves scored only 16 points, falling behind by one.

As the game wound down, the major attraction was the matchup between Minnesota's Kevin Garnett, the $100 million kid who would have been a college junior had he not elected to play in the NBA (Charles Barkley quipped, "Just think how much he would have made if he was any good"), and the Pacers sharpshooter Reggie Miller. With the score tied, Miller twice lofted jumpers over the outstretched arms of the 6′11″ former high school star from Chicago. Both found the bottom of the basket, and the Pacers won the sixth of their last seven games, 94–90. "Reggie got hot," said Bird, whose club improved to 9–6. "He lifted us up. Without him, we walk out the door with a loss." The narrow victory (only the second time all season the Pacers had managed to win a game decided by less than five points) put a smile on the coach's face. "This is why I got back into basketball, the competition at the end of the game," Bird said. "That's what it's all about for me."

While Bird was pleased about being back in the game, Latrell Sprewell was leaving it. At least for a year. The day after being "fired" by the Warriors for attacking and threatening to kill his coach, the NBA suspended him without pay for a year, making a trade to another club impossible. Sprewell was also dumped by Converse, his basketball shoe company. Many wondered why he wasn't in jail. Bird's thoughts were simple: "You just can't have that in our league. It's the same way when guys were bumping officials. I thought they should have been suspended for a year. You have to stop that stuff right away."

December 5, 1997, also marked the first coach-firing in the NBA. Jim Cleamons, the former Chicago Bulls assistant, was terminated by the Mavericks, who had begun the season on a dismal note. General manager Don Nelson replaced Cleamons.

Also on the 5th of December, the Pacers faced the Nuggets and another coach whose job was in jeopardy. Despite his feisty attitude as a player, Bill Hanzlik hadn't been able to transfer that spunk to his team, who had won just 1 game in 14 tries. Nevertheless, Denver nearly upset the Pacers before falling 96–85. Mark Jackson, briefly a Nugget in 1996, led the way with a double-double effort in points and assists. He also turned the game around in the fourth quarter with a clever behind-the-back pass that found Rik Smits along the baseline. His short jumper swished, and the Pacers, who won their fifth straight, never looked back as they ran their record to 10–6.

At Phoenix on December 7th, Bird's 41st birthday, Miller proved he had regained the form that made him one of the best scorers in the NBA. In the most exciting game to date, the former UCLA star took an inbound pass from Mark Pope with 2.5 seconds left in overtime, bounced the ball twice as he darted around Suns guard Jason Kidd, and launched a buzzer-beating 18-footer to win the game. Larry Bird thrust his right arm in the air as teammates mobbed Miller.

"Our guys played their hearts out tonight," Bird enthused. "We've been on the road, and coming here tonight, our guys could have just packed it in, but they came out in the first half and played great defense, and Reggie made the big shot." He also praised Mark Pope, adding, "I always said he [Pope] would win a lot of games for us. Even though he's a rookie, he can make passes like that."

The win came against Suns coach Danny Ainge, a fixture with Bird on the Celtics championship teams from the 1980s. Asked if he missed seeing his buddy, Ainge told reporters, "Are you kidding? I miss my wife a lot more than I miss Larry." Bird added, "You run into ex-teammates all the time in this league. Me and Danny are friends. It's almost like we grew up together. But it's time to go on with our lives."

Seeking their seventh straight win, Indiana traveled to Salt Lake City to face the Jazz, runners-up to the world champion Bulls in 1997. Utah had struggled in the early games of the season without their star guard and playmaker John Stockton, who had arthroscopic knee surgery in mid-October, but he was back for the first time.

When the final buzzer sounded, the Pacers wished he had taken off one more game. His return electrified the Delta Center and inspired his teammates to a near-perfect performance against the road-weary Pacers. Utah outmuscled Indiana, and though Dale Davis fought Karl Malone to a standstill, Reggie Miller didn't help any by arguing a call in the third quarter and getting ejected. Without Reggie, the Pacers were shorthanded in the fourth. More than anything, the Pacers' defense was their downfall. For the first time in 17 games, they gave up more than 100 points, losing 106–97 to drop to 11–7 for the season.

At Portland the day after Michael Jordan moved into third place on the all-time NBA scoring list (behind Wilt Chamberlain and Kareem Abdul-Jabbar), the Pacers lost their second straight 93–85. And after the 3–2 road trip, things weren't about to get any easier with Miami and Washington, both playing well, invading Market Square Arena.

The Heat were coached by Pat Riley. After the 1985 NBA championship series, when the Lakers had beaten the Celtics, Bird told Riley, "You coached a perfect series." As Riley moved first to the Knicks and then to the Heat, Larry intently watched Riley's style, believing him to be an excellent strategist and motivator. "Pat adapts to any style that suits the moment," Bird said. "I'd love to be that kind of coach, to build a team that's able to run the ball when it has the chance but can also play the kind of rough half-court game you need in this league. Pat Riley is the Michael Jordan of our profession." Asked if he'd ever talked to Riley about coaching, Bird demurred. "Never," he said. "C'mon, he's a Laker."

Unfortunately for Riley, whatever strategy he had designed for the Pacers' Dunking Dutchman Rik Smits failed miserably. The 7'4" center, now with "happy feet" in his new Nike basketball shoes, delivered 29 points using a series of jump hooks, soft jumpers, and authoritative dunks that helped his teammates bury the Heat 104–89. One of those dunks came on a down-the-key, in-your-face, thunderous charge to the basket that left fans breathless.

While Indiana improved its record to 12–8 at the quarter mark of the regular season, off-court activities continued to blemish the NBA image. Rod Strickland and Tracy Murray of the Washington Wizards decided to slug it out after a name-calling bout, and their fight cost each of them $25,000 plus a reprimand from the league.

On the court, the Wizards, coached by Bernie Bickerstaff, visited Market Square Arena, but they brought no magic. Rik Smits and Reggie Miller combined for 47 points, and Dale Davis added 13 in his best offensive effort of the season. The Pacers improved to 13–8, good for fourth place in the Central Division behind Atlanta, Cleveland, and Charlotte. The Chicago Bulls, still Pippenless, were a game behind Indiana.

At Toronto in mid-December, they chalked up number fourteen, 108–101, though the game was much closer than it should have been against one the NBA's poorest teams. As Bird chewed his fingernails and fidgeted on the bench, unforced errors hampered his team. Bird showed confidence in the bench, playing Antonio Davis, Pope, Hoiberg, and Rose in the fourth quarter as Mullin and Smits watched from their courtside chairs.

Most experts believed that Indiana had turned the corner. *USA Today* proclaimed them to be the eighth-best team in the NBA: "Larry Bird's influence is starting to show," they reported. No better example of Bird's ability to lead was there than Jalen Rose, who worshipped Magic Johnson. "I would turn on games," he recalled. "And see a 6'9" guy pushing the ball 94 feet at 100 mph. That inspired me." Thus far in the season, Bird was inspired by Rose's play.

When the Knicks came to Indianapolis, Bird was anxious to see how the Pacers would react to what he believed was one of the four best teams in the league. "L.A., Utah, Miami when they get Mourning back, and the Knicks," Bird told reporters, "They look like the cream of the crop."

Bird felt his team was playing better, especially after the debacle at Portland. After that game, he'd intentionally mangled the English language, as he did periodically, to describe the effort. "I told them [Pacers] they had packed it in. They wasn't into it. Guys wasn't into it. Guys wasn't movin', they wasn't setting picks. They was acting like they was into it, but they was giving fake hustle. That happens in this league. It happens too much."

When his words were reported, the players knew he meant business. Normally Bird took time to make certain his English was as correct as possible, but when he butchered the language, that came from the heart. Scoldings using cuss words accompanied by bad English meant "Watch out, Bird is upset." That wasn't something anybody wanted to see. Mychal Thompson, the center from the University of Minnesota who played with Bird in the mid-1980s, once said, "My few rules in life are these: Don't cheat the IRS, don't curse the dead, and don't get Larry Bird mad."

"You've got to be able to read Larry," one player explained. "Watch his face, his expressions, but most of all watch his language. When he's hot, words you never heard are blasting at you." Reggie Miller agreed, but told USA Today, "One of the hardest things is separating Coach Bird from the legend. Because he runs you to death and then you go home and watch Classic Sports [Network] and there he is every single night. There's the great Celtics of old and him playing the Lakers or the 76ers . . . . People always ask how he is as a coach and I'm like 'You guys don't understand, that's Larry Bird out there coaching us.' . . . It's almost like a kid in a candy store."

Though Patrick Ewing's New York Knicks were talented, the team had struggled under coach Jeff Van Gundy. Expected to challenge Miami in the Atlantic Division, they had become a so-so team in disarray. Indiana, on the other hand, was seeking its 13th win in sixteen games. Van Gundy saw the difference, telling reporters, "But who's really surprised? Did someone think Larry Bird couldn't coach? He's a natural."

Though Van Gundy's perception seemed accurate, Bird was still concerned about the effort, or lack of it, of several of his players. During the off-season, he'd made his point by trading Eric Dampier for Chris Mullin. Bird wanted Mullin, but the coach had also become disgruntled with Dampier's tendency to give less than

100 percent. Bird felt the same about Derrick McKey, the University of Alabama product known as "Heavy D," still on the injured list. He considered him a soft player who coasted during games and played hard only when he felt like it.

Unlike many coaches, Bird didn't shy away from scolding his players in public. After the lackadaisical effort in Toronto, he said, "It's not like we have to win by 30 or 40 points, but the guys better give me the effort. Sometimes, some play hard for 10 or 20 minutes, that's all. I need 30 to 40 minutes." Bird used the Knicks as the example. "I'm trying to get the guys to bring their A-game every night," he explained. "Our guys have great respect for the Knicks because they come ready to play."

Against the Pacers, the Knicks were game, but they played like a sleek automobile with one piston on the blink. Ewing, another of Bird's teammates on the 1992 Olympic team, contributed 23 points, but forwards Larry Johnson and Charles Oakley could only light it up for 16 between them. When the final buzzer sounded, the Pacers had improved to 15–8 with an 87–80 win. "We weren't perfect, but we got the win," Larry Bird extolled. "It's a big win and it's New York." Mark Jackson, whose superb play had been the catalyst for the team's early success, took time to assess the team's progress. "We're playing well, picking teams apart and taking what they give us. . . . We're feeling good about ourselves and it shows."

The win came on a night when the Bulls reasserted themselves. In a much-ballyhooed game against the Lakers, possessors of the best record in the league, all Michael Jordan did was to throw in 36 points in a duel with Jordan-wannabe Kobe Bryant. Dennis Rodman, sporting a new hair-dye job featuring a smiley face on the back of his head, snared 14 rebounds as the Bulls sank the Lakers at the United Center in Chicago.

Next up for the Pacers came the Pistons, who had just traded for Jerry Stackhouse. The former North Carolina guard scored a season-high 33 points to lead the comeback charge as the Pistons fought back from a big deficit, but it was two against one as Dale and Antonio Davis came up with stellar efforts for the Pacers. The Dale half of the dandy Double Ds was especially effective, scoring

15 points to go with 10 rebounds as Indiana prevailed 98–90, winning their 14th game in 17 tries. "The Pacers are a terrific team right now," Pistons coach Doug Collins lamented. "And I don't know if Dale Davis has ever played better offensively."

Larry Bird used comic relief (sportscaster Mark Patrick said, "Bird has a sense of humor as dry as Salt Lake City on Sunday") to hide displeasure with the Pacers' ineffectiveness in holding their lead against the Pistons. With his tongue firmly in his cheek, he told reporters, "That's the last time I let Carlisle and Harter coach the second half."

Watching Dale play with intensity brought a smile to Bird's face. He was one to whom the finger had been pointed when Larry talked about players needing to play hard each night. Often Bird thought Davis's mind wasn't in the game. Against the Pistons, it was. "Dale played great," Bird said, believing his recent efforts at motivating the Pacers' muscleman were paying off. "Just great."

With a record of 16–8, the Pacers were four games better than the previous year. "Even after that 2–5 start, we still knew we were a good team," Bird announced. "This streak has just proven that."

That streak reached six straight six days before Christmas, when Indiana outlasted Orlando 95–92. Success from the foul line made the difference, but it was error-free ball in the fourth quarter that pleased Bird. "We lost a lot of games early in the year just like that one there," he explained. "As of late, we've made a lot of plays down the stretch."

The victory came on a night when Patrick Ewing apparently ended his season by dislocating a bone in his right wrist. He joined Hakeem Olajuwon and Scottie Pippen on the sidelines as injuries continued to blunt the play of the greats of the NBA. Ewing's departure spelled immediate doom for the Knicks, but also triggered biting comments from Pistons center Brian Williams: "It's messed up that he got hurt. I know he wanted to make good on at least one of his dozen promises to win a championship." Dennis Rodman added, "They weren't going to win it with him, and now they've got an excuse." Ouch!

Thus far, the Pacers had not only been injury-free with their regulars, but they also were the only team in the NBA that started the same lineup every night. The team's 17–8 record after 25 games was its best since Indiana joined the league in 1976. One of those most responsible for the success was Mark Jackson, who applauded Bird's coaching efforts. "He's on his way to being a great coach in this league," Jackson said. "He has everything it takes to be a great coach. He doesn't bring an ego. He listens. He's willing to learn. There's no question about his coaching future."

8

THE BIRD IN FLIGHT

*"Magic played basketball the way I think you should
play basketball. I loved to play against him,
because it was such a great challenge."*
LARRY BIRD

Larry Bird flew into the national
publicity scene in 1977. Named to the Playboy All-American Team
prior to his junior year at ISU, he ventured to Lake Geneva, Wisconsin, for a dinner honoring the chosen few. Those in attendance
recalled that the only time small-town Larry took off his "Cat
hat" (Caterpillar Tractors) was when the photo session took place.
While in Wisconsin, Bird also sipped a few beers. His passion for
foamy suds was well known, although at the time he resolved
never again to drink out of green bottles after having taken a big
gulp from one and realizing he'd swallowed several cigarette butts
left behind.

In November, Bird made his first of multiple appearances on the
cover of *Sports Illustrated*. He and two lovely ISU cheerleaders,
both of whom had their index fingers touching their lips urging
everyone to "keep quiet" about the Indiana State team, welcomed
readers to the upcoming basketball season. "That cover changed
my life," said Bird, who was labeled the Sycamores' "secret
weapon."

Since many fans across the country had never seen him play, the
cover photo showed them something they didn't know: Larry Bird

wasn't black. Later, he'd travel to New York for another *Sports Illustrated* photo session. The sports information director at Indiana State recalled Bird saying, "They charged $6 for a hamburger and a coke. I could never live there."

Bird's celebrity status surprised him, but Georgia Bird knew what was happening. "He has no concept of how famous he is," Larry's mom said. "But he'll figure it out one of these days. And it will hit him so hard it will knock him down." Sycamores coach Bob King didn't think so. "He's an odd kid. He drives an old clunker and doesn't care about clothes or material things. He'd sidestep all the publicity he could."

After defeating Czechoslovakia in a preseason game when Larry scored 29 points, the Sycamores took dead aim at the Purdue Boilermakers, who had inflicted one of only two losses during the preceding season. The game was a sellout at Hulman Center in Terre Haute, but Bird's shooting touch (4 for 17 in the first half) was as cold as the Indiana weather outside the arena. In the second half, the Birdman warmed up, and by game's end, he'd totaled 26 points and 17 rebounds. ISU triumphed with ease, winning 91–73.

Against Central Michigan in a 93–77 victory, a miracle play Bird made astonished fans. As his gangly body was falling out of bounds behind the basket, the young phenom tossed the ball over the back of the backboard and it fell gently downward through the hoop. "It was one of those 'you can't believe it happened, but it did' plays," teammate Brad Miley said at the time.

Making that shot was commonplace for Larry Bird. He practiced it constantly and bragged about his ability to never miss it. On one occasion, he bet a maintenance man that he could hit 10 in a row. Guess who paid up?

Indiana State won 12 more games before the team lost its first. Much was expected, but when the curtain fell on the regular season, the Sycamores' record was a disappointing 19–7.

The game for the Missouri Valley Conference championship against Creighton was a foreshadowing of Bird's ability to "play hurt" throughout his career. After the team made it to the finals, a teammate jumped on his back in celebration, and Bird could barely walk. A half-hour before the Creighton game, he was being examined by a doctor at an Omaha hospital courtesy of Creighton coach Tom Apke. Doctors suggested painkillers, and Bird reluctantly acquiesced. He scored 29 points, but his team fell short by 2.

Apke spoke to his team before the game. "We knew [Bird] was hurt," Apke said, "but we told our players it wouldn't matter because he was such a great competitor. . . . He could cut off one of his legs and still score 30 points." Bird was so thankful for Apke's assistance with treatment on his sore back that he wrote him a thank-you letter.

ISU's performance in the conference tournament and the fact that Bird was a nationally known player earned the team a shot at the NIT championship in New York. Bird led his team past Illinois State; but Rutgers, led by James Bailey, beat the Sycamores by one point. Afterward, Bird congratulated Bailey and then walked off the court. Moments later, an irate fan jumped on Bird's back, yanking his hair and punching him. Assistant trainer Rick Shaw recalled the incident. "Larry just decked the guy with both fists . . . I was about three steps in front of that . . . I got hit with blood. This guy's nose looked like a Heinz Ketchup bottle. It just exploded . . . I've seen Larry rearrange some dentures before, but this guy was just laying out there."

Bird's boxing performance wasn't surprising to those who knew him. Ever the loyal one, the Birdman had started swinging away during his first year at ISU. On one occasion, he helped a Sycamore football player defend his honor against a bunch of toughs at a local tavern called The Ballyhoo. Later, Bird decked 6'11" DeCarsta Webster when he picked on one of Larry's buddies during practice. "Bird always was looking for a fight," an ISU teammate said. "He'd punch a guy at the drop of a hat." K. C. Jones later labeled Bird a "street fighter." Coach Bill Fitch added, "He's one of the meanest son-of-a-bitches in the league. He has no fear threshold. He may be a 'hick from French Lick,' but he's streetwise. If you bully Larry Bird, you picked on the wrong guy."

Joining the "street fighter" in the collegiate spotlight during the Sycamore season were future NBA stars Sidney Moncrief, Joe

Barry Carroll, Phil Ford, David Greenwood, and a young man named Earvin Johnson from Michigan State. Those players and others of note teamed up to play international foes in Lexington, Kentucky. Coach of the squad was the Wildcats' Joe B. Hall.

The All-Star practices were the first time Bird and Magic Johnson were teammates. "In practice, we played together on a second unit that was beating the first team," Bird remembered. "I loved playing on the court with Magic. Coach got mad at us one day, though. We were playing our game when he said, 'How can we work on this stuff if you guys are throwing these crazy passes and taking these stupid shots?' . . . He was getting angry with us because we were embarrassing his first team."

During a game against the Russians, Bird tried guarding 7'4" Vladimir Tkachenko. He held his own against the giant player, and managed to pass the ball to teammates so well that it dazzled fellow ballplayers and fans alike. One staunch French Lick supporter came to Lexington prepared with a poster. It read: "NBC's peacock flew away, but ISU's Bird is here to stay," a reference to the network's discontinuance of its famed symbol. When Larry saw the sign, he cringed, disapproving when fans drew attention to him.

Prior to Bird's senior year at Indiana State, there was speculation he would turn professional. Indiana Pacers coach Slick Leonard coveted Bird, but Larry made it clear he wouldn't give up the chance to graduate. Ironically, 20 years would pass before the Pacers and Larry Bird finally hooked up.

Hindsight indicated that the Pacers made a critical mistake by not drafting Bird even though he had a collegiate season left. Cagey general manager Red Auerbach of the Celtics outsnookered Indiana by doing so, grabbing Bird as the sixth player chosen in the draft. The Pacers drafted Rick Robey, who never was an impact player.

Auerbach, whom Bird had first seen on television in King Edward cigar commercials, was acting on a scouting report from K. C. Jones, one of his former players. Jones had come to Terre Haute to watch the Birdman, and left believing he had seen Superman. "Larry is double- and triple-teamed every time he gets the ball," Jones wrote. "[On one play] he gets away on a fast break, but there are two guys hanging on him as he goes down the court. Larry fires the ball off the backboard at an angle, simultaneously zigzagging away from the two defenders. They think he's just thrown up a crazy shot. Larry goes right to where he knows the ball would come off the board, and in the air he takes the pass he's just thrown to himself and dunks the ball."

Jones's report was in direct contrast to that of Portland general manager Stu Inman. Before the draft, Inman said of Bird, "He had a beer-drinking, softball image. I just didn't think he could be a bigtime NBA player."

Ironically, being drafted by the legendary Celtics wasn't a big deal to Larry Bird, who was playing golf on the day he was selected and had to be told what it all meant. "The Celtics didn't mean anything to me," he recalled. "I didn't know about the banners or the parquet floor or even Red Auerbach. I didn't know anything about all that Celtics tradition."

One player on the Celtics team was familiar. "I had heard of Bill Russell," Bird said. "In fact, my cousin and I used to play one-on-one over at his house in Shoals, Indiana. . . . We'd take turns. I'd be Bill Russell and he'd be Wilt Chamberlain, and the next day we'd switch. But I had never actually seen Bill Russell play. Bill Russell was just a name to me."

During the summer months before his senior season started, Bird worked in French Lick and assisted at the local Boys Club. He also played slow-pitch softball with his brothers for the 500 Platolene-Carpet Center. The team won the state championship.

The Sycamore team that Larry returned to in Terre Haute was far different than what fans had seen the previous year. The changes started at the top, since Coach King had suffered first a heart attack and then an aneurysm during the summer and was recovering. Assistant coach Bill Hodges was promoted to the head coaching job. Joining him on the bench was ex-Pacers star Mel Daniels, the king-sized center who had been a two-time MVP in the ABA.

The inexperienced Hodges was so excited about his new position that he made a rookie mistake. He told half the players to show up for practice at 2:00, the other half at 3:00. Of course, Bird was there at 1:00, so it didn't make any difference to him.

Six new Sycamores joined Bird for the 1978–79 season: Bob Heaton, a pepper-pot guard and defensive specialist; Carl Nicks, returning to the squad after spending a season at a junior college; Eric Curry, Alex Gilbert, Rich Nemchek, and Scot Turner. Back for Bird's senior year were Brad Miley, Steve Reed, and LeRoy Staley, but an incident before the basketball season began nearly ended Bird's collegiate career. During an interview with a local Terre Haute reporter, he was asked his thoughts about playing for Coach Hodges instead of Coach King. When the article came out, Bird was quoted as saying Hodges "helped" players if they had a conflict between playing basketball and taking a test. The reporter went on to imply that on some occasions, Hodges got the player out of taking the test altogether. When one of his professors chewed Bird out and told him he better never try to escape his test, Larry was enraged, threatening to turn professional and leave ISU.

The incident triggered a basic distrust of the media by Bird that continued through his playing days in the NBA. At Indiana State, he told Coach Hodges he'd stay at the university only if he didn't have to talk to the media one-on-one. Hodges, who admitted his goal for the season was "to not upset Larry," reluctantly agreed.

Later, Bird received special treatment from the Celtics. They permitted Larry to sit on a wooden trainer's table in the middle of a room. All the media hovered around the superstar to ask their questions. After awhile, Bird noticed that 10 minutes was all the time required to answer questions, and reporters came to abide by Larry's "10-minute rule." When time was up, Bird slinked off the table and walked toward the door. Any neophyte reporter from out of town who bothered him with a question was met with the Bird stare and dead silence. Later, as coach of the Indiana Pacers, he reinvented the 10-minute rule. A sign in the media room announced that Bird would be available in his office at 5:50 before games. At precisely 6:00, those sessions were over. As one reporter said, "Everyone knows the drill."

Hometowners familiar with Bird knew his private nature was the reason for his behavior. Like other superstars uncomfortable in the limelight, he was insecure and scared that reporters were going to dig up his past—delving into his father's suicide, his failed marriage, and his relationship with daughter Corrie. "Larry doesn't like he or others to be criticized or cut down in public," a French Lick resident said. "If he never had to talk to the press again, it would be too soon."

"There were just a handful of the press around at first," Bird, the humble one who attempted to distribute praise for his success around to the other players, recalled. "And so it wasn't so bad. Then all of a sudden I'm this big college player and everybody wants to know what I'm all about. I wasn't ready to handle it. I didn't want to tell anybody anything."

Bird also said he was concerned that other players on the Indiana State team were being neglected by the media. "We had just won a game and there were about 15 or 20 people in the [locker] room," he explained on one occasion. "I come out of the shower and they're all waiting for me. I scanned the room, and the other players had their heads down. . . . The press only wanted to talk to me, when the other guys had played just as hard. . . ."

Bird's ban on the press notwithstanding (he once told a reporter, "Why should I care about what you write? I don't read your crap"), the Sycamores got off to a good start in the new season with a solid win over a touring Russian team. Larry did a decent job guarding 7'4" Vladimir Tkachenko, and Indiana State won 87–79. Two more victories were followed by a buzzer-beating win against Evansville. Bird scored 40 points to lead his team. The squad, dubbed "four overachievers and Bird" by a local reporter, then traveled to Florida for a tournament, where Bird joined French Lick friends before the game. He was invited to their hotel room to watch a favorite television program, *The Waltons*, which was popular at the time. One visitor recalled that Bird, ever the homegrown Hoosier, had a large wad of chewing tobacco stuffed under his lip, spitting into a white Styrofoam cup.

Indiana State was successful in the Florida Hatter Classic, against Cleveland State, even though Bird lost his temper over offensive remarks made by a Cleveland State University assistant coach. "Larry the Bird," as the press dubbed him, tried to break Cleveland State's locker room door down, but school officials restrained him.

After six games, the Sycamores, led by Coach Hodges, who explained that his offense was geared around "getting the ball in Bird's hands 75 percent of the time," were undefeated. Bird led the nation in scoring with a 33.3 average, and his team was ranked ninth in the nation. Against Morris-Harvey two days before 1978 ended, Bird scored the magical number of points necessary to break the ISU scoring record. The game was halted and the ball given to Bird. He had intended to give it to his mother, but instead bounced it to Jerry Newsome, whose record he had broken.

At New Mexico, after the team had racked up 17 straight victories, Larry Bird the fighter emerged once again. He tumbled into the stands after a loose ball, and before he could pull himself up, a disenchanted fan bopped him over the head with a rolled-up program. Las Cruces newspapers reported the next day that Bird had "sent the culprit to the 27th row," but Bird sloughed off reporters' questions. Bob Heaton, Larry's roommate, provided the heroics in that game, floating a desperation 55-footer clean through the net as the buzzer sounded. The Sycamores were 18–0; but barely. Bird summed up their play, saying, "We beat teams on guts and determination. We just decided we weren't going to lose."

During halftime of the New Mexico game, Larry Legend not only showed who ran the Sycamores, but who ran the university as well. When President Richard Landini, an avid fan, sauntered into the locker room at halftime with the Sycamores trailing, Bird suddenly yelled, "Get the f... out of here." Coach Bill Hodges was strangely silent, and the president backtracked out the door without a word.

The incident reminded players that it was Bird who was in charge of the team and not Hodges. Throughout the season, the coach deferred to Larry, realizing his superstar knew far more about the strategies of basketball than he did. During timeouts, Bird would often successfully challenge Hodges's game plan, saying, "Aw, let's stick with this, it's working." In effect, Larry Bird was coaching the Sycamores, priming himself for future endeavors.

Midway through the season, Indiana State was ranked second in the national polls to Notre Dame, and "Bird Fever," as one newspaper dubbed it, was in full force. National stories appeared about the Cinderella team—and Larry Bird, who'd risen from working as a garbage collector to stardom, was the center of attention.

Opponents were fed up with all the fuss. Illinois State, the archrival of the Sycamores despite going through the throes of a dismal season, attempted to stop Bird by double- and triple-teaming him at every turn. "The first time down the court," Bird recalled, "I could tell something crazy was going on. There were *three* players on me. I said to myself, 'Why don't I move a little further out,' and three of their players went with me. So we were basically playing four-on-two."

The game plan was a miserable failure, because Indiana State was not a one-man team. Bird only scored four points, the lowest of his career, but the team prevailed 91–72. The win propelled the team to the number-one position in the national polls, something that had never happened in the school's history. Purdue, Indiana, and Notre Dame, the state's "Big Three," could only look on with envy.

National television coverage came to Terre Haute when Billy Packer, Jim Simpson, and Al McGuire broadcast the Sycamores–West Texas State game. Heavy, wet snow that blanketed the roof of the Hulman Center leaked on the playing floor, and a mob of volunteers mopped up the water until tipoff.

The television viewers were treated to Indiana State basketball at its best. Bird was sensational for three quarters-plus, scoring 45 points. With 40 seconds to go, four more points were needed to break his school record, and Hodges decided to leave him in the game. He got the four, along with 19 rebounds that he hauled down in his final regular season game.

The Sycamores' 27th straight win came in the Missouri Valley Conference championship tournament against West Texas State.

The Buffaloes utilized a "box and chase" defense against Bird that proved effective, but the Sycamores prevailed by 10 points.

After besting Southern Illinois, Indiana State faced Illinois State. The Sycamores won easily, but the victory proved costly when Bird injured the thumb on his left hand batting away a loose ball. He left for the dressing room just two seconds into the second half; Illinois State had hope. But ISU proved once again it was not a one-man team, and kept pace until Bird returned, bandaged thumb and all.

The victory spelled ISU's first trip to the NCAA tournament, and the victory celebration was long and loud. Among those dipped into the shower was United States senator Birch Bayh.

When Bird's injured thumb was x-rayed, a small fracture was noted in the tip. Since no plastic or metal shielding was permitted by the NCAA, doctors knew he'd be playing in the tournament with just padding and tape to protect the swollen digit. The injury permitted great fodder for sportswriters, with "Bird's Broken Wing," "Bird's Mum on Injured Thumb," and "Wounded Bird" among the best headlines across the country. Fans telephoned in various remedies, as did political activist Dick Gregory, who suggested a special herb remedy that would quell the pain. "I used this on a big toe injury that I had," he wrote, "It worked for me and it can work for Larry."

Recognition for Bird and Indiana State was still hard to come by (Billy Packer spelled his name *Byrd* in a letter to Coach Hodges). When the NCAA opened play, most felt the small school and its star player would fall victim and head to the sidelines.

But Bird and his Sycamore teammates had other ideas. Known as the "Magnificent Seven," they intended to prove to the basketball world that a "small" school had the wherewithal to make it to the NCAA finals.

Bird's individual awards for his stellar play during the season filled a large trophy case. He won the prestigious Naismith Trophy (at the presentation ceremony, he told the crowd, "You couldn't have picked a nicer guy to win this award"), the Associated Press Player of the Year Award, the Eastman Kodak/National Association of Basketball Coaches Award, and the John Wooden Award.

The shy lad, one who never made eye contact when talking to strangers or the media, became the only player ever to skip the Wooden Award ceremony where the accolades were passed out. He told officials he was busy earning enough credits to gain a diploma at Indiana State, something he had promised his mother he would do.

At the Chicago presentation for the Associated Press award, Bird again showed his disdain for the press. While accepting the award, he asked if a certain Chicago sportswriter who had belittled him and ISU was present. Told he wasn't, Bird said, "That's too bad. I always wanted to see what a real live prick looked like."

Bird wanted to use more than words to describe his hatred for a *Sports Illustrated* reporter named Bruce Newman. In a February article about Larry and his teammates, Newman suggested he was a scared, undisciplined crybaby. He called him unemotional and cold, a true prima donna who actually frightened his coach and fellow players. Worse, the reporter saw fit to hone in on the suicide of his father. Bird had to be restrained from heading to New York to, as he put it, "kick the guy's ass."

The site for the team's opening games in the quest for the NCAA championship was Lawrence, Kansas. First-round opponent Virginia Tech was an easy mark, and ISU won 86–69. The ambidextrous Bird popped for 22 points, many of them of the left-handed variety.

Indiana State's next major test was in Cincinnati against Oklahoma. Bird continued his verbal battle with Billy Packer, who had been downplaying ISU's chances, telling the announcer to stay clear of the Sycamores' next game. T-shirts commemorating that warning were printed containing Bird's words. They were big sellers, as were placards imprinted with "Billy Who?" on them.

How to defend Larry Bird became the cry of the day. Earlier in the year, Drake's Bob Ortegel suggested the best way was to "steal his tennis shoes." Oklahoma coach Dave Bliss told reporters he'd received over 500 suggestions on how to stop the ISU wonder.

"I've gotten more mail than Barry Switzer (coach of the Sooners football team) has gotten about the wishbone," the coach lamented.

With Red Auerbach and Celtics player-coach Dave Cowens watching, Bird put on a show, scoring 29 points and grabbing 15 rebounds. Nothing Coach Bliss tried worked; and by game's end, when Bird was removed from the game, even *Sooner* fans and cheerleaders gave him an ovation. Indiana State fans bellowed out their customary "Amen" chant.

Thirty-one straight victories meant the Sycamores would tackle Sidney Moncrief and the Arkansas Razorbacks in the regional final, with the winner advancing to the elite Final Four in Salt Lake City. "Bird versus Moncrief," the headlines predicted, with Arkansas favored. The game was tight from the opening whistle, and as the seconds ticked away, the two teams were deadlocked at 71 each. Arkansas had the ball, but a traveling violation gave the Sycamores a last-second chance. Steve Reed nearly took the last shot, but at the last moment shoveled the ball to Bob Heaton, who lofted a beauty that hit the rim, bounced around, and then fell softly through the net. ISU, the no-publicity school that surely couldn't, simply had. Indiana State University was going to the Big Dance.

Among those making the trip to Salt Lake City was Larry's mom, Georgia. Friends learned she didn't have the money to go, but a Terre Haute businessman came to the rescue, and she was on her way to see Larry play in the NCAA finals. She joined raucous Sycamore fans cheering for their beloved players, all of whom sported cowboy boots and hats, a tradition started by Mel Daniels.

The Final Four featured Indiana State, Pennsylvania, DePaul, and Michigan State. The latter being a finalist was no surprise to Bird. They had a sophomore phenom who was getting as much ink as Bird, a kid by the name of Magic Johnson. "Before our senior year, I watched Michigan State play against the Russians on television," Bird said. ". . . Magic was just killing them with his rebounding and his coast-to-coast stuff. I said, 'Right there, boys, you are looking at the team that's going to win the NCAA championship this year. Boy, they're good.' "

Banners at the finals were everywhere, one proclaiming "The State Bird of Indiana is Larry." Billy Packer continued to suffer. One T-shirt sported the words, "Al McGuire for President—Billy Packer for Dogcatcher."

After Michigan State had demolished Penn by 34, the Sycamores took the court against Ray Meyer and the DePaul Blue Demons, who featured their own scoring ace, future NBA star Mark Aguirre. Bird dominated the duel with 35 points (he hit 16 of 19 shots) and 16 rebounds, but it was his teammates who shone during the closing seconds. With few ticks on the time clock, Indiana State led 75–74. Ray Meyer called a play designed for Aguirre to take an open jumper, but it came from 20 feet and bounced off the rim. ISU's LeRoy Staley grabbed the rebound, and was fouled. He hit one free throw, and when DePaul struggled to get the ball into position for a shot, the buzzer sounded. It was the Sycamores versus the Spartans in a dream matchup for the national championship.

Hollywood couldn't have scripted it any better: Larry Bird and his gang of small-college wannabes against the Magic Man, Earvin Johnson, and his major-college Michigan State Spartans. Everyone was sure it would be a Monday night to remember—one that would leave indelible images with basketball fans forever. "It's a matchup of two of the greatest players ever to wear a college uniform," Al McGuire, a Bird believer, proclaimed.

Bird's dry, sarcastic wit was never more apparent than when reporters questioned him. He disliked most of the media, and had decided that the best way to deal with their silly questions was to humor himself. Asked what he recalled about playing with Magic in an All-Star game, he replied, "He wouldn't pass me the ball." An inquiry about his thumb produced "It's broke." When queried about whether he wanted to play Michigan State or Penn, Bird replied with tortured syntax, "It don't make no difference to me."

When the Spartans and the Sycamores gathered around the center circle for the most celebrated confrontation in college basket-

ball history in Salt Lake City on March 26, 1979, they played like
one had just awakened from a 24-hour nap and the other hadn't
slept for a week. While Michigan State had a no-sweat game with
Penn, isu's squad had squandered much of its emotion in the
heart-wrenching win over DePaul. Several Sycamores were drag-
ging, and though he wouldn't admit it, Larry Bird's thumb was
killing him. And he knew it would take a superior effort to handle the Spartans. He told reporters, "All I know is that we better
come to play, cuz we'll get blown out if we don't."

Before the game, reports indicated Bird wasn't confident with
his own game. Assistant coach Rick Shaw said Larry was sitting
at a table having his ankles wrapped when he startled teammate
Bob Heaton by saying, "I hope you got it tonight, cuz I just don't
feel it. . . ." If true, it marked one of the few times in his career
when he wasn't ready for a big game.

To his credit, the Spartans head coach, Jud Heathcoate, had
designed a perfect defense for Bird. Reporters dubbed it a *matchup
zone*. Throughout the game, Bird, wearing near-knee-high white
socks with blue stripes on them, was shadowed, and the shots he
did get had to be rushed. By game's end, he had scored only 19
points, and the Michigan State Spartans were the ncaa champions.
The Cinderella story had fallen one game short; Bird sat on the
bench crying, a towel draped over his head.

"We didn't go in with a good game plan," Bird, ever the frank
one, surmised later, disappointing coach Bill Hodges with his criticism. ". . . We thought we had proved that we could beat every
kind of defense, but we had never seen anything like that zone of
theirs. I couldn't do anything at all against it. . . . They really did
a good job on me . . . I think if we played them 10 times, we might
have beaten them twice."

The image of Bird walking off the court after the game was a
vivid one that lingered in the mind long after the final buzzer
sounded. The big guy's emotions were spent, a season's worth of
fighting the fight behind him. Around the country, fans of the true
underdog cried with Larry, aware that the dream was over. "Sometimes the ball goes in, and sometimes it doesn't," Larry shrugged.

That didn't mean there wasn't cause for celebration. The Sycamores' season ended 33–1, and they finished as runners-up in the NCAA tournament. The day after the devastating defeat, smiles started to reappear on the players' faces as they realized what they had accomplished. Fifteen thousand fans filled Hulman Center for a tribute that reporter David Benner (later to become the media relations director for the Pacers) labeled "The Sycamore Variety Hour."

Back in good humor, Larry Bird was a stand-up comedian extraordinaire. He teased players and coaches alike, telling the crowd that Bill Hodges wasn't one-third the coach Bob King had been. "We'd have won the whole thing if King had been around," Bird kidded. Teammate Brad Miley, who professed that it was he who taught Bird how to shoot the jump shot, wasn't spared. "Miley says he's a twenty twenty man," Bird shouted. "Yeah, right, twenty shots, twenty misses." To assistant coach Mel Daniels, who had sat alongside the Birdman on the bench in Salt Lake City and cried, Bird yelled, "Remember the memories about Mel because he can't play a lick."

Bird also chose to make fun of himself, putting everyone at ease as he closed out his college career. After Brad Miley had talked about teaching him the jump shot, Bird grinned, and told his worshipers, "Yeah, I guess that's the one I had last night," referring to the poor shooting performance against Michigan State. The crowd roared; Larry Bird, the hometown hero, had 'em laughing again.

More than anything, the outstanding Sycamore team had proven to Bird the worthiness of the "team" concept, something that would follow him throughout his playing career and into coaching in the NBA. "We didn't have much raw talent at Indiana State," he said later. "But we proved what you could accomplish when you have guys who really believe in each other, who work together, and who know what it takes to win."

Teammate Steve Reed's comments were poignant, especially for what lay ahead with Bird's career as a player in the NBA: "Larry's presence on the court made all of the other players better," Reed said. "Just being around a player of Larry Bird's caliber, you pick up a lot of things. He's such a superb player and such a fantastic passer. I think some of his passing has rubbed off on me. I know I'm a better player now than I ever was."

The days at Indiana State changed Bird's life forever. The mixed-up kid from French Lick had found many caring friends, like Rick and Max Gibson, who treated him like a son and assisted him with every aspect of his life. He discovered two coaches, Bob King and Bill Hodges, who made him a better player, unselfish to a fault. And Bird had survived a marriage to the wrong girl, the birth of a child, and a media determined to uncover every dark secret in his life. To be sure, college days at Indiana State had matured him as he readied himself for the next step: professional basketball. "The entire college experience was great for me," Bird mused. "I learned more about myself and more about people than in the rest of my life put together. . . . And it all happened so fast."

He also realized the importance of receiving his college diploma in June after completing his student teaching responsibilities. "It proved one thing—if *I* can get a college education, there's hope for everyone else. When I got out of high school, I didn't have great grades. . . . So a lot of people laughed at the idea of me going to college. But my mother used to tell me, 'Son, you're going to be the first one from either side of the family to earn your degree.' It was always on my mind: get an education."

Larry Legend had accomplished that goal at Indiana State—and much more. Now he'd get an education of a different sort—one earned by competing against the professionals in the National Basketball Association.

Mop-haired Larry Bird lets a jumper fly during a Springs Valley High
School game against Jasper.

Courtesy Indiana Basketball Hall of Fame

Townspeople in the French Lick–West Baden, Indiana, area dedicated a street to Larry Legend.
Courtesy the author

Controlling the ball in traffic and weaving through defenders, Larry Bird heads for the hoop.
AP/Wide World Photos

Critics said Larry Bird was too slow, lacked quickness, and couldn't jump. He proved them wrong.

AP/Wide World Photos

A battler on the backboards, Larry Bird
prided himself on second-shot opportunities.
AP/Wide World Photos

Larry Bird's deft passing ability astounded
teammates and fans alike. His no-look
passes were a trademark.
AP/Wide World Photos

Larry Bird lays in a left-hander against the Pistons as (left to right) Joe Dumars, Adrian Dantley, and Rick Mahorn look on.

Copyright © Steve Lipofsky

Intensity, concentration, and a perpetual game face were Larry Bird's hallmarks in the triple threat (pass, drive, or shoot) position.
Copyright © Steve Lipofsky

Triple-teaming Larry Bird was not unusual. Here he's surrounded by
Magic Johnson, Kareem Abdul-Jabbar, and Michael Cooper.
Copyright © Steve Lipofsky

Three-time NBA Most Valuable Player, Larry Bird is honored by
commissioner David Stern.
Copyright © Steve Lipofsky

Sixers–Celtics matchups featuring Dr. J
versus Bird became legendary, and grew
into one of the great sports rivalries of the
1980s.

Copyright © Steve Lipofsky

Despite their on-court rivalry over the
years, Bird and Magic became friends,
especially after Larry played in Magic's
All-Star game.

Copyright © Steve Lipofsky

9

REGGIE AND THE BOYS

"[The temptation to suit up] will be hard,
but I'll manage. Michael would probably love to see
a 40-year-old like me out there."
LARRY BIRD

Even before the 1997–98 season started, the won-lost record of 58–24 was written on the blackboard in the Indiana Pacers locker room. That challenge seemed lofty at the time, and most experts doubted it was possible.

In late December, the day before Indiana matched up against David Robinson, Tim Duncan, and the rest of the San Antonio Spurs in Texas, USA *Today* had positioned the Pacers in the number-three slot among the elite teams of the NBA, just behind Seattle ("rolling along without a care in the world") and Los Angeles ("the bench has been the difference"). The Pacers ("the most balanced team in the league") were ahead of Chicago ("Mr. Rodman has been Mr. Good Citizen"). Rounding out the top 10 were Miami, Atlanta, Utah, Houston, San Antonio, and Phoenix.

Though the exciting play of Miller, Smits, Mullin, and Rose (who continued to surprise) ignited the Pacers, it was Bird's leadership that made the difference. While most fans remembered the Birdman as a great basketball player and were impressed with his coaching ability through the first part of the NBA season, it was his ability to interact with people that was his finest characteristic. Though he could be cantankerous at times, he had changed little from the Midwestern-born yokel who cared for freedom and the American way. Through the years, he could count his enemies on one hand. Few had a bad word to say about the gangly warrior who had inched his way through life using street smarts as his guide. That credo had required loyalty to his family and to coveted friends, who thought of Larry as just one of the boys—who asked for no special attention or privileges.

Bird's ability to read people had been an asset from his early days. "If a person is a friend of his, they're a friend for life," a boyhood chum from French Lick said. "But if they prove to be a phony, Larry will throw them away like spoiled meat."

During his playing days in Boston, he was revered by players and fans alike, but those who worked at Boston Garden were true worshipers. "Spider," a longtime Celtics employee, was especially close to Bird. So were the security guards, the maintenance men, and the other behind-the-scenes bluecollar workers Bird befriended. Often, after hearing a tale of woe, a few bucks would be forthcoming from Bird, or a simple thank-you if that was what was called for. When there was a birth or death, Bird might make an appearance, especially if he'd made a promise to do so. If Bird gave his word, that was it, whether there was a contract, a handshake, or simply an "I'll be there."

That type of straightforwardness had appealed to the Pacers players from the moment they met with him for the first time. "He explained what he wanted, and what we could expect from him," Mark Jackson recalled. "He let you know exactly where you stood." Reggie Miller admired Bird's hint of arrogance. "He's got that," Miller said. "And it's more than confidence. . . . You have to have an arrogance, a sense of confidence. He had that when he played. . . . He knew he was going to win."

"Larry's honest and he's smart; and if he tells you something, he won't change his mind," Walsh said. "I'd rather bet on him with no experience than three-quarters of the guys in this league with experience."

Most observers felt Bird's mettle would be tested most severely with Reggie Miller, the tempestuous superstar. After several years as an NBA All-Star, the former Olympian's game had hit the doldrums during the 1996–97 season. "He looked like he'd lost his confidence," Pistons coach Doug Collins observed. "And that's lethal for a shooter."

A dependable 20-points-a-game man, Miller's numbers had dropped off during Coach Larry Brown's final season. Worse, Reggie had failed to produce the offensive thrust needed as the game clock wore down. When the game was on the line, Miller frequently seemed confused, unable to break free for his patented poetry-in-motion jumpers, or to take a feed darting down the line.

With Rik Smits (a certified mechanic with an affection for rebuilding classic muscle cars and collecting Roadrunner memorabilia) on the sidelines for much of the season, and no one else available to aid Reggie's scoring efforts, Miller became moody and lost his enthusiasm for the game he loved. Realizing each game meant double- or triple-teaming, Miller ended up doing what other frustrated superstars did: he pouted. Worse, the former UCLA star took his anger out on officials, blaming them when an errant shot banged off the rim. "Reggie Miller was a pain in the ass much of last season," one official barked. "*He* missed [shots], but it was *our* fault."

Miller's work ethic had never been questioned. Among all NBA players, he was front and center with those who gave 100 percent every night. But Reggie's flash was gone as the 1996–97 season wound down. Fans who had screamed "Reg-gie" during his glory days suddenly became critical and unforgiving.

As the summer months of 1997 began, two events triggered roaring emotions in Miller. When arsonists torched his $2.9 million, 14,000-square-foot castlelike home in northeast Indianapolis, he was devastated, and even considered quitting basketball. Racial overtones lingered in the air, although authorities had no proof that Miller had been singled out. The Pacers stalwart lost personal memorabilia that was irreplaceable—but worse still, it dented his psyche, causing him to withdraw and become suspicious of the world in general. The police's inability to find a suspect (the crime remains unsolved) brought Miller to say he was considering retirement.

Seven days before the fire, Reggie had been at the opposite end of the emotional spectrum when he heard Brown was leaving. Though Miller thought highly of the diminutive coach, he believed his taunting and yelling at players had created an atmosphere not conducive to championship play.

Miller had hardly digested the news when he heard rumors that Larry Bird was being courted as the new Pacers coach. He was ecstatic. He wondered if it could be true, knowing that if Bird could coach with the high degree of enthusiasm he exhibited as a player, the Promised Land might lay just ahead. When Bird was hired, Miller was thrilled. Shortly thereafter, the fire at his home had taken its toll.

While Reggie considered giving up the game he loved, Bird had other ideas—and a meeting cemented a friendship that stretched beyond the player-coach relationship. Bird told Miller that retirement was a copout, and Reggie was impressed. "He told me I was in the public eye, and that this was my city and my team," Reggie recalled. "He said, 'Don't let one bad apple ruin it for you,' and that made me feel good, that he believed in me that much."

From the first day of training camp, Miller was his old self. He knew the addition of Chris Mullin complemented him, and the Miller-Mullin-Smits tandem required defenses to contend with three scoring threats. Exhibition games proved the theory, and when the NBA season dawned, so did Reggie.

During the first 25-plus games, Sir Reginald was in high gear. "Reggie blows through the lane, leaping to the glass for a reverse layup," Pacers radio announcer Mark Boyle roared during one game. "Reggie blows down the lane, nailing a one-handed layup," television announcer Jerry Baker added later. Best of all, his sidekick, Slick Leonard, bellowed out his trademark "Boom Baby" when Miller hit a three-pointer from beyond the key.

Miller's renewed enthusiasm for basketball and his tireless effort brought smiles to his coach's face. "Reggie works hard, real hard," Larry, his southern Indiana twang apparent, explained. "And he's got his confidence back. I was a shooter, I know what that feels like. And believe me, Reggie can shoot with the best of them."

Though Bird became disgruntled early in the season when Miller's trash-talking to officials hurt the team, Reggie was a happy camper. "If anyone on the team is ecstatic to have Coach Bird come here, it's myself," he explained. "Anytime you can learn from someone who has definitely lent so much to the game, it is only going to work in your favor."

Best of all, Miller regained his shooting touch. He'd always possessed near-perfect form to launch the rainbow efforts from three-point land, but in the early games of the new season, those shots were dead-center. Miller's philosophy was simple, especially during an off-night. "You shoot and shoot," he said. "Balls go in and out, but a shooter always believes the next one will go in. If I get in a bad streak, I'll just keep firing. I know I'll get my share."

Learning from Bird had been a plus for Miller. "Working off screens, setting my game up, late-game situations, knowing the game clock, all those things I've learned more about from Coach," Reggie admitted. "Playing for a living legend is really something."

With 25 games under his belt, Bird was no longer considered a rookie coach. He had weathered a poor start, juggling players like a magician, and brought continuity to a team that had been streaky the year before. Against San Antonio in late December, the Pacers sought their seventh consecutive win—but the Spurs' twin towers, David Robinson and rookie sensation Tim Duncan, had other ideas.

On the same night, Chicago Bulls coach Phil Jackson won his 500th NBA game and San Antonio surged to an early lead, fell back when the Pacers rallied, and then turned on the steam in the final quarter. David Robinson smoked Rik Smits for a season-high 39 points, clearly outplaying his taller rival. Duncan added 18 points and 17 rebounds to offset 25 from Miller.

To make matters worse, Bird had one of his worst coaching nights of the season. The Birdman's substitution pattern was questionable, and worse, he decided to play Derrick McKey, just off the injured list. McKey was clearly struggling, so much so that his performance was embarrassing. He stumbled badly driving for the basket, had shots blocked several times, played porous defense, and threw up bricks for free throws. His play—along with that of Chris Mullin, who suffered a horrible shooting night, and Dale Davis, whose muscular body was shoved around unmercifully by Duncan—had Bird scratching his head and rubbing his cheek, two nervous habits that conveyed the coach's displeasure.

Though Bird laid off blame by saying, "It's tough when the Spurs have the two big guys; usually you don't face teams with guys like that," he was clearly unhappy with Indiana's performance. And perhaps with his own.

When the Orlando Magic visited Market Square Arena the day after Christmas, Chuck Daly's squad was still missing superstar guard Penny Hardaway, who befuddled Daly as much as Shaq did Del Harris, the Lakers' coach. Harris had thought a reporter was kidding when told O'Neal, who'd already missed five weeks of the season with a strained abdominal muscle, had injured his right wrist punching a heavy bag. He wasn't. The headline in the *Los Angeles Times* read, "Shaq Scores Knockout. Of Himself."

Without Hardaway, Orlando was no match for the Pacers, especially when the Magic were also missing Rony Seikaly, who had the flu. Smits took full advantage of the situation, posting 16 of his 20 points in the first half. "We got off to a fast start and things came together," Smits said. "Definitely one of our best games of the year."

And what did Orlando coach Daly think of Larry Bird's efforts with his squad? "Larry's adapted his style very well," the 67-year-old Hall-of-Fame coach said. "The Pacers are very well coached. You face one of the top teams in the league with five of your top eight out and you expect to get hosed, but Larry's got his team playing great."

Reserve Fred Hoiberg had one of his better games in a Pacers uniform. He stunned the Magic with five straight three-pointers, totaling 20 points in all. "Freddy played very well, both ways," Bird opined. "He was scrappy, and we need him to play like that."

Eighteen and nine for the season (same record as the Bulls, third-best in the NBA), the Pacers took on the other Florida NBA team two nights later. Instead of victory number 19, the Miami Heat gave the Pacers a wake-up call. "Wait a minute fellas," they reminded Indiana, "You still have a long way to go." The final score was 101–90, but more devastating to the Pacers was being beaten at their own game: defense. Alonzo Mourning had rejoined Pat Riley's club several games earlier. He and his teammates smothered Smits, Miller, and Mullin, the Pacers' three offensive amigos. Smits and Miller were a combined 4 of 17 from the field on a night that coincided with the debut of a McDonald's french fries commercial featuring Grant Hill and Larry Bird. It also saw Michael Jordan score 47 points and Rodman grab a career-high 29 rebounds against Atlanta as the Bulls moved into first place in the Central Division.

Miami especially relished the win, considering it a payback to Reggie Miller, who taunted the Heat during the final seconds of the Pacers 104–89 victory in Indianapolis in mid-December. "At the end of that game, he looked at our bench and said [in effect], 'We can beat you any time,' " guard Tim Hardaway recalled.

Reggie didn't repeat his mistake December 30th against New Jersey. He and Chris Mullin tossed in 23 points each, as the Pacers broke the game open in the third quarter en route to a 109–91 win. Keith Van Horn of the Nets made his rookie debut against Bird's charges, scoring 17 points on the same night Chuck Person hit nine three-pointers for the Spurs and Michael Jordan rang up his NBA record 788th consecutive double-digit game. Coincidentally, Jordan's efforts cracked Kareem Abdul-Jabbar's record during a week when Jabbar was charged with assault and battery for beating up a Los Angeles man after a traffic altercation. Jordan's effort came despite a bizarre note he received at halftime stating his mother had been taken ill to a hospital. Fortunately, it was just a hoax.

The Pacers victory positioned them a half-game back and in third place in the Central Division behind Jordan's Bulls and the Atlanta Hawks. After a 2–5 start, they had gone 17–5. "I'm pleased," Bird said, "but we do have a long way to go."

———

Indiana welcomed the new year with a renewed determination to extend their season deep into the playoffs. "Can this team win the NBA championship?" Bird was asked. "Hell yes," he said without hesitation.

Bird's comments came during a season in which as much news was being made off the court in the NBA as on it. A cover story in

USA *Today* was right on target with the headline, "Power Play: The NBA and Its Players Grapple for Control." With talks regarding renewal of the collective bargaining agreement between the players and the league on tap for the spring, a sense that Commissioner David Stern and league owners were tightening their grip on control had left the players uneasy. "Our relationship was always a little testy," Karl Malone surmised. "Now it's getting a little worse."

The focal point of discussions regarding collective bargaining was what was known as the "Bird Rule." In 1983, the Celtics wanted to extend Larry Legend's contract, but salary-cap rules prevented it. An exception was made, and Bird was signed when the league and the union permitted teams to go over the cap to sign their own free agents. Bird was the first to benefit, signing a seven-year, $12.6 million deal.

Many pundits believed the new rule would lead to the downfall of the NBA because salaries paid to coveted players escalated into the stratosphere. But worse, those who weren't worthy benefited to excess. Bird agreed, telling columnist Conrad Brunner, "It's sort of ruined the league, hasn't it? I thought at the time it was good for everybody . . . but it hasn't really been that great for the league. . . ."

Whether Bird will ultimately be better known for his days as a Celtics player, as the Pacers coach, or for his attachment to a controversial free-agency rule remains to be seen, but the ironies abound. That a man who thought making $100 a week as a sanitation worker was big bucks, and who played the game of basketball much more for the love of it than love of money, should be mentioned every time multi-million-dollar contracts were debated bordered on the amazing.

Bird's Indiana team opened the new year against Washington at the Wizards' brand new MCI Center. The Wizards had rebounded from a poor start to hit the .500 mark and were determined to become a significant force as the season progressed. In their new arena, Washington was a perfect 8–0. "It's our new home," Chris Webber said, "And we defend it." Those words inspired the Pacers, especially Reggie Miller, and Indiana blasted the Wizards

99–81. "We wanted to give them their first loss," Miller stated. "We wanted to go down in history."

On the night fellow rookie coach Rick Pitino's Boston Celtics matched their victory total for 1996–97 (15), Indiana won its 18th game in its last 22. "Bird's got 'em going," Wizards coach Bernie Bickerstaff said. "They're really playing well." Not only that, Bernie, but Larry continued to show why he was the ultimate players' coach. During the final seconds of the game, Bird whispered something to trainer David Craig, who turned to Pacers public relations director David Benner and told him to save the game ball. When Benner asked why, Craig said, "Larry wants it."

The mystery was cleared up minutes after the game. When Bird ambled onto the team bus, he presented the ball to Austin Croshere, remembering that the rookie had just scored the first points of his NBA career. "Talk about impressive," one player remarked. "Larry never forgets the little guy."

Accolades for Bird's coaching tactics with the Pacers continued to pour in. The *Miami Herald* reported, "Bird is quickly getting the reputation as a players' coach. He doesn't scold players during games, and he doesn't fill timeouts with frantic dialogue. He is blunt with them during private moments and demands the same effort in practice, win or lose." The newspaper quoted Rik Smits as saying, "He'll let you know if he's upset with something; he just flat-out tells you. But he lets you play and learn from your mistakes."

That was in keeping with a Bird philosophy that had impressed trainer David Craig. "He lets the players be the players they can be. He doesn't want robots. Basketball is a game of reaction, the game must come naturally, and Larry wants the players to use their natural instincts. He wants them to play at their optimal ability. They appreciate that."

On the third day of the new year, Smits and the Pacers faced Toronto. The Raptors, who had reportedly tried to trade star guard Damon Stoudamire to New Jersey, succumbed 89–77 as the Pacers earned their 10th victory in 12 games and 8th straight at Market Square Arena. Despite the victory, Bird wasn't pleased. "We didn't come out like we have been," the coach lamented.

"The starting unit, other than Smits, wasn't into it. The bench [Fred Hoiberg and Antonio Davis combined for 20 points] came in with some energy and helped us tonight." Nonetheless, Toronto coach Darrell Walker was impressed. "Indiana is a very deep, very physical, very good team. They're one of the top two or three teams in the East. They're solid at every position." Damon Stoudamire, hoping a trade might free him from the shackles of a team that lost its 28th game against only four wins, saw the Pacers win more simplistically. "This must have seemed like practice for them," he told reporters.

A half-game behind the hard-charging Bulls, who were riding high led by Michael Jordan's average of over 40 points a game in the past 10 days, the Pacers prepared for their January 6th game with Phoenix and speculated about the upcoming All-Star Game. Even though fans' voting hadn't been kind to any of the Indiana starters, several had a chance to be named to the team. "Last year I had a great year, and the team sucked," three-time All-Star Reggie Miller barked. "Now, we're having a great year, . . . so I think we should have three [players] on the team, especially if we finish out the month strong."

For his part, Larry Bird said he wanted no part of the All-Star affair. "I have other plans," he told the Associated Press. Asked what he would do if he was named to coach the team, he replied, "I'll send Rick and Dick." Bird's comments about the All-Star affair were surprising since he had been a showcase player in the game during his Celtics days. Nonetheless, he wanted to avoid the event. "I don't like the All-Star games. I don't want to do it," he explained. "I hope we have the best record because it puts us in the best position for the playoffs, but I have no desire to coach the All-Star team."

Mark Jackson and Reggie Miller preferred to talk about their coach. "We've adopted the attitude of our coach," Jackson said. "All business. Go out, practice, work hard, prepare, and take no prisoners. . . . We're very dangerous." Miller echoed Jackson's comment. "No question, there is something very special going on."

Talking of such lofty goals sometimes produces overconfidence, the Achilles heel of all sports teams who start reading their headlines and believing them. Boosted by the adoring press clippings, Bird's Indiana squad believed they could beat Danny Ainge's 19–10 Western Conference contenders by just showing up and going through the motions.

Wrong! On the night Dallas beat Denver in a battle between the league's two worst teams (Dallas had lost 15 straight, Denver 13), the Suns awakened the Pacers with an 81–80 loss that should have never been. Though they played shorthanded (Dale Davis was on the sidelines with a sprained left ankle), Bird's boys fell behind in the first quarter with what could only be labeled a lackadaisical effort, and teetered on the brink of oblivion throughout the game. A fourth-quarter surge brought them close and provided a chance to win, but overall the performance was lackluster.

Two chief reasons for the loss were clear. Smits, named the NBA Player of the Week for his superb play, had one of his worst games of the season. His 7′4″ frame towering over the smaller Suns players, Smits should have controlled the paint. Instead, he allowed Clifford Robinson and other Suns to push him around, forcing him to miss 8 of 12 shots.

Miller, who had hit a closing-seconds winner in Phoenix earlier in the year, was also disappointing. The sharpshooter was anything but sharp, missing 12 of 15 shots. His cold touch was epidemic. His teammates shot just over 30 percent for the game.

In addition to the poor play of Smits and Miller, Coach Bird was unable to get his Pacers to adjust to Danny Ainge's motion offense, or to pass the ball to Smits in the post, where he had his great height advantage. "Bird was clearly outcoached in this game," a Phoenix reporter said. "Ainge must have a big smile on his face."

Indiana's last-gasp attempt to win the game provided a glimpse of Bird's inability to convince his Pacers in whose hands the ball should be at crunch time. With 5.5 seconds left, and the Pacers trailing by one point, Bird and his coaches designed a play where Smits set a pick instead of getting the ball himself. Reminiscent of other Pacers losses in 1996 and 1997, the team seemed unsure of themselves when they took the court. When Smits's pick was a halfhearted one, Travis Best, the left-hander whose poor play in the final quarters of games had raised Bird's ire, ended up with the ball. His running shot was off-balance, and bounced off the rim. Bird took Travis aside in the locker room, trying to boost his confidence by telling him he had taken a good shot, but the bottom line was a miss by a player who probably shouldn't have been shooting in the first place.

The Pacers had lost a game they should have won, and critics wondered if Bird would be able to inspire the Pacers toward better play at the end of close games. Danny Ainge realized what could have helped the team. "Thank goodness Larry wasn't in the game," he said, his face aglow with a winning smile.

PART

III

10

CELTIC GREEN

"The way I see it, if I put two hours in by myself, then someone who is working out with somebody else has to put in four hours in order to beat me. That's the way I've always gone about it."
LARRY BIRD

The smartest decision Larry Bird made as a professional basketball player was choosing Boston-based attorney Bob Woolf as his agent. When Woolf asked why he was singled out as the lucky one, Bird smiled and said, "Well, Bob, the other guys were just too smart for me so I chose you."

Though many would follow, Bob Woolf was the first agent to negotiate a sports contract between a player and management, having advised catcher Earl Wilson regarding his contract with the Detroit Tigers. Known for his flamboyant personality and resplendent wardrobe, Woolf possessed a tough outer crust and protective quality that endeared him to more than 500 sports figures he represented in the early 1980s.

While Bird made the final decision to hire Woolf, he had actually been chosen by what became known as the "committee," a group of four Terre Haute businessmen assigned the task of making sure that no one took advantage of their hometown boy. "We've got a Jew, a Catholic, and a Presbyterian on the committee," one of the advisers remarked when asked about the diversity of the group. The group's goal was to make certain Larry was paid a competitive wage, one comparable to the contracts of other first-round draft choices. "Hell, all Larry wanted," the businessman said, "was a garage full of six-packs and some way that a six-pack could automatically be replaced each time he took one out. We had to protect him."

From the 65 agents who were considered by the committee, Woolf and Cincinnati attorney Reuvan Katz, who represented Reds stars Johnny Bench, Pete Rose, and Tony Perez, were selected as finalists. Katz was second because of his lack of representation of basketball players. Woolf, who became a true father figure for young Bird, had experience, having negotiated contracts for such NBA stalwarts as Calvin Murphy and Otis Birdsong.

After a get-acquainted dinner, the deal was struck and Bob Woolf represented Bird in negotiations with the Celtics. He would propose a fee once the final figures of the deal were in place. If the committee felt his fee was too high, they could reject it. In effect, an agreement to agree was in place, something nebulous that risked all sorts of misunderstandings. Whether the committee had failed remained to be seen, but the fact that they were outnegotiated by the very agent they chose for Larry was surprising.

Bird's utilization of a hometown committee reinforced the Celtics' worry that they had taken a great risk in drafting the Indiana State star. They were well aware that Bird had been unable to handle the big-city nature of Bloomington, Indiana, a city of less than 100,000, even when the university was in session. How could Bird deal with Boston, a metropolis a thousand miles away from his family and friends? One NBA general manager surmised, "The Celtics have taken a hell of a chance. Bird's a country boy. . . . He's been shielded from the press, kept away from everyone. That was foolish. How's he gonna deal with Boston? He's in for a major transition."

But Bird knew that. During the summer before his rookie season, a reporter had asked him who he preferred to play for, the Pacers or the Celtics. "I told him the Pacers, but I really wanted to play for Boston," Bird admitted. "I was lying like hell because I was scared to death to go to Boston. I had never been out of Indiana except to play basketball and then I'd come right back home." Bird also provided a glimpse into his mind-set at the time when he said, "All I want out of my game is to play five years and have a million dollars in the bank. That's my goal."

Boston management had predicted that Woolf would be Bird's agent, so they were prepared to deal with his confrontational manner. His s.o.b. qualities didn't make him popular with Celtics management, who viewed Woolf as a leach who should be stomped on. During Bird's first visit to Boston Garden (he received a standing ovation when he entered the arena), Auerbach reminded Woolf who was boss. They left a locker confab fuming and fighting. Negotiations over Bird's contract were going to be as heated as a presidential debate, complete with all the mudslinging associated with politics.

Auerbach decided to launch the first missile, leaking to the press a report that Bird wanted a million dollars a year for six years to play for the Celtics. The Hick from French Lick was portrayed as a spoiled kid who didn't appreciate his chance to play professional basketball for a team that was rich in tradition. Auerbach's offer at the time was $400,000 per year. Woolf and the committee thought they'd ask for $1.2 million per year, knowing his market value would be in the $600,000 to $800,000 range.

Back home in Indiana, Larry Bird felt abandoned by the Celtics. Auerbach did his best to defend his position by informing the press, "I've made Bird my final offer, that's it. If he doesn't want to play for the Celtics, hell with him."

That didn't mean the contract being offered to Bird wasn't impressive. "The money was never a big factor," Bird had declared in explaining why he didn't leave Indiana State after his junior year. "The only time I ever remember being aware of the kind of money that might be available was when I read something in the paper about David Thompson [North Carolina star] signing a new contract for $800,000," Bird said. "I thought, 'Wow, $800,000!' I was pretty impressed with that, but it was something I couldn't relate to my own situation." Understanding *why* was the key to money matters and the Larry Bird of the future. "You've got to understand that all I ever heard as long as I'd been playing was about everything I wasn't or everything I couldn't do," Bird would explain later regarding his naiveté with money. "It was always: *He's from a small town. He can't run. He can't jump. He can't play against bigger guys. He's a step slow. He can't play defense.* It was the same way with money: *He doesn't deserve it."* Those words from a man who thought $3.50 an hour was big pay, one who thought he had the world on a string when he brought home $500 a month working as a sanitation employee in French Lick.

"Larry Bird never had money," a friend recalled. "To him it would become a status symbol. He figured that if you made a lot of money, then everybody would say you were a great player. Larry might not admit it, but he wanted big money to show people how good he was."

While Bird and Bob Woolf were deciding how to deal with the irascible, cigar-smoking Auerbach, Red escalated the feud. Asked about the chances that Larry would never play for Boston, he told reporters, "I could eat [the draft choice] if I had to. If I do, he'll never get the contract I've offered." Auerbach's public statements made Bird livid. Never one to choose his words carefully, he told friends that "[expletive] Auerbach" was "crazy" and that he'd "never play for him." Bird's tendency to include cuss words in his vocabulary was well known, though his mother and grandmother had tried to break the habit.

After discussing the Celtics mess with Woolf, Bird told him, "Don't worry. If they call, fine. If not, fine. I'm going fishin'." That was easy for Bird to do, but Woolf was quickly becoming the most hated man in his hometown of Boston. One time he asked for directions to a meeting, only to be met with an icy stare and told that he'd get the directions only if he signed Bird to a contract with the Celtics. Those encounters didn't worry the savvy agent as much as the volumes of hate mail that flooded his office daily. Boston newspapers dubbed the standoff, "The Hundred Day's War."

Two changes in Celtics management brought things around. Dave Cowens resigned as player-coach, and team owner John Y. Brown, the Kentucky Fried Chicken king and husband of celebrity talk show host and former Miss America Phyllis George, sold his shares to businessman Harry Mangurian. The logjam in negotiations was broken, and soon Celtics fans were dancing in the streets and reading newspaper headlines that proclaimed "Celts Set to Feather Bird's Nest," and "Auerbach to Cry Woolf Again for Bird's Contract."

The feathered nest called for Bird to receive $600,000 for the 1979–80 NBA season and the next four. In all, his $3 million plus contract was the highest in the history of sports for a rookie. Red Auerbach, in an effort to mend fences, told the press, "Larry signed for a lot less than he would have gotten elsewhere. He truly wants to be a Celtic."

June 8, 1979, was the date set for the signing, and the 23-year-old kid from the cornfields of Indiana flew to Boston for the occasion. Once all the hoopla was over, Bird wanted to return home, but that proved more difficult than expected. Before taking an early-morning flight, Larry decided a morning jog around Bob Woolf's neighborhood would be nice. The newest member of the leprechaun brigade arose at 6:00 A.M. and trotted down the paved streets in the plush area where the Boston attorney lived. Forty-five minutes later, he realized he was lost, not having paid attention to the route he'd taken. If not for a passing motorist who befriended Bird, he might still have been standing on a street corner waving his hands when the new season began. "Some guy picked me up," Bird admitted. "I told him I was lost. He said, 'That's a hell of a way to begin your career here.' " If Bird had left it at that when asked about the incident by reporters, he would have saved himself and his hometown from embarrassment. Ever the honest one, Bird continued on, explaining, "Somehow I got back to Mr. Woolf's house. I guess I'm still a hick from French Lick." Newspaper accounts the next day displayed that remark for all to see. Larry Legend-to-be moped home to disgruntled friends and family who couldn't believe he'd berated himself and them.

Though money had been a dealbreaker in the negotiations with the Celtics, Bird saw things differently. "Don't tell Mr. Auerbach, but I'd have played for nothing," he explained when asked about the size of his contract. Soon the $600,000 figure would be expanded. Bob Woolf negotiated deals with 7-Up, Spalding, and Converse that brought in revenues of more than $400,000. The shoe contract was an interesting one. In college, Bird had driven Indiana State team managers nuts by switching brands (Converse, Adidas, Pony) nearly every game.

Shortly after receiving his first check, Bird purchased the headstone for his dad's grave. Later Bird said of his dad, "I wish he was here. I would take care of him and give him anything he wanted."

When Bird's mom visited Boston for the first time, he gave her a new watch, and a sparkling ring with two pearls on it that she had always dreamed about wearing. "Georgia was just so proud of Larry," a family friend said. "She loved him so much."

Bob Woolf learned about Bird's values when they went house-hunting. Instead of buying a home in an affluent neighborhood, he chose a three-bedroom house in a middle-class area. "Who would I talk to?" Bird had asked Woolf when the real estate agent showed him houses in a neighborhood filled with wealthy businessmen, doctors, and lawyers. Later, Bird showed his frugality when he told Woolf he'd appreciate help furnishing the house, but only "one room at a time."

That philosophy was reminiscent of Bird's behavior when it came to buying a home for his mother in the French Lick area. Georgia had fallen in love with a home that cost $55,000, but Larry wasn't ready to act, telling a friend, "I know a lot of guys go off the first year they come into money and buy everything in sight. Then they find out they didn't have as much money as they thought they did." While Larry agonized over the decision, the selling price of the house rose to $80,000. Bird's response: "Mom, forget it. We ain't gonna pay more just because I'm a ballplayer."

If not for friend Max Gibson, many believe Georgia would never have left her house on Washington Street, where she had lived since 1972. After refusing to buy Georgia her dream home, Larry built his own home among the rolling hills and countryside surrounding Abbeydell Road on his father's parents' property, which he bought for back taxes. His idea was to position a trailer on the property, rent it out, and give Georgia the income so that she could pay for food and utilities while living in his house. Gibson talked him out of that, and all of Georgia's bills were sent to Max, who took care of everything. Even so, relatives reported that Larry actually chastised his own mother for running up grocery, utility, and phone bills while he was making more than a million dollars a year playing for the Celtics.

Nearly 20 years later, Bird's affinity for being frugal hadn't changed. Despite his $4.5 million contract and partial ownership in the Pacers franchise, Bird recoiled when Crooked Stick Golf Club in Indianapolis told him he could join, but would have to pay membership fees and dues like everyone else. He was already a member at The Country Club of Indianapolis, one of the perks of his Pacers contract, and wasn't about to fork over any money to Crooked Stick out of his own pocket.

That story coincided with Bird's thoughts about having an expensive car. Offered a Mercedes, he said, "I'll be glad to drive it if someone wants to buy it for me, but I can't see spending $70,000 on a car." Asked to wear what he considered an ugly shirt as an endorsement, Bird, who as a player had only permitted his wife a trip to Los Angeles after compiling enough frequent flier miles, replied, "If it's free, I'll wear it."

Bird's frugality didn't mean he wasn't free with his money when it was called for. Celtics executives recalled that Larry had footed the bill several times for an aging equipment manager so he could accompany the team on road trips. "Bird will spend money," a friend confided. "But he hates to waste it."

Accompanying Larry to his new home in Boston was Clinger, a Doberman puppy. He had a tougher time in Bird's rookie year than Larry did. After a stint in an obedience school, Clinger was hit by a car, taken to the hospital in an animal rescue ambulance, and housed in a special suite once it became known he was Larry Bird's prized dog. He was treated by a bevy of doctors, one of whom inserted a pin in his hip. True to his celebrity status, Bird never received a bill.

Larry had his own way of describing his Boston entrance. When asked how it felt, he said simply, "I'm still the hick from French Lick. I lead a simple life. I'm just a small-town kid gone to the city."

The city he'd chosen, Boston, was rich in basketball tradition; but the NBA was going through a transitional period, one marked by enormous expansion. Fifteen years earlier, there had been only 9 teams in the league. By 1971, there were 12 competing for advertising and fan dollars with the rival ABA, which also sported 12 teams. Five years later, the NBA featured 18 teams, the ABA 8. During Bird's final year of college, the leagues merged, and the NBA had 22 teams competing.

More than being a part of expanded player rosters, most of which had been diluted of talent through expansion drafts, Bird surfaced in the NBA at a time when a new white superstar was badly needed. In 1979, when he made his debut, more than 70 percent of the NBA players were black. Moreover, the retirement of John Havlicek and Jerry West, and the decline in the careers of Bill Walton and Rick Barry, meant the league lacked a legitimate white superstar for fans to cheer. Other top players such as Dave Debusschere, Jerry Lucas, Billy Cunningham, the VanArsdales, Don Nelson, and Bill Bradley had also retired by the time Bird laced up his shoes in the NBA. Clearly, a new white hope was needed.

Nowhere was this more evident than in perennial big market cities like New York and Boston, where the Knicks and Celtics had reigned for years. League officials were concerned that in New York the white gate was nearly nonexistent since the Knicks had gone from having an equal balance of whites and blacks in the mid-1970s to having no whites during the 1979 season. Even their coach, Willis Reed, was black. Some pundits labeled the team the Niggerbockers, a cruel racial slur.

The Celtics team Bird joined was also in transition. They had won the NBA championship in 1976, but Philadelphia cut them down the next year in the semifinals. In 1978, Auerbach's celebrated Celtics fell to 32–50, and links to the great Boston teams of the past—once armed with Bob Cousy, Bill Russell, and Dave Cowens—seemed like a distant memory. "My God," Phil Jackson of the Knicks exclaimed. "The Celtics' magic is gone."

Most noticeable by his absence was John Havlicek, a.k.a. "Hondo," the cagey scrapper from Ohio State who had combined with Dave Cowens to make the Celtics a perennial contender. Disappointed by Auerbach's reticence to pay him his worth, and troubled by foot problems, he'd called it quits. That meant the team's most popular player (especially with the white fans), one who had links to eight Celtics championship teams, was now gone. Auerbach knew a replacement was needed, and Bird was the heir apparent, the savior who would not only bring racial balance to a team, but also become a legitimate superstar to mold the Celtics of the 1980s.

Though the racial makeup of the Celtics was seven blacks and five whites in 1979, Auerbach knew there was a divisiveness between the two races. "It was as if I had two different teams," he admitted later. "Of course, Don Chaney was an independent cuss, but otherwise our team was split right down the middle." Celtics vice president Jeff Cohen said, "Boston is the most racial city in the country. And when we began losing, people suddenly became aware of a player's color." Bill Russell, arguably the finest center ever to play the game, knew that. Even when he was dominating play in the NBA as the Celtics waltzed to title after title, Bob Cousy and John Havlicek got all the headlines. "I never felt like I got my due in Boston," Russell lamented. "People there loved the white guys. I got used to it, but I didn't like it."

When Bird entered training camp, 8 of the 15 players in camp were white. "My job is to get a ballclub out there the town will like," Auerbach admitted, apparently unaware that his statement meant he cared more for the color of his players than their abilities.

Bird never permitted himself to consider his appointment as the "great white hope" to both the Celtics and a league sorely in need of a white superstar. He'd always been comfortable around blacks, having played playground ball as a youngster in junior high against those who worked at the French Lick Hotel. "They were great," Bird recalled. "I couldn't believe how good they were."

Later, Bird became friends with the University of San Francisco seven-footer Bill Cartwright, a player he'd met during an All-Star game in college. Jim Wisman, his roommate at Indiana University for the three weeks he was a Hoosier, thought he knew why. "Larry got along with black players great because they came from similar backgrounds," he recalled. When Bird, who was highly revered by black players like Ray Tolbert, Eddie Johnson, Ricky Pierce, Cliff Livingston, and others who respected his ability and cared little about his race, was asked about Wisman's statement, he said, "I'll never think of myself as some great white hope. . . . On the whole, blacks are the best basketball players in the world. I think it's because they're hungrier. They crave success. A lot of white kids are too spoiled. They get cars and other luxuries."

Doubting Thomases were everywhere as Bird began his pro career. One writer who'd seen Bird play three times said, "He's slow afoot and deficient in individual defense. . . . He could be an excellent goalie on a zone defense but may develop a sore neck watching faster forwards speed past him." Even general manager Jerry West of the Lakers, who knew a thing or two about the game, was dubious, telling reporters, "Boy is he slow. . . . It's a shame he couldn't be as quick as other guys out there." To those naysayers, Mel Daniels countered, "To me, Larry will be on the same par as the Doctor [Julius Erving] in a year."

Larry Bird's prediction? Asked what he expected, he said, "I pass good, so I'll probably pass a lot. I doubt that I'll be a big scorer in the pros."

In the middle of August 1979, Bird traveled to his new home away from home on the eastern seaboard. Fortunately, two other new arrivals—one a player, the other a coach—meant the Celtics had potential for the new season. Taking over the reigns for the Beantown team was Bill Fitch, the first Celtics "outsider" to be hired by Auerbach. He had been the coach at Cleveland, where he'd built the expansion team into a contender before experiencing a fallout with management. Fitch was known as a no-nonsense basketball taskmaster (Auerbach believed that was sorely needed with the Celtics) with an expertise in preparing for an opponent.

Fitch and Bird locked horns from day one at rookie camp. ". . . Right away I realized that [Coach Fitch] intended to show me who was boss," Bird remembered. "When we started the scrimmages, he was doing everything he could to test me. He wanted to aggravate me, and he just couldn't do it. He'd make me guard this player, then another one. He'd put me here, then he'd put me there. He tried to run me until I was ready to drop."

The other newcomer, whom Fitch yanked away from free agency, was M. L. Carr, a veteran swingman from the Pistons who had led the league in steals the prior year. Carr was projected as the sixth man Boston required to contend and to recover from the dismal 29–53 record during the previous season. Carr looked forward to practicing against Larry Bird, the bigshot kid from Indiana. "I wanted to see how tough he was," M.L. recalled. "First time down the court, I popped him with a forearm to the chest. Next time down, he popped me."

Injured finger and all, Bird was a positive influence on the Celtics from day one. Scrapping for balls and his neverending shooting drills rubbed off on everyone else on the team. "In 10 years, I never saw anyone throw himself around like that," Norman Frank, owner of the training camp at Milbrook, Massachusetts, said. "Most of those guys were always worried about risking their careers. But Bird had all the guys diving for balls."

"The white boy can play," veteran Cedric Maxwell proclaimed. M. L. Carr backed up Maxwell's words, saying, "Rookies just don't come in the way he did; making creative passes, joking confidently, and going out and backing up his words with his play."

The Celtics training camp was not without incident. "I knew some of the veterans would be testing the rookies, and I was right," Bird recalled. "Cedric Maxwell walked in and said to one of the guys. . . . 'Hey, . . . look, that's our savior over there.'"

Bill Fitch showed the Celtics he was boss, and the players either understood or took a hike. "That very first day Curtis Rowe was jogging at half-speed," Bird recalled. "Fitch said to him, 'Just take that jog up there by the door on the left, take a shower, and get out of here. You've been cut."

Bird saw through Fitch's action that day as being his creed for the season. ". . . I had him pegged," Larry said. "He wanted to make sure he was in total control. He wanted me to listen to everything he said, so I just went along with the program . . . I think that once he found out that I was tough and always played hard, I don't think he had any problem with me."

Bird's first encounters with the marquee players on the Celtics provided a real challenge. "[Cedric] Maxwell really wanted a piece of me," Larry declared. "He had all these veteran-type tricks and we would go at it every day. . . . Before practice, M. L. Carr would say, 'Hey, rookie, let's go.' . . . . Dave Cowens always wanted to play, and I had a hard time with him at first. Eventually I stopped him. I stopped M.L. And I stopped Maxwell. . . . I had to. Just to get them off my back."

Besides veterans Cowens, Maxwell, and Carr, Chris Ford and Nate "Tiny" Archibald were Celtics teammates during Bird's first year. His first game as a professional, at least in the exhibition season, was against the Philadelphia 76ers and all-time great Julius Erving. "I just couldn't wait to play against him and see how good he really was," Bird said. He scored 18 points in 28 minutes, and the Celtics lost 115–90.

During the exhibition season, the Celtics played the Indiana Pacers at Terre Haute. Bird played sporadically, totaling 17 points and 16 rebounds. Asked what had surprised him most about professional basketball, Bird grinned and said, "All the girls hanging around."

Bird's first season in the NBA was dotted with the promise of great things to come—but like all young players, he struggled in the beginning. On opening night against the Houston Rockets at Boston Garden, the rookie was plagued by foul trouble, but contributed 14 points and 10 rebounds in 28 minutes of play. Boston won 114–106. Bird said his main problems were the absence of a shooting touch and an inability to handle Houston's tough defense. Never one to look for excuses, he nonetheless remarked that the ball used in the NBA (narrow-seamed Wilson brand) differed from that utilized in college (wide-seamed Spalding ball). "Once I get more used to shooting that ball, I'll be all right," Bird said. Of the stiff defense he encountered, Bird was blunt. "It's so much better in the pros," he explained. "And in college I always followed my shot. In the pros, you can't afford to because your man is steaming downcourt."

Despite Bird's learning process, his impact on the Celtics was immediate. Boston broke from the gate 11–3 instead of the dismal 2–14 of the year before. Portland coach Jack Ramsey saw the obvious difference in the team, noting "Bird makes his teammates around him play better—that's the sign of a great player." Teammate Tiny Archibald said, "Larry is a tremendous passer. He always looks for the pass first. He did it from the first day of training camp. As a result, everyone started to move without the ball."

To Bird, passing was contagious. "That's the way we played at Indiana State," he professed. "One will want to make a good pass, then the next guy wants to make one. Pretty soon everybody's doing it." Yes they were, and the Celtics blasted out to a 20–6 record. Bird was the savior. Indeed he was.

His rookie season was full of firsts for Larry Bird. The first triple-double came on November 14, when he had 23 points, 19 rebounds, and 10 assists. Three weeks later, he took the floor against the Lakers and Magic Johnson, their first encounter since the NCAA Finals. Headlines like "The Magic Man versus the Bird," and "Can the Magic Man Pull a Bird Out of His Hat?" promoted the game.

Through the years, the two men forged a mutual respect, but their different approach to the game distanced the relationship. Magic saw things clearly, telling reporters, "He [Larry] thought I was Hollywood, egotistical and stuck on myself . . . I thought he was the country guy who couldn't relate to me and the other guys." Bird retorted, saying, "He's showtime. I can't play the game smiling and joking. I'm too serious."

Just as Indiana State couldn't beat Michigan State in the NCAA finals, Bird's Celtics couldn't overcome Magic's Lakers, and the Celtics lost 123–105. Magic had 23 points to Larry's 16, but in the fourth quarter Bird meant business, knocking Magic to the floor when he tried to dart down the lane for a layup. Johnson immediately confronted Bird, and the two had to be restrained. "If he thought I was going to lay down for him he was crazy," Bird remarked. "He wasn't going to back down, and I wasn't going to back down."

Comparisons regarding the two players were already being made, though they had been in the league less than two months. Tommy Heinsohn, the former Boston coach and current broadcaster, proclaimed, "Magic is the better athlete . . . and is quicker. But I think as a basketball player, Bird is better."

Both men were named to the All-Star squad, but Bird, standing with the other greats of the game and wondering what he was doing there, made the most impact. Several passes were of the unforgettable nature, especially a behind-the-back beauty on a fast break that had fans and players alike oohing and aahing. Though Bird didn't win the MVP award, one sportswriter explained, "He just won the game." Trivia buffs noted that Bird hit the very first three-pointer in All-Star competition.

By season's end, Boston had the best record in the league. (Before the season, Fitch asked the Celtics to write down how many games they would win. Bird guessed 47; the team won 61.) And Larry Legend, who averaged 21 points and 10 rebounds a game, was named Rookie of the Year by a 63–3 margin over Magic. The Celtics swept Moses Malone and the Rockets in the first round of the playoffs, but then were unceremoniously dumped by the 76ers, who featured Julius Erving, Caldwell Jones, and Daryl Dawkins. "We had the best record, and they put us away like nothing," a bitterly disappointed Bird said.

Coach Bill Fitch still saw the emergence of a potential superstar. "He had an uncanny ability to see the floor," Fitch explained. "I call him 'Kodak,' because his mind takes an instant picture of the whole court." Atlanta coach Hubie Brown marveled at Bird's play, saying, "He's a complete player, . . . a beautiful player to watch. He epitomizes how the game is supposed to be played." Tom Heinsohn summed up his thoughts about Bird by saying, "It's like someone went into a cave in French Lick and there was a block of ice. They chipped away and out popped this prehistoric basketball player."

Bird's realization that he could play in this league had come in a game against Phoenix after the All-Star break. He threw 45 points at the Suns and never looked back. That didn't mean the season hadn't drained Bird. "I just stayed home and slept for three or four days," Bird recalled after the playoffs. "I really felt bad about getting beat so early."

That for a kid who nearly didn't attend college and was judged by all the experts as being too slow to play in the NBA, one whose name was third on the list in the voting for MVP in the 1979–80 season behind two other fairly good ballplayers named Kareem Abdul-Jabbar and Julius Erving.

Larry Bird's next three seasons saw him continue playing at a high level. Sensing they had the makings of a championship ballclub, the Celtics made some moves to provide Larry with a better supporting cast. The first improvement arrived when Auerbach landed center Robert Parish in a trade. Then the Celtics guru garnered the University of Minnesota's lanky center Kevin McHale in the NBA draft. While they became perfect complements to Bird, Tiny Archibald and M. L. Carr, their first days as Celtics made Bird wonder about both players.

Of seven-foot Robert Parish's running ability, Bird said, "You didn't know whether to laugh or feel sorry for that guy. . . . By the time he'd get to midcourt [in practice], he'd be so far behind everyone that he'd have to turn around and go back the other way. . . . Everybody on the team was saying, 'Who is this guy? He can't even get up and down the court.'" Kevin McHale, Bird recalled, had nearly sat out the season over salary disputes. He'd packed his bags for Italy before signing with the Celtics, causing Fitch (the ex-Marine Larry dubbed "the Drill Sergeant") to call the skin-and-bones McHale "Spaghetti Man."

After an adjustment period, the Celtics jelled—at one point winning 25 of 26 games. They finished the 1980–81 season with

62 wins and a division championship when they were able to defeat archrival Philadelphia 98–94 in a deciding game. Bird shone through with 24 points, and the accolades poured in once again. Auerbach, after lighting his trademark cigar, reflected on his prized player. "I didn't realize how quick he was," Auerbach said. "I had no knowledge of his rebounding abilities. I knew he had a court presence on offense, but I didn't realize he had one on defense, too. And I had no sense of his leadership qualities, or his ability to motivate other people." Auerbach praised Bird's toughness. "I had no great insight into his character, or his personality, or his willingness to play in pain. I have never had an athlete in my 39 years in the league who liked to play more than Larry does . . . I call him a pro's pro. Knock him down, he'll get up again. He won't take any crap from anybody."

Bird's mental and physical toughness proved worthy in the playoffs in 1981. Against Chicago, three years before Michael Jordan made his debut in a Bulls uniform, Larry's fierce competitive spirit impressed Auerbach. During the fourth game, with a chance to sweep, Kevin McHale replaced Bird in the lineup. As he walked by, Bird whispered to McHale, "Kill these guys." Later, Bird hit a three-pointer that he called at the time, "the best shot of my life." It buried the Bulls, and enabled Boston to face dreaded Philadelphia for the conference championship.

When the Celtics fell behind three games to one, they were given up for dead. They won Game Five, but then had to return to the Spectrum in Philly, where they had a dismal record. In an effort to break the spell, Fitch told his team to dress at different lockers and warm up at the opposite end of the court than usual. Though the team fell behind early, they rallied and nipped the 76ers 100–98 to tie the series.

In the seventh and deciding game, Bird started a furious comeback from an 89–82 deficit by stealing the ball from Dr. J. With the game clock ticking down, Boston took the lead; and when Bird's pressure forced the Sixers' Bobby Jones to throw an errant last-second pass to Erving, the Celtics were the conference champions. "Bird was brilliant," Philadelphia coach Billy Cunningham exclaimed.

That didn't mean Bird hadn't worked his butt off matching up with Julius Erving. "My personal rivalry with Erving was growing," Bird recalled. "It's still the most exciting confrontation I've ever had at the forward spot. . . . The most important thing I had to do while guarding Dr. J was to get help. When he started going along that baseline, you knew what was on his mind. He wanted to dunk. Once he got a step on you, there was nothing you could do. Any daylight at all and Dr. J would jam it through." Bird also disputed reports he trash talked with Erving. "That was M. L. Carr from the bench," Bird said. "Believe me, I never said a word to Dr. J on the court."

In the finals, Boston bested Houston in six games to win their 14th NBA championship. In the final game, Houston had rallied to make it close when Bird faced a three-point shot from the corner. "This has got to be *it*," Bird recalled. "It's all in my hands. . . . When the ball went through the net my heart started pounding. I mean that sucker was really beating fast." After the game, Bird posed with Auerbach, grabbing Red's cigar and putting it in his mouth. "To this day, I love that picture more than any photo I have," Bird said.

The series was filled with outstanding performances from both teams, but it was a Bird shot in Game One that was the most memorable, one of those shots that fans and players would talk about for years to come. In the fourth quarter, Bird threw up a 25-footer over defender Robert Reid, who stood and watched the shot as it careened off the rim of the basket. Larry, however, had already followed the rebound to the right side of the hoop, where he floated into the air to retrieve it. The momentum carried him toward the baseline—but in a split-second, realizing a right-handed shot would nick the backboard, Bird switched the ball in midair to his left hand, and threw up a left-handed shot that floated toward the basket. Bird's rear end bounced on the floor just as the ball went in. Reid and the other players stood in disbelief. "I still don't believe it went in," Reid said 10 years later.

That play and others inspired Auerbach to call Bird "a 6'9" version of Bob Cousy." Bird's assessment of his own game was brash. "At times," he told reporters, "I think I'm the best player in the league. Now I figure three out of four nights I'm gonna play better than anybody else in the game."

———————————

During the 1981–82 season, Larry Bird excelled, but his team's attempt to win another world championship was derailed by the 76ers. Over the summer months, which he spent in French Lick, Bird was determined to bring back the glory to Boston Garden.

Quinn Buckner, the outstanding defensive guard from Indiana University, joined the club for the new season, joining a roster full of veterans including Bird, McHale, Parish, Maxwell, Ainge, Archibald, Rick Robey, and M. L. Carr. Bird was especially fond of Ainge, the ex-baseball player whose feistiness matched his own. He often teased Danny about his first practice with the Celtics the year before, when Ainge had gone 0 for his first 19 shots.

Bird blazed to his quickest start ever, and in March set a Celtics scoring record with 53 points against the Pacers. But Boston was a "team of individuals" that year, according to Bird, who was injured much of the season, and the team won only 56 games to the Sixers' 65. Worse, they were swept by the Bucks in the play-offs. "It was embarrassing," Bird recalled. "We never got it together that year."

Bird hated losing. "Sitting in the locker room after being swept by the Bucks was the worst feeling I've ever had playing basket-ball," he said. "I had known great moments, had won a champi-onship, and had had a lot of good games, but at that moment it seemed like the end of the world."

Over the summer months, Bird dedicated himself to improve-ment. He practiced on the new basketball goal he built at home, and began running harder than ever. "I also did a great deal of thinking about what went wrong," Bird remembered. "And I tried to think of ways to improve our club."

Bird's regimen that summer was tougher than boot camp. Most of the work was done in solitude. "Even when I was young," he explained. "The way I liked to practice was by myself or with no more than one other guy. . . ."

K. C. Jones replaced Bill Fitch at the helm of the Celtics for the

1983–84 season. For Bird, adjusting to Jones was easy. Though he admired Fitch, the fiery coach alienated nearly every one of his players with a hard-fisted, never-bend attitude. K. C. Jones was the opposite, interested more in team play characterized by permitting the players to freelance more, with fewer restrictions than Fitch had imposed. Bird also admired Jones as a person. Later he said, "I try to treat people like K.C. did. I think he's a great man. He stands for all the right symbols."

Added to the Boston roster was sticky-fingered defenseman Dennis Johnson, acquired in a trade with Phoenix. Gone was Rick Robey, Bird's roommate, whose night-owl antics were in contrast to Larry's propensity to hit the sack early and avoid the nightlife.

Bird extolled the virtues of Dennis Johnson. "D. J. is simply the best player I've ever played with on the Celtics," he said. "Kevin is great. Robert is great . . . . But when I look at other teams, there is always a player on that team who seems to symbolize the whole team. When I think of our own team, the guy I think of is D. J. . . . The guy will do anything to win."

From the first game against Philadelphia in the preseason, the Celtics proved they were ready to compete for an NBA title. First Cedric Maxwell threw the ball at Moses Malone's head, and a fight erupted. Minutes later, Bird tangled with Mark Iavaroni, punching him in the mouth. After peace was restored, Malone and Bird went after each other. Then Bird and Iavaroni had to be restrained. Finally, Auerbach climbed down from the stands and challenged Moses Malone. "Hit me, you [expletive]," Red bellowed.

The exhibition game at the Boston Garden was a sign of things to come. The Celtics played tough, hard-nosed basketball, and Bird was battling like never before. "How are you supposed to play Bird now?" 76crs owner Harold Katz asked. ". . . If he doesn't like the way you are playing him, he'll belt you."

When the regular season ended, the Celtics meant to challenge for the title. They won their last nine games of the year, and figured to meet nemesis Philadelphia in the second round. New Jersey took care of that, however, by upsetting them in the first.

The semifinals in the Eastern Conference matched the Celtics and the Knicks, led by talented forward Bernard King, who had averaged 44 points a game in the previous series. Bird ended any thoughts New York had of winning, averaging 30 points a game to lead Boston. After the seventh game, Bird said, "Some days everything just clicks, and I could tell early in the first quarter I was going to play really well. I was in the kind of groove where I knew I could do anything I wanted to at any time . . ." Bird later explained his philosophy in big games. "In a situation like that, I try to take it one quarter at a time. If I have a good first quarter, that's over with. Then the second quarter. Then the third, and so on."

The Celtics went on to beat Milwaukee in the conference finals in five games, avenging their disappointing loss the previous year. In the NBA Finals, they faced the Lakers and Magic Johnson, and basketball fans everywhere were licking their lips in anticipation of the showdown.

Of Johnson, Bird remarked, "You really can't compare us. He's more flashy and can make more things happen than me, make them happen quicker. . . . He's a perfect player." Johnson replied, "It's no personal battle. Larry's definitely the best player at this time. . . . He's the best, so you've got to bring your best. The boy is bad."

After three games, the Lakers led two to one. "We played like sissies. I know the heart and soul of this team, and today the heart wasn't there, that's for sure," no-excuses Larry scolded after the Game Three loss. "We got beat bad and it's very embarrassing." Egged on by Bird's inflammatory words, the Celtics made certain Game Four was a donnybrook. Motivated by their leader, Boston responded with a no-holds-barred effort that nearly sent several Lakers to the hospital. Early in the game, Kurt Rambis tried to glide down the lane, only to be thrown to the floor by Kevin McHale. Bird, who had definitely sounded the call to battle, got into the act with a jarring block that sent Michael Cooper flying into a group of photographers. When Kareem Abdul-Jabbar elbowed Bird, Larry came roaring after him, and the two superstars stood jaw to jaw before being separated. "I've never quite seen Larry like that," Jabbar said later. "He would have killed to win that game."

Fortunately, Bird didn't have to. Instead, in overtime, number 33 sealed a Boston victory with 16 seconds left by posting Magic in the paint, and then recoiling away from him for a soft jumper that was dead center.

Game Five, which went to the Celtics, was played at Boston Garden, where Red Auerbach—known for being a prankster during his career (he once set off the fire alarm in the opponents' hotel so they had no sleep)—had the thermostat turned up to 97 degrees. Lakers players, used to playing in the air-conditioned atmosphere of the Forum in Los Angeles, were gasping for oxygen on the bench. "People came dressed in ways I had never seen at an NBA game," Bird said. "T-shirts. Shorts. Women in halters. Men with no shirts."

Bird was unaffected by the tropical temperature. "I love to play in the heat," he said. "I just run faster to create my own wind."

The Celtics won that game, but Los Angeles squared the series at three games each as fans marveled at Magic's no-look passes and Bird's soft touch off the glass. In Game Seven, after Bird had chastised his teammates by saying, "We need 12 heart transplants to win," Celtic rebounders overwhelmed the Lakers. Boston won its second championship of the Bird era and gave Bird a measure of revenge against Magic five years after Johnson's Michigan State Spartans had beaten Larry's ISU Sycamores in the NCAA finals.

"The winning feeling is indescribable," Bird proclaimed. "You look up at the clock and it is 11:30 or 11:45 and you're saying, 'I wish I could freeze this time for 24 hours.'"

Though Magic Johnson dished out an astounding 95 assists in the series, Bird was the dominant player, averaging nearly 28 points. Larry Legend collected the MVP trophy, one he placed next to the league MVP award that he won and stored for a time in the back of his mother's pickup truck. In five short seasons, Larry Bird had reached the top of the mountain; he was the finest player in basketball. He also continued to endear himself to all the fans in his home state. "This one is dedicated to Terre Haute," Bird exclaimed, later adding, "Dedicating the NBA title to them was the best I could do to make up for the loss to Michigan State. In their eyes, at least, I had finally beaten Magic."

BIRD TALK

*"To get the best out of people you have to push the
right buttons. It's more common sense than anything. . . .
With this group, I have to give them confidence
and I had to manage them."*
LARRY BIRD

During the first few months of the
1997–98 season, Pacers players were subjected to what quickly
became described as *Bird talk*, or *Birdisms*. From early childhood, small-town Larry had developed his own vocabulary, one
designed to protect him when he wanted to portray himself as a
true hick from French Lick. The masquerade or "camouflage," as
it was described by former Boston executive Dave Gavitt, was
intended to throw people off by hoodwinking them into believing
poor ol' Larry was a bit on the slow side.

Use of words and phrases such as "gawsh," "them guys," "if I
had my rathers," "he's ran hard," "ain't," "don't have no," and
"pitcher" instead of "picture," crept into his speech patterns from
time to time. Bird admitted to a longtime friend that he loved to
play with people's minds, making them wonder if he was brilliant
or a country hick who could be taken advantage of. Boston journalist Bob Ryan saw through his facade, and once told him,
"Larry, we've just spoken for a half-hour and you haven't used one
double negative."

Sportscaster Mark Patrick was surprised when he listened to Bird at a Miller Beer outing. "Larry said he didn't want to do it, hated speaking, but then he got up and gave a remarkable talk to all those beer distributors," Patrick recalled. "He talked like a polished professional, and he was as deft with his words as he was with his passes when he was a player."

Those who knew Bird well were aware of his keen intellect, which was enhanced by an astonishing memory. Many times he had amazed sportswriters by recalling detailed incidents from games played 15 years earlier. "One time I asked Larry about a shot he hit against the Lakers," former teammate Dennis Johnson said. "And he says, 'You mean the one after you double-dribbled the ball out of bounds?' I couldn't believe he remembered that."

Bird loved to tell people he "had read one book in 20 years [a John Kennedy biography]," but that didn't mean his brain wasn't soaking up everything around him. Donnie Walsh had seen evidence of that when they originally discussed the new coaching position. "I couldn't believe how much he knew about the Pacers," Walsh recalled. "Little things too. From nearly every game they played last year."

Bird's photographic memory, the one that had caused Bill Fitch to dub him "Kodak," flew squarely in the face of his dunce image. Who was this man—the one famous for the verbal solecisms, or the one who once amazed a teammate by recalling the name of a song being played in a 1986 game just before he hit an open jumper to win a close game? Alan Cohen, one of three Celtics owners during Bird's heyday, saw the savvy side of Larry Legend. "In 1991, Larry negotiated his own contract. I must admit I was intimidated. To me, Larry has never been the hick from French Lick. He likes people to think he is sometimes." That about the same guy who, prior to a 1990 ceremony honoring Magic Johnson, had to ask someone to help him tie his tie. Fortunately, wife Dinah saved him by providing several tied ties in his carry bag. "Ain't she wonderful?" Bird exclaimed.

To Bob Ryan, the question was complex. "It is quite possible that nobody knows the real Larry Bird," Ryan proclaimed. "He may not even know the real person himself." A family member of Bird's said it another way. "Larry's a tough one to call," she said. "He's like a chameleon. Oftentimes, when he surprises me by doing something I hadn't expected, I want to say, 'Will the real Larry Bird stand up?' Even Larry's mom had a tough time. She used to tell me she never could figure out Larry."

Most observers believed Bird's paradoxical ways stemmed from being the child of an alcoholic. "He gets by without saying much," a longtime friend said. "He's very insecure, doesn't trust people. He's suspicious of anything he can't control." Red Auerbach had words of warning for anyone who underestimated Bird. "He looked like a country bumpkin, but when you looked into his eyes you could see he was no dummy. He knew what he wanted in life and what he needed to get there."

While his use of poor English and a sarcastic tone were defensive mechanisms he'd learned from childhood, he used humor to mask feelings and keep people at bay. In effect, as Terre Haute attorney Tom Newlin said, "Larry had built a shell around himself. Only wife Dinah and a few close friends have ever been allowed in." Magic Johnson was one of those, having made friends with Bird after they filmed two television commercials, one in French Lick in the summer of 1984. "The more we talked, the more I liked him," Johnson recalled. "Especially his sense of humor. I started a T-shirt company, and sent him a few samples. He wrote back, "Thanks for the shirts. P. S. Get a job.""

Bob Woolf, Bird's longtime agent, said before his death, "Larry's so different in private than he is in public. It's a shame more people don't know that side of him. I really love the kid. He's so down-to-earth and so intelligent. . . . But he's shy around strangers, especially reporters."

Bird's appearance contributed to an image that was misleading.

Perhaps it was the receding chin and the slack jaw that made him appear "dumb" at times, or the absence of a noticeable lip line that caused a casual observer to think Bird had no teeth. Combined with the remedial language and his lope-along gait, Larry on occasion had a lost look about him as if he were trying to figure out what to do next. Just when that image appeared, Bird's glistening blue eyes would suddenly flutter, a meaningful expression would cross his face, and he appeared in tune with everything before him.

Several times during his rookie coaching season, television cameras captured the paradox. One moment viewers could witness him wiping the sides of his mouth with his right hand, apparently deep in thought. The next, he'd be gazing out in space with a blank look on his face as if to say, "What's going on here?"

Regardless of all of the comments and observations, one thing was clear: Pacers players were in love with their new coach. "Larry's been great," reserve center Mark West said. "This is a season I'll never forget."

Continuing their pursuit of the Bulls, who were trying to repeat their three-peat magic of the early 1990s, Indiana traveled to Houston on January 8th to play Rudy Tomjanovich's Rockets. Fortunately, the team caught a break since none of the Rockets' Big Three—Hakeem Olajuwon, Clyde Drexler and Charles Barkley—were in uniform. Indiana was a prohibitive favorite—but instead of blowing out the Rockets, the Pacers starting five stunk up the place. Smits looked like anything but a potential All-Star and NBA Player of the Week. He was called for silly fouls, failed to position himself securely in the paint for easy lobs from the guards, and shot like a beginner. By game's end, he had just two points. Miller, Mullin, Jackson, and McKey, subbing for the injured Dale Davis, didn't fare much better. Their lackluster, going-through-the-motions play allowed the spunky Rockets to stay in the game.

Bird—nattily dressed in a brown sportcoat, bright blue shirt, and gold paisley tie—sat on the bench perplexed, chewing gum at a feverish pitch, his hand to his chin as if to say, "I can't stand watching this." A minute into the second half, he had had enough, and yanked all five starters. On the way to the bench, Reggie looked like a pouting kid who had just had his favorite toy taken away. "I wanted to get five guys out there who could get the job done," Bird said later.

Bird's bold move earned him additional respect from Pacers officials and the media covering the game. The Dallas morning newspaper lauded the coach's decision, suggesting that Bird was a coach who wouldn't tolerate modern athletes who gave less than 100 percent. "He's a throwback to the old college coaches," one reporter said. "Nice to see that."

Bird's ability to publicly scold his starters indicated how much respect they had for him. None seemed offended, but rather appeared to be willing to put individual goals and ego behind what was best for the team. Miller said, "If I'm having an off-night, I *should* be on the bench."

That type of attitude was rare in a league where multimillion-dollar players who acted like prima donnas were the rule, not the exception. Bird's leadership abilities were a breath of fresh air that team management applauded.

Nobody appreciated Bird's approach more than the second five on the team. Craving minutes, they knew Bird would give them a shot if they kept working hard. That was all they could ask.

The Houston game was no exception. With Jalen Rose, a life-saver all season, scoring a season-high 18 points; Travis Best, becoming a greater offensive threat as the season progressed; and Antonio Davis, the bluecollar worker on the boards leading the way, the Pacers kept the scrappy Rockets at bay. Indiana never trailed, though the game became a nailbiter in the final few minutes. Houston's mistakes cost them a chance of winning, and Indiana escaped with an 87–80 victory that buoyed their record to 22–11, just a half-game behind the surging Bulls in the Central Division.

Two nights later, the Pacers completed what television announcer Jerry Baker called the *Texas two-step*. The team ventured to Dallas to play the lowly Mavericks—coached by another Celtics legend, Don Nelson. By his side was son Donn, destined to take over the team when his father retired from basketball in the year 2000.

Though Don Nelson, who had tried 12 different starting line-ups since taking over the club, did his best to inspire the Mavs by waving his arms frantically along the sidelines, Indiana had too much firepower for Dallas. On the night when Utah Jazz coach Jerry Sloan recorded his 600th career triumph and Scottie Pippen brought a smile to Bulls coach Phil Jackson's face by scoring 14 points in his first game back after foot surgery, the Pacers prevailed over the 6–29 Mavericks, 84–79.

Significant to the win was a Reggie Miller shot that came after a timeout with the score tied 77–77 and 1:07 left on the clock. Realizing the mistake they'd made in the Phoenix game when Travis Best ended up with the ball in his hands as the final seconds ticked off, Larry Bird and his two sidekicks called Cross 4, a play set up for Reggie to come off a Smits screen and then lob the ball into the "big fella" (as sportscaster Mark Boyle called him).

Miller disagreed with the call, arguing that he should be given a chance to ice the game with a three-pointer. "I wanted the ball in my hands," Miller later said. "I told Larry I wanted the last shot. We had one play drawn up, but we ended up running another play." In the huddle, Bird, adapting to making critical decisions under pressure, remembered his days in Boston when *he* wanted the ball at crunch time. After some thought, he figured out a way to make everyone happy. If Dallas, who had possession, scored, then Cross 4 was the play. If the Pacers held them without a basket, Reggie's play was on.

Mark Jackson tried to inspire his teammates toward the hoped-for stop. Walking onto the floor after the timeout, he asked them, "How much do we want to have Reggie take the shot?" Then he and his teammates proceeded to stop Dallas, setting up Miller Time.

Jackson controlled the ball as the Pacers set up their offense. He glided down the key to the right of the basket, then spotted Reggie all alone ("Out there smoking a cigarette," he said later) behind the three-point line on the left wing. He rifled a pass toward Miller, whose form in burying the three was perfect despite Don Nelson's waving his arms wildly, realizing no one was guarding Reggie.

Bird applauded Miller's effort, but didn't hide his displeasure when Reggie followed it with his own version of the Texas two-step, a smart-aleck, in-your-face gesture that infuriated the Dallas bench. "We'll remember that," Nelson said. "We'll remember."

The win was the Pacers' 23rd against 11 losses, and kept them a half-game behind the Bulls, who beat the Warriors on their home court. Pippen's return and Dennis Rodman's latest hairdo (small curls resembling leopard spots that made it appear he had ringworm or some other dreaded disease) triggered a lackluster win against Golden State. A showdown between Chicago and Indiana at the United Center on February 17th was beginning to loom large between the two Central Division rivals.

Phil Jackson, who had seen his team return to championship form, chose to be philosophical about the future of the five-time NBA title holders, and the game itself. "We're coming along, but I'm more interested in seeing what teams are going to rule the years ahead," he told Chicago beat reporters in the hallway outside the visitors locker room at Madison Square Garden. "I may take a year off to look at the changes in the game. I thought I saw a brief glimpse of the future in Boston and New Jersey. There's a lot of frenetic play, trapping defenses, running up and down the floor. Players playing in shorter shifts. And I think the big guys are falling by the wayside. You see a lot of teams playing with centers that are 6'10", so they can help out with defense."

Jackson's remarks came the day before the Pacers were seeking win number 24 against the revamped Pistons—and a day after a proper scolding from Larry Bird. Though Mark Jackson had said after the Dallas win, "Our goal is to win a championship," the Pacers had suffered through four consecutive subpar performances that had their rookie coach shaking his head. "We're getting into a pattern here I don't like," Bird lamented. "I know you go through stretches of the season where you don't play as well as you like, but we've got to get out of it and get back to the way we're capable of playing."

Bird's sour mood produced additional assessments of the Pacers' recent performance. "This team has to decide how far it wants to go," the coach said. "We're looking for a championship year, and while a month ago I would have said we could beat anyone on any given night, now I'm not quite so sure."

The coach decided a pregame meeting with Mark Jackson and Reggie Miller was in order. "He told us how important the Pistons game was," Jackson reported. "That we needed to turn things around."

Both players proved to be up to the task. Against Detroit, the Pacers couldn't stop Grant Hill from scoring a season-high 37 points, but Jackson (16 points, 11 assists) ran the offense superbly, and Miller responded with 25 points. More importantly, Reggie helped his chances of becoming an All-Star in February by once again coming through in the clutch. With 46 seconds left, and Grant Hill having just hit a three to bring the Pistons close at 96–93, Miller darted around the court, got himself open, and drained an NBC (nothing but cotton) "take-that" three. Once again, having the ball in Miller's hands had proved fruitful in the waning seconds of the game. "What have I learned in the first half of the season?" Bird was asked after the Pacers 100–93 victory. "That Reggie wants the ball in the last few seconds of the game."

That night, the Twin Towers of San Antonio combined for 50 points as the Spurs moved into a first-place tie with Utah in the Midwest Division. Chicago led in the Central, Miami in the Atlantic, and Seattle, though losing unceremoniously to the Bulls at the United Center (Michael leading the way with 40 points), ruled the Pacific.

After 35 games, Indiana's 24–11 mark, the best start in the team's history, was fourth-best in the league. Bird was grinning once again as he looked toward a weekend game with Sacramento followed by his first visit to Boston.

When the Kings came to Indianapolis, the game took on added significance because the Bulls had lost to Philadelphia and Indiana had a chance to take over first place. Though Rik Smits had been less pivotal in recent games, the Pacers center, still hopeful of an All-Star invitation, had continued to be the most important factor in Indiana's turnaround. Media relations director David Benner, whose association with Bird went back to the days when Larry was burning the nets in high school, said, "Besides Coach Bird's demeanor, which involves his never holding a grudge, the play of Smits has been the difference. Sure we've added Chris Mullin, and others have stepped up, but without Rik we were a mediocre team last year. Now we can contend for a championship."

Against Sacramento, Smits did more than step up—he basically wiped out the Kings' chances for an upset in the first few minutes. Scoring at will with a series of hooks, soft jumpers, and dunks, the Dutchman had 10 of the Pacers' first 15 points. By game's end he had notched 20, and with the assistance of Jalen Rose's career-high 23, the Pacers cruised to an easy 117–92 win—their 14th victory in 17 games. "Guys have been talking about winning and going into first place," Rose said. "This is a great morale builder and a stepping stone."

Bird's kids, Conner and Mariah, weren't impressed. They just wanted their daddy to take them home. During the final few minutes of Bird's meeting with the media, the two youngsters bounded into the interview room, hugging their Pacers mascot dolls and yelling, "Daddy, Daddy. Are you done yet?" Glancing their way, Dad grinned as he shook his head and pointed toward the door.

Standing at 25–11, with first place wrestled away from the Bulls, the Pacers headed to Boston for the most anticipated game on the schedule. Returning to the parquet floor in Beantown (The Fleet Center had replaced the revered Boston Garden) for the first time as a coach against the team that had passed him over for Rick Pitino, Bird tried to be nonchalant about the visit. "We're hoping to come out of there with a win," he said. *Indianapolis Star* columnist Bill Benner saw a bit more drama in the return, writing, "It may have been the most heralded arrival here since Paul Revere galloped through the streets on horseback and informed the populace that the British were on their way. Only this time, Bostonians were happy—indeed, elated and ecstatic and even euphoric —to see this particular enemy coming." Reggie Miller echoed those thoughts, telling Benner, "This was a lot like when Michael came back against us at our place . . . the magnitude, the press, the ambiance."

Media coverage for the event, which was televised on NBC, was at a fever pitch. Bird, in accordance with his seasonlong policy, refused to do one-on-one interviews; otherwise he was cordial with the media.

Having been accorded recent acclaim in *Sports Illustrated* for his efforts in leading the Pacers to new levels, Bird also had received applause from his players. "It's not what he says, it is how he says it that is making a difference," Travis Best told the Associated Press. "He doesn't scream at you, he doesn't embarrass you when you make a mistake. He just looks at you, and you get the message. Then when the time is right, he'll talk to you calmly and explain what he wants."

Mark Jackson's take on Bird offered another perspective. "The one comment that he made, that made me understand that he had a clue, was that coaching is overrated, and that's the truth," the Pacers guard said. "You take your players, allow them to get into the best condition, the best shape possible. You give them the x's and o's, you prepare them, you have fun, and on game days you trust them to come up with results." He added, "You give them confidence and then you sit there and relax like you're a genius. He's done a wonderful job of that."

The night before the Boston game, Bird was philosophical about the Pacers' early-season success. "As ballplayers, they've done everything I've asked," the coach stated. "They've been excellent to work for. I always say I work for them, because it's their team. It's up to them if they want to go out and give the effort every night."

Besides that refreshing attitude, Bird was showing leadership in other ways. Often the team would have a shooting contest before practice where players, coaches, and trainers kicked 20 bucks into the pot, meaning the winner could eat filet mignon each night for a month. Once, in San Antonio, it had come down to just two people—Bird and Derrick McKey, who had swished his shot from halfcourt. Money was on the line as the Pacers coach took his position. Before the lighthearted competition, he had told everyone, "You don't want me to get in, because if I do, I'll win, and it'll tick you guys off so much you won't practice hard." After such a boast, the airball that Bird launched from halfcourt shocked everybody. "He missed everything," Rik Smits laughed. "I mean he missed bad. It was terrible, not even close." It also created suspicion and led to speculation. One-upping a player wasn't Bird's style, especially when McKey, struggling to regain his form, needed a confidence builder.

Whether Bird missed on purpose no one would know, but his low-key effort was producing results for a team in disarray a year earlier. "That's a solid team they've got over there," coach Bernie Bickerstaff proclaimed. "They're experienced, and they're well-coached. What they're doing is no fluke."

When the Pacers faced Boston, all 12 roster players were ready to play. Allocating meaningful playing minutes hadn't been easy, but Bird had gone 10, 12 deep in most games. "I figure we've got 12 players getting a paycheck," the coach explained. "We might as well get out money's worth."

Sports Illustrated's Phil Taylor was more impressed with Bird's ability to get his team to move the ball. "The Pacers now have a much more fluid attack, predicated on ball movement that at times is dazzling," Taylor wrote. "On one sequence against the Wizards, the interior passing between Mullin, McKey, and Smits, which led to Smits being fouled on a dunk attempt, was reminiscent of Bird's Celtics days with Robert Parish and Kevin McHale."

No one but Bird knew what went through his mind as he walked onto the parquet floor. No matter—he played the bally-hooed affair low-key. Even when the organist greeted him with a poor rendition of "Back Home in Indiana," Larry didn't acknowledge the tribute.

Boston fans were frenzied. Amidst posters that read "Bird Flies Again," "No Matter Who Wins, Bird Can't Lose," "Bird Returns to Nest," "Clone Larry," and "We Love Larry," he was greeted with thunderous applause. Though his face seemed taut with embarrassment, Larry acknowledged his adoring fans, many of whom had witnessed his magical play during 13 seasons in Celtics green.

For a minute-plus, Bird whirled around waving at the worshipers, sharply dressed in a charcoal suit, white shirt, and gold tie.

Since his former frontline buddy Robert Parish was to be honored at halftime when his number oo would be retired, Bird appeared quite dapper.

Bird's boyish grin continued through the warm-ups as he watched his Pacers ready themselves to play Rick Pitino's young Celtics. Irony abounded in the confrontation, since Pitino had taken the coaching job that Bird said he had been offered. Several months after Pitino and Bird had been hired for their respective positions, Bird and the Celtics espoused different versions of whether he had been offered the job. Larry said he had, but the Celtics front office begged to differ.

Quite by happenstance, the matter was apparently cleared up. During a sideline interview, Auerbach was asked by NBC reporter Jim Gray his opinion of Larry as a coach. "He's a very good coach," Red responded. "Has complete control. Knows how to motivate. We offered him the job before Pitino came into the picture. There was no response, so we went ahead." Nuff said; the god of Celtics basketball had spoken.

Though Bird seemed to downplay the game, he told NBC's Bill Walton (another ex-teammate) that "this is the biggest game of my life." The network's pregame tag added to the excitement, with Greg Gumbel gushing, "Larry Legend is coming back, but he isn't wearing green." Later, Gumbel called Bird "the hero with the common touch," but then chiseled that compliment down a bit by saying, "Bird was as exceptional on the court as he was ordinary off it."

With all of the subplots playing out, it was a wonder the two teams remembered they had a game to play. Bill Walton had said the Pacers had the best chance to unseat the Bulls in the East, but in the first quarter the team played as if it were a schoolyard pickup squad instead of an experienced playoff contender. Walton also said that the Pacers had taken on Bird's identity, the persona of their coach, but in the first 20 minutes they played like they had never met their coach.

True to his plan, Pitino had decided that the slow-stepping Pacers were susceptible to a press. He questioned their ballhandling abilities, and in the second quarter his young minions harassed the veteran Pacers into several inbounds errors.

While Pitino had a game plan, Bird seemed confused trying to counter the pressure that was embarrassing his players. Bill Walton had called Bird the best player he ever played with, but Larry didn't have a quick remedy for Pitino's press—and the Pacers fell behind. Losing to the Celtics would be bad enough for Bird, but being outcoached before his adoring fans and a national television audience was quite another thing.

To Bird's credit, he continued his pattern of sitting on the bench, seemingly nonchalant, occasionally wiping his hand over his nose and mouth, or puckering his lips when a stupid play made him want to leap onto the court and strangle the culprit.

By halftime, the Pacers, led by Jalen Rose, whose heroics included a behind-the-basket turnaround flip for two points that astounded the crowd, took a slight lead. Contrary to Bird's calm outer demeanor, Pitino stalked the sidelines in blue pinstripes waving and yelling and acting like a college coach, which was exactly what he had been a year earlier.

During the break at halftime, Robert Parish was honored. Bird left the locker room, where he had chastised the Pacers for their poor play, and joined McHale, Cornbread Maxwell, Red Auerbach, and master of ceremonies Tom Heinsohn in paying tribute to the Celtics center who played a pivotal role in the championships in the 1980s.

When the tributes ended, Bird disappeared and Parish and Auerbach pulled the ropes that lifted his uniform number to the rafters, joining Bird's own number 33 in its rightful place of honor. Parish, "The Chief" (named by Maxwell because he thought Parish resembled "The Chief" in the film "One Flew Over the Cuckoo's Nest"), seemed as embarrassed as Bird had been when his number was retired; but as the song "Hail to the Chief" was played, he smiled and waved and did all the right things. The sellout crowd of 18,624 (scalpers got $1,000 for courtside seats) cheered and hollered, and then settled back to see if their Celtics could knock off Bird's Central Division leaders.

When Bird returned to the floor, he was once again overwhelmed with applause, as he was each time the huge television screens depicted great moments from his career to the tune of Lynyrd Skynyrd's *Free Bird*. Several times during the game, fans were entertained with Bird floating in midair for a game-winning jumper, or Bird slashing down the lane for a layup, or Bird diving to the floor chasing a loose ball. One can only wonder what Pitino thought when he heard chants of "Lar-ry, Lar-ry, Lar-ry," as he was preparing his team during timeouts.

On nearly every trip down the court in the second half, Bird experienced the ecstasy and then the agony of a tight NBA game. A great play was followed by a pitiful one, and the Celtics stayed close. Then Smits and Miller returned to the lineup, providing offensive firepower. First Rik and then Reggie began to score at will, and the Pacers led by 10 with 1:53 to go. Several times, Miller ducked around a pick and rolled to the basket. "That's just what Dennis Johnson used to do for Larry Bird in the 1980s," Bill Walton explained.

Two key plays led to the final outcome. Reggie hit a clutch three-pointer with 1:19 remaining, and then Derrick McKey, still struggling to find his previous All-Star form after Achilles heel surgery, stopped the Celtics' budding star Antoine Walker from holing a jumper in the paint. When the Pacers brought down the rebound, the Celtics were sunk. As the clock wound down in the 103–96 Pacers win, their 26th of the season, Bird's frozen face began to thaw with relief that "the biggest game of his life" was finally over.

The victory was important to Bird for another reason. It signified a three-peat, Walton reminded viewers, since Bird's Pacers had handled former teammate-turned-coach Danny Ainge in Phoenix and also Kevin McHale's Timberwolves in Minneapolis earlier in the season. Bird's pride in winning at Boston outshone those triumphs, but all three were important.

The most memorable image was Reggie Miller grabbing Bird in a bear hug, congratulating the coach almost as if he were a brother. Rik Smits summed up the team's feeling. "This was a big day for Larry," the tousle-haired 7′4″ center said. "We wanted to make it special for him." Bird was practically speechless, telling reporters, "Coming back here and getting this win is just unbelievable. Everything feels good right now, but then again, I'm numb." Then he added a line that transcended the game itself. "I love my team. I love to watch them and I love to coach them. It's been an awesome experience." "How many NBA coaches ever said that?" a Boston reporter asked.

If he hadn't returned to his senses two days later, a trip to New York to play the Knicks provided smelling salts. Two nights after Lakers announcer Chick Hearn marked a milestone by broadcasting his 3,000th game, the Spurs won for the 16th time in 18 games, and Seattle continued to enjoy the best record in the NBA, the Pacers visited Madison Square Garden to play the beleaguered Ewing-less Knicks.

On paper, the game was a mismatch, since the Pacers had a center named Rik Smits who was programmed to devour his shorter opposition and prove to the New York media that he was worthy of All-Star selection. Smits sought also to add further evidence in his free-agent-to-be year that he deserved a new contract worth millions.

Unfortunately, Smits's dream night turned into a nightmare. By the time the Dunking Dutchman took a seat on the bench in the fourth quarter, he had missed six of nine shots and had snared just four rebounds. The Pacers limped home to Indiana on the short end of a 97–89 score. Since Chicago beat Charlotte, Indiana's tenure in first place in the Central Division was short-lived.

A day earlier, Wizards star Chris Webber had been arrested for several traffic violations and possession of marijuana, in other NBA news; but the story of the game in New York was that Reggie Miller produced a disappearing act in the city that made him famous. Actor Spike Lee didn't have to rag on Miller in the fourth quarter. Reggie not only went scoreless, but he wasn't able to hoist a single shot. Memories of the past season cropped up in Pacers fans' minds, a season in which Miller had often let the team down.

Kudos to the Knicks players were spread around. Five players landed in double figures, and Jeff Van Gundy's smiling face after the game reflected his satisfaction with the victory. "It was the hardest we played this year," the coach explained. "Our team defense was very good."

For his part, Bird believed the game was lost on the boards. "Sometimes it boils down to getting some rebounds," the downtrodden coach said. "That's been one of our problems all year long." Smits, both Davises, and Derrick McKey should have been listening. They were outrebounded by Mark Jackson.

With a 26–12 record, the Pacers returned to Market Square Arena to face Karl Malone, John Stockton, and the Utah Jazz. Jerry Sloan hoped to climb the mountain with his team one more time and put championship rings on Malone's and Stockton's fingers. To date, the Jazz had responded and were only percentage points behind San Antonio in the Midwest Division.

Utah jumped out to a 15-point lead in the first half behind 61 percent shooting, and it appeared it might be a long night for the Pacers. But heading into the third quarter, with their coach fussing and fuming and chewing his gum furiously, Reggie Miller, Rik Smits, Antonio Davis, and Mark Jackson took over. Miller's three-pointer with two minutes left in the period brought the Pacers to within six, followed by a quick spurt that propelled the team to a one-point lead starting the final period.

With 2:59 to play, Smits hit a 10-footer, and the Pacers led 98–96. A Jabbar-like hook by the big guy extended the margin to four, before the Dutchman was fouled and converted two critical free throws. Superb Indiana defense prevented two attempts by the Jazz, and a 106–102 win was the result over a team that had gone 10–1 in their prior 11 games.

Mark Jackson's season-high 18 assists put his teammates in position to score, and Antonio Davis took advantage by racking up a season-high 23 points. "We kept playing as a team," he explained. "Even when we were down 15. That's the mark of a great club." Of Davis, Bird added, "It's about time, isn't it? He played like a man tonight. He played so good it was unbelievable."

The Pacers' 27–12 record kept them a game and a half behind the Bulls, who nosed the Nets when Jayson Williams was called for goaltending on the final play of the game. While Indiana and Chicago continued their fine play, Denver's Nuggets failed in an attempt to avoid losing their 23rd consecutive game to tie an NBA record. A loss at Phoenix sealed their fate, and they stood 2–38 in a week in which the Pope made an historic visit to Cuba only to be knocked out of the headlines by a sex scandal that threatened to bring down President Bill Clinton.

Indiana's 39th game of the year was a return match with the Celtics on January 24th. With six games remaining until the All-Star break (Bird continued telling the press he wouldn't coach the Eastern Division All-Stars even if eligible—"I'll be in Florida taking it easy," he said. "The commissioner won't be able to find me"), the two teams battled in what was becoming one of the NBA's most intriguing rivalries. Bird didn't hide his feelings about the game. "I want to beat them so bad, I can taste it. I've got a lot of friends back there, and I want to show them I can do something other than play."

The Pacers recognized Bird's passion, but unfortunately they came out playing as if they wanted him to lose. For the better part of the first half, they performed like preps. Boston's young bunch played like a college team, racing up and down the court and making fools of the veteran Indiana team. All the while, Larry sat stoically on the bench as his stomach cried out for Maalox.

The Pacers of the year prior would have surely lost the game, but Bird's crew was proving a hypothesis he believed true. One of his basic coaching philosophies was that a deep club with confidence somehow finds a way to win. When one or two or even three players were having an off night, the role players stepped in. Through the first half of the season, that had resulted in victory after victory on nights when the starters had little to offer.

Bird's thoughts were a direct result of his playing days, when the Celtics won three world championships with him, Kevin McHale, Dennis Johnson, Robert Parish, and seemingly a cast of thousands. Bird learned then that in order to win consistently, a team needed players to step up, one and two at a time—and that if they could, the team could be successful over the long regular season and into the playoffs.

Against Boston, the team needed a lift. With everybody having a subpar evening, it was time for a veteran to take command. One did—Reggie Miller, who singlehandedly carried the Pacers back into the game in the third quarter. Dashing to and fro, and moving without the ball to get open, he cashed in 13 of his game-high 32 points when Indiana needed them most. Then he added a critical three-pointer with 4:51 left to give the team the lead for good, and they went on to post a 95–88 win over the hustling Celtics.

Bird was diplomatic. Of his team's reputation as the NBA's "Comeback Kids," he said, "I knew a bad game was coming. But we've worked awfully hard to get where we are. . . . We came out and played good basketball in the second half." The Celtics' Antoine Walker, a budding superstar who totaled 22 points to lead his team, offered his assessment: "They picked it up defensively in the second half," he extolled. "They're a tough team on their home court, and you need to put them away when you have the chance."

Mark Jackson, whose spectacular nearly court-length pass to Rik Smits in the final minutes produced a bucket and a free throw, deflected the credit for the victory in Reggie's direction. "Reggie was the difference," he said. "He put pressure on their defense instead of settling for jumpers."

Rick Pitino was impressed with Bird's Pacers. "Larry's learning all the time," the ex-University of Kentucky and New York Knicks coach explained. "I think after a time, a team becomes a reflection of their coach. If Larry had begun coaching with a bunch of rookies and young players like I did, it would take him much longer to produce a winner. But at Indiana, he inherited veterans, and it hasn't taken him much time to mold them into a good team. What I see most is a collection of good players who are playing great at times. That's the Bird effect. He did that as a player and he's doing it as a coach."

12

CELTICS CHAMPIONSHIPS

*"I like fast-paced basketball, pressure defense, and
emphasis on team play. Get the ball off the board,
up the court as quick as possible, get it to the people
who can put it in the hole, and play good defense."*
LARRY BIRD

Larry Bird began the 1984 season
with the Boston Celtics by attempting to punch the great Dr. J,
Julius Erving, in the mouth after the two began shouting at each
other during a shoving match under the basket. The league fined
the pair $7,500 each for their behavior, the largest fine handed out
by the NBA up to that time.

The quick-tempered Bird had carried his propensity for retaliation with him ever since childhood, when he fought with his
older brothers. The same treatment was in store for NBA players
who guarded him too closely or baited him with trash talk. Bird
excelled in both areas. On defense, he hammered his opponents,
all the while taunting them to try to throw them off their game.
He once told Laker nemesis Michael Cooper, "I'm going to take
your skinny butt down low," which he proceeded to do, and then
scored.

Former Indiana University star Ray Tolbert said Bird would
score over his outstretched hands, and then wink as he ambled
down the court. "Didn't block that shot, didja?" Bird roared,
proud that the white guy who everyone said couldn't jump had

leaped high enough to score. The Lakers' James Worthy saw that side of Bird. "He'd say, 'Get down,' or 'In your face,' or 'You can't guard me,' " Worthy explained. "At first I thought he was a jerk, but later I realized that was just part of his game. He was always measuring and analyzing his opponents, and he would do so from the moment he stepped on the floor." Worthy admired Bird's pregame preparation. "Before a game, he'd eye you at the other end, checking tendencies and mannerisms. He could tell if you weren't right. He could tell, sense the vibe. If you came out on him and really didn't bump him or weren't aggressive with him, he knew he had you. If you showed any signs of doubt, you were through with Larry."

"He'll do anything to win," former Seattle coach George Karl said, echoing commentator Matt Goukas, who said Bird would "cut your heart out to win." "He's a killer," NBA great Dominique Wilkins agreed, recalling a 1982 incident when he first met Bird. "I attempted to shake hands with him, but all I got was a cold stare. You look in his eyes and you see a killer." Bill Fitch said, "Larry Bird would kill to win at a game of jacks." Bird's retort: "Hey, I could be a nice guy too. I just don't have the time. There are games to be won." Some, like Isiah Thomas, thought Bird was a dirty player. Thomas arrived at that opinion, he said, "after Larry gouged at my eyes while we were scrambling for a loose ball."

Bird's propensity to talk trash surprised many people, but Julius Erving blamed it on Beantown. "Boston has rubbed off on Bird. Maxwell, M. L. Carr, all those guys do it. And so Larry started too. Those guys talk a lot of junk. I don't think Larry needs it. He's too good for that."

John Salley, who scuffled with Bird during his days with the Detroit Pistons, added, "Larry was a big-time trash man, but he was quiet about it. He'd say 'I've got 20 [points] and we got another 30 minutes left,' or 'I can't believe Chuck [coach Daly] put you on me.' " Larry Legend defended his tactics, saying, "I'm just playing the only way I know how. I don't talk any more than anyone else."

Bird's tough nature carried over to his teammates when the 1984 season began, and the Celtics won 15 of the first 16 games.

Larry was spectacular, winning two games with buzzer-beaters. Against Portland, one second showed on the clock when he launched a rainbow effort near the out-of-bounds line in the left corner. The ball arched over the top of the backboard and nestled in the net as Bird fell to the floor. Bird's explanation for such heroics was predictable: "I guess my concentration gets better when the game gets close. Some days I've shot as many as 2,000 times. That's why I like to take the last shot in a game even when we're down by a point."

Bird professed not to be nervous as the final seconds ticked by. "I know I do things down the stretch without even thinking about it," he said. "I'll go back and see it on film, and say, 'Damn, that was a big shot I made.' . . . Then I think back to what I'm feeling at that point in the game, and I remember that I felt calm, more calm than at any other time in the game."

Bird was certainly calm in a game against Atlanta in New Orleans. By halftime, he had 32 points. Then 40. Then 50. As time ran out, Bird crept ever closer to the 60 mark. He missed a three-pointer that would have put him over, but then Dennis Johnson nailed him with a perfect pass, and Bird's swish from short range gave him the magical 60. Afterward, Bird's reaction to the achievement was modest. "It was just a freaky thing," he said. "I scored big, but I didn't rebound well and I didn't pass that well." Quinn Buckner remembered the game. "Larry was so good that night the Hawk fans were high-fiving it," he said.

By season's end, Bird's superb play had propelled the Celtics to a 63–19 record. M. L. Carr summed up the team's strategy by saying, "All we did was get the ball to Larry and get out of the way."

In the first round of the playoffs, Boston met Cleveland, whose fans thought Bird was too cocky. Every time he touched the ball, they yelled a mock "Laa-rry, Laa-rry," but Bird ignored them and led his team to victory.

That didn't mean Bird believed the Cleveland fans were wrong in their assessment of him. "I try to carry myself a certain way on the court," he explained. ". . . It's not that I don't have respect for my opponent . . . [but] you've got to act like a Celtic. . . . All I know is that I play all-out."

After beating Isiah Thomas and the Pistons, the Celtics once again faced the Sixers. Bird survived an injured elbow and Charles Barkley's big-mouth boasts as Boston marched into the finals against the Lakers—again.

A 148–114 trouncing of the Lakers in the first game startled most who thought the series would be close; but Los Angeles rebounded, and with Bird suffering through a horrible stretch of shooting, the Lakers prevailed in six games to win the world championship. Bird won the NBA MVP award for the second consecutive year, but clearly was disappointed. "Your goal is to win a championship, and if you don't win it, you're a failure."

––––––––––––––

Bird had been told to rest his injured elbow during the off-season, and he couldn't practice shooting until mid-July. A few days after resuming his regimen on his home court, Bird picked up an old, deflated basketball and heaved it the length of the court into the basket. His brothers were astounded, but even more so when Bird repeated his fullcourt shot. "That's the most amazing thing I ever saw Larry do," brother Jeff exclaimed.

When the new season approached, the Celtics roster included Bill Walton, the former hippie who had led the Trail Blazers to the 1977 world championship. Bird knew the redhead was a team player who could be a valuable asset for the club, and had been an admirer of his ever since North Carolina State and UCLA had hooked up in the 1974 NCAA finals. Larry (age 18) watched the game on television. "[Walton] was doing everything he could to be a team player," Bird said. "I loved the way he passed and rebounded and his technique was flawless. . . . If you can say I had anything close to an idol in basketball at the time, that player was Bill Walton."

Walton felt the same way about his new teammate. During a visit to Larry's home in French Lick, Walton said, "When I got to Larry's house, I took out a jar and scooped up some dirt from the driveway court where Larry used to play as a kid. I carried it in my gym bag all year long . . . and when the season was over, I went to my parents' home and sprinkled it over the court I played on as a kid and stomped it in. That ground is now sacred."

Both Walton and Bird had physical ailments that concerned the Celtics, however. Toward the end of the summer, Bird had reinjured his back, and days prior to training camp he could barely walk. "I'd always had a little stiffness and soreness there, but things got bad during the summer . . . ," Bird said. "I was home running and playing ball and doing some work around the house, when one day—bam-o. My back went out. For two weeks I just stayed in bed."

Bird's explanation was logical, if not entirely accurate. Often Bird told half-truths either covering up a mistake or seeking to avoid embarrassment. He was a great rationalizer who felt that little white lies, or even medium-sized ones, never hurt anyone. On one occasion, he said, "I'm basically an honest person . . . I don't lie to people, but that doesn't mean I tell 'em the whole story or everything that's on my mind."

In reality, Bird had had back problems for years. At Indiana State, he was constantly fighting pain, but the Bird mettle played through it. With the Celtics, back discomfort was a constant challenge—one that he had been able to withstand until "some work around the house," as he called it, proved costly.

Despite Bird's wealth, he scrimped whenever possible, saving money like a person who had $10 in his checking account. The word *frugal* fit Larry perfectly, especially when it came to paying for any chores he felt he could do himself. That attitude, coupled with maintaining the image that he wasn't a prima donna afraid of hard work, led to the injury. Having decided to build a fence around his property in French Lick to ward off gawkers who frequented the area, Bird opted to shovel gravel himself to fill the post holes. He overdid the task, and injured his back.

A visit to a physician in Michigan provided some relief; but in the third game of the Celtics preseason against the Lakers, he played less than 10 minutes. Celtics management was terrified that they might be Bird-less for the season.

Bird's value to the Celtics was apparent. Alan Cohen, one of three owners of the franchise, said, "There's an old saying, 'If someone sneezes, the world catches cold.' Well, when Larry sneezed, everyone on the Celtics worried about the flu. Anything bothering Larry was cause for great concern."

Bird downplayed his back injuries. He was from the old school, and that meant going to work regardless of the discomfort. He remembered his father pulling a work boot on over a foot so swollen he could barely walk and then leaving for the jobsite. If Dad could do that, Larry figured he could do anything. "I'll always respect my father for that," Bird said. "He never backed away, no matter how tough it got." To mend Bird's back, physical therapy from Boston-based Dan Dyrek was required. "I asked Larry how much he wanted to play," Dyrek recalled. And he said, "Forty-eight minutes. Hell, Doc, that's not even an hour."

Dyrek's therapy was successful, and soon Bird was back in a Celtics uniform. Always anxious to silence critics, Larry pummeled the Pistons with 47 points shortly after the season opened. He shared the headlines with Danny Ainge, whose quip inspired Vinny Johnson's famous nickname: "If that guy in Chicago [Bears lineman William Perry] is called the Refrigerator, then you gotta call Vinny the Microwave. He really heats up in a hurry."

With Walton blocking shots and amazing even Bird with his pinpoint passing, the Celtics won 17 of 18 games. Kevin McHale knew the reason why. "During that season, Larry had 'the look,'" he said. "It meant 'Give me the ball and get out of the way.'" Bill Walton saw it another way, saying, "That '86 team could play any style, but if nothing worked, we just gave the ball to Larry."

At midseason, the All-Star game featured not only the East-West matchup, which meant Bird versus Magic, but also the first three-point shooting contest. If Larry was apprehensive about his chances, he didn't show it, walking into the locker room and proclaiming, "We know whose name is on the first-place check. Which one of you gets second?" Kevin McHale, who told reporters that even though he "played second fiddle to Larry, that's still a pretty good fiddle," knew Bird was correct, telling reporters, "When I found out Birdie could make ten grand by shooting basketballs in one afternoon, I knew it was all over."

McHale was right. In the finals, Bird—who was making $1.8 million in salary and thousands more in endorsements—psyched out Craig Hodges by telling him beforehand, "Now I know who's going to finish second. . . . The money's got my name on it." Then

Bird, whose shot seemed to spring out of his hands like a rubber band launched it, hit 18 of 25 shots, including a final "money ball" to beat Hodges. The same day, the diminutive Spud Webb won the dunk contest.

When Bird, a fine shooter despite having mangled a right index finger during a softball game, won the contest the next two years, the prize became known as "the Larry Bird Fund," which he with tongue in cheek designated as his favorite charity. Bird's ability to hit the three-point shot came despite his disdain for the idea. Throughout his career, he made fun of it, saying, "A basket, any basket, should be worth two points, but as long as they have it, I'll keep shooting it."

Later, Knicks trainer Mike Saunders learned firsthand about Bird's prowess *banking* three-pointers. During shooting practice before a Knicks-Celtics game, Saunders bet Bird, who had been draining them in practice, that he couldn't bank one in the game. Bird responded by banking a beauty during the fourth quarter, then passing the Knicks bench yelling, "Ten bucks, Mike. Ten bucks."

And Bird could hit not only triples, but home runs. One day he astounded Celtics coach K. C. Jones, who promised to end a practice if someone could drop a shot from midcourt. "I can still see it," Bill Walton said. "Larry took two deep-knee bends, two dribbles, and hit nothing but net." The shot didn't surprise Boston reporters. They were used to hearing Bird challenge them by saying "Shoot for money?" at Boston Garden before practice. That meant Bird bet a dollar he could hit a shot from long range. Ninety-nine percent of the time he did, and the reporters forked over the dough. He was "the ultimate pool hustler turned gym rat," *Boston Globe* Columnist Dan Shaughnessy said.

As the season wound down, Bird captivated fans in Portland with an incredible *left-handed* shooting performance. He did virtually everything (except writing) right-handed, but on his way to a 47-point, 14-rebound, 11-assist game, he hit 10 shots with his left hand.

The Celtics record of 67–15 (40–1 at home) marked them as one of the great regular season teams of all time. Bird, who later called his teammates "one of the great beer-drinking championship teams in the history of the NBA," commented, "We were always focused. Hell, we even quit drinkin' for two months, which wasn't easy . . . I still think that team was the best one ever assembled."

Bird collected his third consecutive MVP on a near-unanimous vote. Sportswriter Bob Ryan was in awe, writing, "At different times, he passed like Cousy, shot like Havlicek or Sam Jones, rebounded like Russell or Cowens, and had an aggressiveness reminiscent of Heinsohn."

At playoff time, the Celtics faced the Bulls, the first series to pit Bird against Michael Jordan. "[Jordan] had come in and beaten us once when he was a rookie," Bird said. "And I told the press that he was the best player that I had ever seen." Jordan did nothing to change Bird's mind in the playoff series in 1986. In the first game, Jordan hit the Celtics with 49 points. The next day, he broke the playoff record with 63 points. "Michael is the most exciting, awesome player in the world . . ." Bird said. "I think it's God, disguised as Michael Jordan." Later he added, "Michael Jordan was—and is—a completely different type of player than I had ever seen before. He was literally on a different level. Michael had the whole package. He can run, jump, block shots, and play great defense. Most of all, he was a great competitor."

Bird's words were never more true than in the playoff game when Michael scored the 63 points. But in the second overtime, the outcome rested on a play Larry made after one where Jordan failed to come through. With time running out, Jordan danced through the Celtics defense and faced a wide-open 13-footer. His jump-shot form was perfect, but the ball ricocheted off the rim into Celtic Robert Parish's hands. Jordan's expression was one of disbelief as he backtracked downcourt.

Bird, once described by coach Hubie Brown as "a total menace," took Parish's pass and ambled up court. In contrast to Jordan, whose gait was like a thoroughbred's, Bird seemed awkward dribbling the basketball. But bounce it he did, and when he entered the Bulls' front court, his facial muscles became taut as he panned the defense looking for an opening. Fifteen thousand-plus fans rose from their seats, anticipating a Bird move using a pick or a screen. His eyes flashing in anticipation, Bird started left, but then out of the corner of his eye, he spotted Robert Parish's seven-foot body positioned perfectly to shield his defender.

For a split-second, Larry was open, and he cocked his elbows as if to shoot. But instead of grabbing the glory, he hoodwinked the two defenders who were leaping high to deflect his shot, and fed a pass around their outstretched arms to Parish, who had executed the perfect pick and roll. He emphatically dunked the ball as Bird's face lit up with a huge grin.

Having disposed of the Bulls, the Celtics faced the Atlanta Hawks, featuring Dominique Wilkins, the NBA scoring leader during the season. At one point in Game Five, Boston led by 41 points, 102–61. "It was the finest exhibition of basketball I've ever seen," Doc Rivers said, a thought echoed by Atlanta coach Mike Fratello. Later, Danny Ainge called the game, "The way basketball is supposed to be played." He was right. After leading at halftime, 66–55, the Celtics went on a 12–6 run before exploding for 24 straight points. Mike Fratello was in shock, saying later, "All you can do is take a timeout and make substitutions. The league doesn't let you make trades during games." The final score was 132–99. "That final quarter was as close to perfection as you're ever going to see," Larry Bird recalled.

After sweeping the Milwaukee Bucks, the Celtics faced Bill Fitch's Houston Rockets, who had handled Magic and the Lakers in the semifinals. In Game Five, with Boston ahead two games to one, Rockets center Ralph Sampson picked a fight with Jerry Sichting, Bird's fellow Hoosier. Though Sichting (6′1″) looked like a midget next to Sampson (7′4″), the two fought as if they were of equal height. Bird's thought on the altercation was a beauty. "I can't believe [Sampson] picked a fight with Sichting. Heck, my girlfriend could beat Ralph up."

Fortunately, Game Five was memorable for other reasons. Later, many pundits labeled it "The greatest game of the decade," one marked by another memorable moment in Larry Legend's career. It occurred when Bird outfoxed his former coach Bill Fitch, whose strategy had been to keep Bird covered on the perimeter. Most times, two or even three Rockets descended on Larry, negating his ability to score from outside. With less than three minutes left, Houston defenders surrounded Bill Walton, who had positioned himself perfectly in the post. Fitch waved frantically, trying to attract attention, realizing Bird was open. Walton sensed it also, and he shoveled a pass to his teammate, who immediately lofted a jump shot. Fitch's face paled, and he never bothered to watch the shot. He backtracked to the bench, realizing the inevitable as Bird's shot singed the net. The Houston crowd was as quiet as a sleeping baby. Larry Bird had yanked their hearts out. "That was a great series," Bird said. "One of the best ever."

Attempting to wrap up the championship in Game Six, K. C. Jones called a practice session, but had to stop it midway through. "The intensity level was just incredible . . . I had to call it off before they killed each other . . . These guys went at each other like Muhammad Ali and the gorilla."

Bird was more psyched up than anybody else. "I never quite had a feeling like that in my life," he said. "I was so pumped up for that game, I think I hit my max. I was never fired up for a game like that again. . . . And I'll never forget walking off that court with my heart pounding so hard I thought I was going to have a heart attack."

To say that Bird buried the Rockets all by himself would be a slight overstatement, but by halftime he had totaled 18 points, 8 rebounds, and 8 assists. Houston's Jim Peterson was amazed. "I never saw anyone demoralize a team [singlehandedly] the way he did," he stated. "That's why he's the MVP of the NBA. I saw him take on five guys by himself. At times, he doesn't need teammates."

How confident was Bird of the outcome of the game? "I changed my uniform at halftime," he said later. "And that's something I never do. I was playing so well and feeling so great that I just took that uniform off, stuffed it into my bag, and got a new uniform out, so that way I would have two championship uniforms [to keep] instead of one."

That type of confidence spelled sayonara for Bill Fitch's Rockets. The former Boston coach was in awe of Bird in the series, but Hakeem Olajuwon said it best when he told reporters, "It was men against boys. And Bird was one helluva man." The Celtics won, 114–97.

Never had that been more true than with a mystifying shot that Larry Bird hit against Milwaukee in the 1986 playoffs. After having sealed the game in the closing minutes by canning four straight three-pointers, Bird, sporting a patchy blonde mustache that needed cropping, held the ball in the corner with three seconds to play. He started to heave it over his head and amble toward the locker room, but then suddenly he turned toward the basket and launched a one-hander. Without hesitating, Bird walked off the court, never glancing behind him as the ball arched squarely into the net.

Larry Bird's 1986–87 season was encapsulated in one image, perhaps the single one that will never be forgotten by sports fans who either witnessed the feat firsthand or will watch it on television whenever the great moments in sports history are replayed.

"The Play" occurred in Game Five of the Celtics' matchup with their new archrivals, the Detroit Pistons. Before the series, Bill Laimbeer, one of Detroit's bad boys, had summed up his teammates' attitude toward Larry Bird by saying, "We don't like him too good." This remark and others like it had required that Bird's unofficial bodyguard (Indiana state trooper T. H. Hill) accompany him to Detroit for two games of the series.

Game Five was at Boston Garden. Bird hit a fallaway shot, and the Celtics led by three with a minute and change to go. Two quick baskets by the Pistons reversed the tide, and the Celtics, down one, called timeout. They set up a play for Bird, but the Pistons' Dennis Rodman, a constant nemesis for Bird in the series, nicked the shot. It hit Jerry Sichting and ricocheted out of bounds.

With five seconds left, it appeared the Pistons had the game won. Although Detroit coach Chuck Daly was screaming for a timeout, Isiah Thomas decided to inbound the ball before the Celtics could set themselves.

Bird's momentum after his unsuccessful shot had landed him on his rear end—but he quickly jumped to his feet and ran to cover Joe Dumars, who was positioned near the foul line. When Thomas saw Bird coming, he passed the ball instead to Bill Laimbeer, but Bird anticipated Thomas's move and changed direction.

In the seconds that followed, Bird reached out and tipped the ball toward the baseline, wrapped his hands around it, managed not to touch the out-of-bounds line, and lunged for the basket all in one motion. As the crowd held its breath, Larry saw that Dennis Johnson was racing toward the basket from the left side. Instantaneously, Bird zipped the ball left-handed toward Johnson, who took it in perfect stride, ducked under Joe Dumars's outstretched arms, and kissed the ball off the glass.

When the ball rolled around the rim and finally dropped in, the Celtics had a miraculous win, and Larry Legend had added to his growing myth. The *Boston Herald*'s headline the next day said it all: "Steal of the Century." Isiah Thomas said he learned a valuable lesson from his Celtics counterpart: "Bird's mentality zeroed in, focused," he said. "He swooped [the ball] up, and boom, he's gone. Layup. Game. . . . That was part of my growth. My maturation."

Game Six went to the Pistons, but the Celtics prevailed in Game Seven to win the conference finals and the right to meet the Lakers. Blemishing play in the outstanding series was an infamous remark attributed to Isiah Thomas, though it was actually made by Dennis Rodman. According to ESPN producer Bill Fairweather, one of only two reporters to hear the comments, Rodman said, "Larry Bird is a very, very good basketball player, an exceptional talent, but if he were black, he'd be just another good guy." Sitting nearby, according to Fairweather, was Thomas, who was asked about Rodman's remark. When he agreed, reporters made Thomas the fall guy, since Rodman had not yet achieved the celebrity status he would enjoy in the 1990s.

Bird admitted that he didn't believe the comment was a big deal ("That's his mouth talking, not his heart," Bird said) until the press ran with it. "All over the country, writers and broadcasters were taking sides," he wrote in *Drive*. "[They were saying] Rod-

man's a jerk. Rodman's not a jerk. Isiah's a racist. Isiah's not a racist. Bird's overrated. Bird's not overrated. Sociologists and political columnists were jumping into it. It was completely crazy." Later, Bird and Thomas appeared together at a news conference to squelch the rumor that Bird was upset over the remark. Larry was conciliatory, but friends said he had trouble understanding why Thomas had supported Rodman's offensive remark.

Anticlimactic to Bird's incredible steal and Thomas's headline-making statement were the finals, which Boston lost to the Lakers in six games. Bird's performance was subpar; he was a worn-out warrior. "I'm going home and resting up," he told reporters. "I'm going to lift some weights and come back a better player than ever before."

Later, Bird reflected on the finals against the Lakers and Magic Johnson. "If [Magic and I] had grown up together or if we were teammates, I think we'd have been best friends," Bird proclaimed. "I feel he's the greatest all-around team player in basketball. I have always looked up to him because he knows how to win. I've always put him a step ahead of me."

LARRY'S ALL-STARS

*"I've never really understood why more players don't make
the effort to become good free-throw shooters. It just
takes practice and hard work. And concentration."*
LARRY BIRD

Indiana's win against Boston on
January 24th produced a 28–12 record—the first time the Pacers
had hit the .700 mark, and a dramatic improvement over the
team's 19–21 record of the previous year. It also made the Utah-
Chicago game at the United Center the next day even more important to Bulls coach Phil Jackson: If his club prevailed in a repeat
of the two teams who battled for the 1997 crown, Jackson would
coach the Eastern Division All-Stars. If the Bulls lost, Larry Bird
would be the nominee, based on the better winning percentage.

Three hours before John Elway and the Denver Broncos upset
the Green Bay Packers in Super Bowl XXXII by a score of 31–24,
Jerry Sloan's Utah Jazz whipped the Bulls. Michael was human
with 30-plus points, but Karl Malone led a balanced Jazz attack
that prevailed. Bird must have been pacing around his home in
Indianapolis, saying, "Damn. I wanted our team to do well, but
maybe not this well."

Go figure. Who would have predicted when the season began
that Larry Bird would be in a position to decide whether he
wanted to coach the All-Star team? Most pundits had picked the
Pacers fourth or fifth in the division. Instead, they were leading

their conference with a better season record than 26 of the other 28 teams.

Now that Bird was the official choice to coach the All-Star team, speculation arose as to whether he would shun the limelight and travel to his seaside home in Florida, or accept with reluctance and be in New York during what he had hoped would be his All-Star break. One who thought Larry would head east and not south was Donnie Walsh. "Bird lives up to his obligations," Walsh told *Indianapolis Star* reporter Mark Montieth. "It's a hell of a tribute to the coaches and our players. It's a great honor for our franchise."

If Bird traveled to New York, he would be the second Pacers coach to be chosen, Bobby "Slick" Leonard having coached in 1970 in the ABA All-Star Game. "Bird needs to see what it's like," Leonard said. "It's a hell of an honor." Assistant coach Rick Carlisle's thoughts about Bird and the potential assignment were apropos for the occasion. "Larry will appreciate it more as the years go on, particularly if he stays in coaching and sees that this isn't easy," Carlisle theorized, realizing that his boss had yet to see the downside—losing streaks and poor play that made coaches want to commit hari-kari. After all, how many individuals who had never coached a basketball game—not pee wee, grade school, junior high, high school, college, the pros—could take the reins and win 70 percent of his first 40 games? Chris Mullin saw the situation another way. "The way Larry attacks a challenge, nothing he accomplishes is a surprise to me," the five-time All-Star said. "If he wanted to be an actor, I wouldn't be surprised if he won an Oscar for his first movie."

Admiration for Coach Bird was evident the Monday morning after his selection as All-Star coach. When he loped onto the Market Square Arena floor for practice, the players gave him a thundering round of applause. His face lit up, pride clearly showing through. "We knew how much it meant to him," Travis Best said. "He didn't want to let on, but we knew it."

Overnight, Bird's attitude toward coaching the All-Stars had changed. "It is an honor and I'd be selfish if I didn't do what I need to do," he explained. "All-Star games are better now, more orga-nized, but I still don't like all the fuss." Though Bird would miss a few days in the Florida sunshine with his family, reporters sali-vated over the prospect of Larry Legend coaching Michael Legend in early February. At NBA headquarters in New York, Commis-sioner David Stern was delighted. Bird's appearance at the All-Star Game would add to the glamour of the event and provide fans from a small-market city like Indianapolis with a sense of pride in the game.

Once Bird and the Pacers returned to work with the regimen of the regular-season games, they concentrated on how to beat the Washington Wizards. Despite Chris Webber's arrest for traffic violations, resisting arrest, and marijuana possession, he was still a formidable opponent. Whether he and his teammates could defeat the Pacers remained to be seen.

On the day the President of the United States gave his State of the Union message while legal scandals surrounded him, and an arbitrator heard evidence in the plea by Latrell Sprewell to lessen his suspension for attacking P. J. Carlesimo, the Pacers played well enough to earn an 85–84 win thanks to a three-pointer from Reg-gie with 36 seconds remaining.

Indiana's 29th victory of the year preceded a trip to the City of Brotherly Love to meet ex-Pacers coach Larry Brown and his unpredictable 76ers. Dubbed by veteran sportscaster Joe Smith as "the worst last-place team in the NBA," Philadelphia sported second-year sensation Allen Iverson and former New Jersey bad boy Derrick Coleman.

Reggie Miller once again provided last-second heroics, which should have been unnecessary because an official had blown a call with a few seconds left in regulation. Complaining about calls by the men and women who controlled the game wasn't normal behavior for Bird. All season long, he had kept his cool with offi-cials, picking up only two technical fouls—but in this case, he made an exception.

Bird's outlook regarding whistleblowers was exhilarating. "If they make the call," he had explained in late January, "they're not going to change it. There's no use me being on these guys all the time. If they make two or three bad calls in a row, yeah, I'll challenge them."

The coach's thought process was based on prior experience. "If you go back and watch the tape, a lot of stuff that we're complaining about they usually make the right calls. Sure they miss some, but overall I think they do an excellent job."

Bird's view was severely tested in the Philadelphia game. Time was running out with the score tied when Travis Best, who had played one of his finest games of the season, steamrolled down the court dodging 76ers. With 6.3 seconds remaining on the clock, the left-hander launched an unsuccessful scoop shot from two feet before tumbling to the floor. No whistle blew, and Bird sank to his knees at midcourt with his head in his hands before complaining to the refs. "They missed the call," Bird said later. "But what's the use?"

But Reggie made certain Bird left the CoreStates Center (formerly known as the Spectrum, but the players hated it so much they called it the "Rectrum") with a smile on his face. The Pacers sharpshooter made the closing seconds of overtime Miller Time by hitting an off-balance three-pointer from the left side of the court to provide a three-point lead. When the 76ers' Jim Jackson's three hit nothing but backboard, the Pacers had earned a 93–90 win to bring their season record to 30–12. Over the previous 35 games, they were a remarkable 28–7.

Against the Cavaliers on January 30, Bird's players were led by his reclamation project, Jalen Rose. Celebrating his 25th birthday, the formerly baldheaded Michigan Wolverine who had let his hair grow during the Pacers winning streak sparked his teammates after they trailed by 13 at the half. Bird believed that Rose's confidence had been shattered during the prior season, and he worked hard to restore it. "Jalen has as much talent as any player in the league," Bird espoused. "He just doesn't realize it at times." An intense player subject to pouting, especially when Coach Brown had chastised him every time he made a mistake, Rose had sparkled under a coach who let his players play and wasn't constantly barking at them from the bench. Pacers players didn't need to keep turning their heads toward Bird with the expectation of a verbal barrage.

Against Cleveland, with the game still in doubt, Rose hit two critical shots that brought a wide smile to his coach's face. After canning a three-pointer from the right perimeter, Rose found himself two possessions later with another effort just inside the three-point line on the left side. Unfortunately, standing in Jalen's way was the Cavs' giant center Zydrunas Ilgauskas, who had stretched his arms to a height of at least nine feet. Nonplussed, Rose merely floated a rainbow shot over the big Lithuanian that seemed as if it would never come down. When the ball nestled in the net, even Jalen looked surprised.

Having brought the Pacers close, Rose now watched Reggie Miller once again provide clutch shots down the stretch. After a second three-pointer sealed the victory, Miller did his version of a dance that appeared to be a combination of Michael Jackson and George Michael. The Pacers' 89–83 win earned victory number 31, and all Larry Bird could do was stand on the sidelines and shake his head. "Is this really happening?" he had to be asking himself as he scratched his ear. "Or is it simply a dream?"

Around the country, sportscasters were amazed at the Pacers' resurgence. ESPN's David Lloyd told viewers, "Beware of the Indiana Pacers. Especially in the second half and especially if they are behind. They are like cornered rats, only taller."

Having won their fifth straight, Indiana traveled west for a three-game road trip preceding the All-Star game. As the calendar flipped to the first day of February, the Pacers took on the Los Angeles Clippers just hours after the Lakers had demolished Michael Jordan and his Bulls a few miles away at the Forum. With 1:08 remaining, and the score 96–92, Reggie Miller nearly became the villain of the game instead of the hero by throwing a terrible pass that the Clippers intercepted. But Derrick McKey stripped the ball from Rodney Rogers, and Miller atoned for his mistake with a deadly three-pointer that led to a 99–92 win. "It should not come down to my shot to decide the game," Miller explained. "We kind of relaxed, and you cannot do that against a good offensive team like the Clippers."

While Miller's exploits continued to make headlines, it was the Pacers defense that was the big factor in their six-game winning streak. Five of the opponents had been held to less than 40 percent shooting, and none had cracked the magic 100-point mark. "We're helping out, working with each other," assistant coach Dick Harter, an incessant gum chewer, explained. "That's the difference."

At Sacramento two nights later, the Pacers continued their onslaught by pummeling the Kings, 115–93. The victory, their seventh straight, was a breeze, so much so that the starters earned a seat on the bench in the fourth quarter. Reggie Miller admitted after the game that he and his comrades had a special feeling about the season. "This is a veteran ballclub," Miller stated. "A lot of guys are in the twilight of their career. Everyone understands that the window of opportunity is closing."

Kings coach Eddie Jordan believed Miller and his gang were destined for an NBA title. "You name it and the Pacers did it to us," he said. "I know Larry doesn't want to hear this, but they are probably the best team in the league." Later, Jordan was more specific. "They are big, unselfish, they've got shooters, they've got rebounders, and they know how to play together," he added. "They have the right chemistry and they are on a mission. We were just a bump in the road for them."

Bird appreciated Jordan's comments, but urged caution. "We got a long way to go and we better know that. . . . Hopefully, we'll get our heads on straight, and don't get them swelled up too much, and keep plugging away."

Bird's thoughts came on a day in which he continued piling up the honors. Already having been named the NBA's Coach of the Month for January, he added to his legend by being named one of eight nominees to the Naismith Memorial Basketball Hall of Fame. The Pacers coach tried to downplay the honor. "I'm pleased," he said, masking true pride in the achievement. "But I don't think about that stuff too much. It's been forever since I played." Whether Bird would be selected seemed to be a foregone conclusion, and Chris Mullin believed it was slam dunk. "To me, the Hall of Fame and Larry Bird are like one and the same," he explained. "They go together."

With a 33–12 mark, the Pacers traveled to Seattle to play one of the only two teams with a better record. The Sonics, with Vin Baker now firmly established as the replacement for Shawn Kemp, were flying high, and Bird knew the road test against a team many felt would be in the NBA Finals would serve as a yardstick heading into the All-Star break.

When the final buzzer sounded, Indiana collected its 13th loss, but they played the Sonics tough. A Reggie Miller 18-footer with 1:08 to play brought them to within five—but then Baker, who entertained with a variety of shots on his way to a career-high 41 points, closed the door with a fadeaway jumper.

The subject of Bird's postgame press conference was Mr. Baker. "He was getting too low in the box, and with those long arms, he's unstoppable. . . . Sometimes you wish when you play them, you wish Shawn Kemp was in there. Not that Kemp's a bad player, but Baker is awesome."

If nothing else, the loss showed the Pacers were mortal. This time they were unable to recover from a deep hole, one that found them down by 15 points at 91–76. The only consolation was that on the same night, the Bulls were blasted by Utah, despite 41 from Michael Jordan.

At the midpoint of the season, the Pacers stood 33–13, a half-game up on Chicago. More importantly, they led Atlanta, Cleveland, and Charlotte by five or more games. By anyone's standards, their play had been outstanding, and Bird had proved he could motivate, inspire, and, more importantly, communicate with his players—nearly a lost art in the NBA.

Reggie Miller had regained the luster lost during the last season, Rik Smits was playing the best ball of his career, and Chris Mullin had added points on the board and leadership. Mark Jackson was the force that kept the team playing like a well-oiled machine, not only with his ability as a playmaker, but with skillful defense. "He's probably our MVP," Bird said of "Jack," who, like Bird, was not a good individual defensive player but became a capable

one playing Dick Harter's help defense. "Jackson's done everything we've asked of him," Bird said.

Off the bench, Jalen Rose had been superb, proving his worth
as one of the league's better utility players. Travis Best, Fred
Hoiberg, and Derrick McKey, slowly recovering from his injuries,
had contributed.

If there was a disappointment, it came from the inconsistent
play of the Davises, Dale and Antonio. Rebounding was their duty,
and neither had established a consistent performance level that
guaranteed the Pacers board strength on a nightly basis; especially Dale, whose physical prowess couldn't overcome a lack of
basketball savvy. "We're in trouble if Dale doesn't start rebounding," Bird admitted. "That's a real weakness for us."

Nevertheless, others in the league were saluting Bird and his
players. Miami's coach Pat Riley said, "The Bulls and the Pacers
are on one level, and the rest of us in the conference on another."
Knicks head coach Jeff Van Gundy echoed the thought, explaining, "Larry's team is as good as the Lakers, Chicago, and Seattle.
They may be the best team in the league."

Whether the Pacers players were convinced that they had a
legitimate shot at a championship was another question. Was the
first half of the season, played nearly injury-free, a fluke? Could
the team sustain its high level of play? Or would Indiana fall into
bad habits in the second half and find themselves slipping from
their lofty perch? Chris Mullin looked at the team's chances with
a realistic viewpoint, knowing all too well what could happen.
"Our margin of error, any team's margin of error, is very small,"
he admitted. "This team has climbed up one side of the mountain.
Now we'll see if we can stay there." Reggie Miller agreed, saying
that in the first half of the season, "We like to sneak up behind
people, take our billy club, hit them in the back of the head, put
them in the trunk, and move on. Whether we can do that in the
second half of the season remains to be seen."

More than anyone, Larry Bird knew how difficult it was to
keep the winning edge. Throughout his years with Boston, that
was the number-one challenge; especially when the other teams in

the league dedicated themselves to beating a team with the rich tradition of the Celtics.

———————————

His name was Kobe Bryant, and he was 19 years old. On February 8th, instead of driving to the local mall with his teenage friends to buy a new CD or readying himself for a basketball game against playground foes, Kobe waltzed onto the revered court at Madison Square Garden prepared to compete against the best the NBA had to offer.

In the 48th All-Star Game, Bryant was the bright new star, the one picked to be the latest "new Michael Jordan." Armed with the ability to vault off the floor like a pogo stick, and a variety of alley-oop moves that left even showtime crowds at the Forum in Los Angeles gasping, Bryant—son of former NBA player Joe "Jellybean" Bryant—was a showstopper with a light-up-the-world smile, ready to strut his stuff.

The youngest player ever to compete in an NBA All-Star Game, Bryant was one of several new stars to influence the game. While such established greats as Charles Barkley, John Stockton, Hakeem Olajuwon, Patrick Ewing, and Clyde Drexler were home soothing their wounded pride or nursing nagging injuries, the new breed of kids like Bryant, Kevin Garnett, Antoine Walker, and Jason Kidd joined superstars Jordan, Karl Malone, Reggie Miller, Shaquille O'Neal, and Shawn Kemp in professional basketball's grandest exhibition game.

On the sideline coaching Sir Michael, Reggie Miller, Rik Smits (the only white player among the honored twenty-four), and the rest of the Eastern Conference All-Stars was Larry Bird, who had played in the contest 12 times during his Boston career. Instead of taking his wife and kids to Florida and hitting the links, or cruising the inland waterways that weaved through the Naples area, Bird readied himself for his coaching assignment.

Before the big game, Bird entertained the media with his dry wit in an attempt to fend them off. "I'm not a good coach," he told the wide-eyed reporters. "I just sit there and let the players play. What's so tough about that?" Asked what he thought of New Jersey's rookie Keith Van Horn, Bird quipped, "It's an honor to be compared to him." And at a Manhattan steakhouse, Donnie Walsh almost required the Heimlich maneuver when Bird joked, "This would be a good time for me to resign."

When game time rolled around, Bird was still trying to develop a game plan that would give the superstars enough court time. "I intend to play everyone the same amount of minutes, but with 12 players, and 48 minutes, it averages out to 17.1 minutes per player," the coach explained. "And if I give Michael Jordan 17 minutes, I'll get killed." Asked if Jordan, known for being the ultimate b. s. artist, should play the whole game if this was his final All-Star performance, Bird was philosophical. "If it really is his last one, he deserves a lot of minutes. If he's fooling us, he doesn't deserve any minutes at all."

Talk about Jordan's potential retirement had made front-page news for two weeks, ever since Bulls general manager Jerry Krause stated that coach Phil Jackson would definitely not be back for the next season. Of course, if Jackson wasn't the coach, Jordan wasn't a Bull, as Michael had said on several occasions. Jackson's precarious situation, especially for a man who had produced five world championships for Krause and company, was a mystery— but it provided a dose of reality for coaches like Larry Bird. All knew their welcome could be worn out in short order, especially if they lost, or even if they won as expected. Doug Collins had discovered that, having been fired at Detroit after a winning season a year earlier.

Bird and the other NBA coaches also knew that if a superstar decided a change at the top was in order, it was a done deal. Grant Hill demanded the departure of Collins, much as Penny Hardaway had with Brian Hill at Orlando, and Magic Johnson had when he wanted Paul Westhead fired as coach of the Lakers. "Screw the superstar," one NBA assistant coach admitted, "and you can count your days."

Heading into the All-Star Game, that was one thing Larry Bird didn't have to worry about. *His* superstar, Reggie Miller, loved him, especially after Bird telephoned him shortly after his appointment as coach with an "I need you" message. Asked by NBC's Jim Gray when he quit looking at Bird as superstar, Miller answered, "The first time he made me run to the suicide line in training camp."

Reggie wasn't a starter in the All-Star Game, but he played well, hitting several threes—much to the chagrin of the Madison Square Garden crowd in general and dapperly dressed Spike Lee, Miller's nemesis, in particular. Rik Smits also gave a good account of himself, showing off his deft shooting touch. His nifty behind-the-back pass to Jayson Williams of the Nets for a lay-in had the Eastern All-Stars pounding their fists in joy.

Kobe Bryant, encouraged by Lakers superfan Jack Nicholson, also lived up to his billing. Throughout the first half, he and Michael Jordan exchanged superlative plays in a duel that was the highlight of the game. In the third quarter, Bryant performed some magic that had even Michael shaking his head. Zipping down the right side of the court dribbling right-handed, he suddenly spanked the ball behind his back off the court and then tapped it just slightly so that it careened around his body back to him. With not a hitch in his giddy-up, Kobe launched a Kareem-like right-handed skyhook that hit nothing but net. NBC commentator Isiah Thomas said the feat captured not only oohs, but prolonged aahs from the crowd. Cameras caught Larry Bird smiling as he shook his head. He and Rick Carlisle looked at each other as if to say, "Can you believe that?"

Most of the game, Bird never left his seat. All he did was watch the minutes-played column, and kept his word by permitting all of his players to play equally. The exception, of course, was Michael, to whom Bird had a further kinship. During the game, Larry was featured in a new Gatorade commercial whose theme was "I wanna be like Mike." Several basketball stars and other celebrities sang parts of a whimsical tune, but just as the commercial faded out, there was Bird in a shirt and tie announcing, "I'm not going to sing." Coupled with McDonald's ads, and others, Larry Legend was adding several hundred thousand dollars to his already over-flowing coffers. He'd come a long way from the days in French Lick when he was the poor kid who sold pop bottles for a nickel.

Bird coaching Jordan was a match made in heaven, or at least Hollywood, and Larry allowed Michael to take over the show. Before the game, Bird had said, "My feeling is that you design a couple of plays and then let the players do what they do best, play basketball. Pat them on the back, encourage them, and then see what happens. In the fourth quarter, that's the time they all want to win, so then you've got to have your best players on the floor."

That meant Michael. As time wound down with the Eastern squad clearly in command (final score: 135–114), Bird, resplendent in a gray pinstriped suit, sent Jordan back in the game. In what Isiah Thomas called "the ultimate playground game," Jordan not only began swishing three-pointers and a variety of loopty-loop shots, but mesmerized the television audience by trying to make a free throw with his eyes closed. The effort was unsuccessful, but the point made: Jordan appeared to be leveling the playing field by providing himself with a handicap.

By game's end, there was no doubt who was the most valuable player. Michael had captivated his peers and fans alike, though George Karl made it a no-brainer by not playing Kobe Bryant in the final few minutes.

Bird departed Madison Square Garden and New York, a city he despised, with fond memories. "It's something I'll never forget," he said. "The players were great." Despite his polite response, Bird privately told friends he'd rather have been in Florida. Though the pomp and circumstance of the event was impressive, Bird's shy, boyish demeanor was clearly evident when he stood with hands folded below his waist as the player introductions unfolded. His face was hollow; barely a smile shone through. "I did my duty," he told one reporter. "But I'm glad this whole thing is over."

Through the years, Bird established good relationships and longtime friendships with many of the superstars in sports, but it was the role players he never forgot. To him, the 12th man was as important as the starters, and Bird went out of his way to help them whenever he could.

That was evident in college, when he was adamant that a little-used reserve score in a game. With the outcome already decided, Bird worked furiously to get the ball to his teammate. Time and time again, he fed the ball; and time and time again, the reserve failed to score. Realizing what was happening, players and fans alike chuckled as Bird tried his best to help the teammate. He never did score, but Larry had showed his passion for helping others.

During his days in Boston, Bird befriended players like Rick Carlisle, Greg Kite, and Eric Fernsten (for whom Larry arranged a shoe endorsement deal even though he rarely played), none of whom were blessed with pure talent. "I was a very marginal player," the Pacers assistant coach said. "And Larry always had a way of making guys like me and Greg feel we were a part of the mix. We would come out of a timeout, and he'd make a point of saying to me, 'When they double-team me, I'm coming to you, so can you knock that shot down?' It was his way of letting you know he had confidence in you. You'd think, 'If Larry Bird sees something in me, it must be there.'"

During the early part of the season, Mark Pope, a native Nebraskan who played high school ball in Washington state, became like a little brother to Bird. The new Pacers coach relished Pope's work ethic and his desire to get better. Whether he'd ever become a great player remained to be seen, but Coach Bird appreciated his love for the game. "He gets better every day," Bird explained. "And he gives me 100 percent."

And more. Mark Pope was the Larry Bird-Chris Mullin-like gritty player on the Pacers' team. He was the first to take the practice floor and the last to leave. He was an incessant practicer, whether it was his jumper, right- and left-hand hooks near the basket, or free throws. He never wanted to quit practicing. Pacers coaches had to drag the flat-topped, babyfaced Pope off the court. When he wasn't practicing at Market Square Arena, he was racing up and down the court at The Indiana Academy, the team's practice facility. He'd even taken an apartment nearby. When Pope's shooting touch was off, or he wasn't happy with his performance at a practice session, he punished himself by running the stairs at the arena. That brought back memories of a certain superstar at Boston Garden. "I've never seen a harder working guy in the NBA," Rick Carlisle proclaimed. "Reminds me so much of Larry."

Mark Pope's trip to the "bigs" was pure fiction. The 6'10", 235-pound Washington State product played two seasons for the homestate Huskers before transferring to Kentucky. After sitting out the 1993–94 season, he played for Rick Pitino at Kentucky, where he became a valuable reserve off the bench.

Despite his lack of star-quality statistics at the University of Kentucky, the Pacers selected Pope in the 1996 draft. He displayed enough talent to keep them interested, but after being cut, he decided to play in Turkey. A partial season in Istanbul preceded a return to the Pacers fold in 1997. Bird took a shine to him—and with Derrick McKey and first-round pick Austin Croshere on the sidelines with injuries, Pope made the final cut. That meant the guarantee of the league minimum ($242,000), and gas for his 1987 Nissan, but also an apartment with no furniture. Still, he was having so much fun, he said early in the year, "I just wake up every morning and think, I've gone to heaven."

That didn't guarantee playing time in regular-season games, however. Though he was a ferocious practice player, constantly battling Pacers veterans, Pope was destined to be a benchwarmer, especially when McKey and Croshere reappeared. Early in the year, in an effort to get more playing time, he'd challenged Bird to one-on-one. The rookie had lost that bet, as well as a shooting contest where he'd egged the coach into promising not to cut him if he won.

Though Pope continued making rookie mistakes that included too many unforced errors, he never gave up. Through the year, he relished every game minute Bird gave him and more. "It's not a glory job [playing so few minutes]," Pope explained during the season. "But I'll do anything. If coach wants me to run out there with my jock over my shorts, that's great."

Another hard-working Pacers player who was beloved by Bird was forward Chris Mullin, the transplanted Golden State Warrior. Mullin was a shorter, deceptively similar clone of Bird, sans the strength and power, playing with a heart full of love for the game and for the competition. Mullin was a five-time NBA All-Star who credited his then coach Don Nelson with saving his life after he had hit the skids and become an alcoholic. Bird loved him because from day one, he fought and scratched for every point, every rebound, every assist. He developed a reputation as a hard-nosed, no-nonsense player who would do anything to win—one who expected no quarter, and gave none.

During their playing days, Bird and Mullin were a mutual admiration society. Both were scrappers and excellent shooters who vied for the NBA free-throw percentage title nearly every year. In 1986, Bird, who won the championship four times (during the 1989–90 season he shot 93 percent and hit 73 in a row), nailed seven of seven in his last game to nip Mullin.

Despite losing the free-throw title to Bird, Chris Mullin played championship basketball for the Warriors, a team that rarely contended. "Playing against Chris, you always had to watch him," the new Pacers coach explained. "He gets things done and knows how to make the plays. He makes everybody better, instead of just worrying about his points. He can have the ball in his hands and make other people look very good." Mark Jackson, a teammate of Mullin's at St. John's University, added, "I've watched him since college and nothing has changed. He stays in the gym the longest and comes in the earliest. He brings us a pure shooter who's a competitor, a guy who knows the game as well as anybody."

Mullin's trade to Indiana after 12 seasons with Golden State was a dream come true. "This is the perfect place for me," the 34-year-old said. "There are hoops everywhere—at the firehouses, in empty parking lots, on houses. Everybody's got a hoop hanging up somewhere. Indiana just lives this sport. It's unbelievable."

Bird began eyeing Mullin immediately after he was named coach of the Pacers. "When I started to think about retooling the club, Chris immediately came to mind," he said. "We needed a third scorer, a smart player who's a winner. That's Chris." Sitting side by side at the press conference announcing Mullin's acquisition, the former 1992 Dream Team teammates were all smiles. "Larry has been a teacher for me for years," Mullin said. "Without his really knowing it. Now, I'll learn from him on a daily basis."

Like Mullin, Bird never hesitated to find an edge with his comments. Against Atlanta in the 1985–86 playoffs, high-flying Dominique Wilkins strode to the free-throw line with a minute remaining and the game tied. When the Hawks superstar glanced underneath the basket, there was Bird giving him the choke sign. Wilkins missed both free throws.

Bird's shenanigans stretched to teammates as well. When Scott Wedman joined the Celtics as a free agent, Bird instantly disliked him. "My first year there, Larry was relentless, he really was," Wedman recalled. "I don't know if he'd ever admit it, but I don't think he was too thrilled about my making more money than he did."

Wedman soon learned the consequences. "I never had been around a team that talked trash like they did, and it was constant from Larry. He would score on me in practice and then say, 'He's too slow. He's too short. He can't guard me.' I was absolutely stunned." Wedman discovered a side of Larry Bird he detested. ". . . It was almost like hazing. Everything he did was good-natured, but it was at my expense. He was having a good time. I wasn't."

Bird's treatment of Wedman, other Celtics players he disliked, and opponents he ridiculed, seemed a paradox—for Bird said he resented the rude way he'd been treated by Kent Benson during his ill-fated freshman year at Indiana University. "I'll never understand why Larry acted like he did," a former Celtics teammate professed. "I guess it was just his insecurity. Larry never let anybody get close to him. And if you got on his wrong side, watch out."

Scott Wedman found that out. During the 1982–83 season, there was talk of a player strike. "We had to have a vote to see if we would strike, and Larry wouldn't raise his hand," Wedman said. "He said he wanted to talk to his agent first. I said, 'What's the matter, Larry? Can't you think for yourself?' He never said a word, but on the way out of the meeting, Rick Robey [teammate] came up to me, and Larry called to him, saying, 'Don't talk to him, he's not our friend.' "

Bird's hold-a-grudge attitude against Wedman continued, but as time passed Larry sensed his potential contribution to the team and began to lighten up. "After a time, Larry was better," Wedman said. "About every six months he'd actually give me a compliment."

Bird's treatment of Wedman was caused by his hard-edged view of the game. After becoming coach of the Pacers, he opined that modern NBA players were "too soft," comparing them to the tough guys he played against in the 1980s. "Players just aren't as physical as they used to be," Bird said. "The whole league has changed."

Bird also believed teams in the 1990s were too coddled, had it too easy. That extended even to the transportation used to speed them from game to game. Later in the season, Bird asked Donnie Walsh to fly the Pacers on commercial airliners instead of the souped-up charter jet that had all the amenities of first class. Bird believed flying coach and going through baggage claim would remind the players how fortunate they were while building a bond between them that could only come from adversity. Walsh was unable to acquiesce to Bird's wishes since the team had a charter agreement, but the coach's point had been made.

TEN DEEP

"Leadership is getting players to believe in you.
Leadership is diving for the ball, and being able to
take it as well as dish it out."
LARRY BIRD

From day one with the Pacers, Chris Mullin was everything Bird had hoped for. He set the tone for the hustling Larry knew was imperative to a winning season. Mullin's intensity spilled over to the other players; he dove for loose balls, pushed and shoved for rebounds, and played defense with guard dog intensity.

Mullin also knew the value of his role to the team. Though he'd started every game in the first 30, the burr-haired veteran let Bird know he'd give up his spot to Derrick McKey, returning from injury. "I'll help the club any way I can," Mullin said.

Mullin did help the club against Orlando, the Pacers' first foe after the All-Star game. His sticky-fingered defense (Slick Leonard said, "Mullin's hands are everywhere, he must lead the league in deflections") drove the Magic's small forwards Derrick Strong and Bo Outlaw crazy. His passing was crisp, and he drove home two three-pointers on his way to 12 points. When teammates Reggie Miller and Rik Smits added 16 apiece and Jalen Rose contributed 12 more, the Pacers overwhelmed Orlando 85–66, giving up their lowest point total of the year.

Even though the Magic were shorthanded—Penny Hardaway was out with a knee injury—Orlando was clearly a step short to the Pacers machine, which continued to feature more teamwork than any other club in the league. "That's the difference," Indianapolis radio talk show host Darrell Francis said on a night that saw Washington Wizards forward Tracy Murray score an NBA season-high 50 points against Golden State and Portland's Isiah Rider get suspended *again*. "The Pacers go 10 deep. Nobody else does that. And they play together. The chemistry is outstanding. Nobody takes bad shots and nobody passes up a good one."

The win came on the front end of a grueling span of four games in five nights preceding a date with the Bulls in the Windy City. That schedule was a portent of things to come, with 18 home dates and 17 road games left, 24 against Eastern Conference foes and 11 against the West.

In Miami, Bird proved that even on a night when he left Rik Smits on the floor too long and lost him to foul trouble, the Pacers could prevail. Antonio Davis, whose path to the NBA included stops with the Greek Basketball Association and the Italian League, replaced Smits early on. He was a physical force on the boards; an intimidator on defense; and an offensive threat who at one point produced a pump fake at the top of the key, darted around his defender, cradled the ball in his right hand, and attempted a slam dunk that resulted in no basket, but a foul. Bird was silently cheering on the sidelines, knowing that if Tony played like that, the Pacers fortunes would vastly improve.

Davis's outstanding play, and 30 points from Miller, earned a 110–101 win, the Pacers' 35th against 13 losses. After the 2–5 start, Indiana was 33–8.

Two nights later, Indiana entertained coach Don Nelson and his beleaguered Dallas Mavericks, who had posted just nine victories. When the Pacers raced off to a 22–6 lead, they appeared headed for their 36th victory of the year. But Dallas continued to peck away, and the margin was down to 10 at halftime. In the third quarter, Indiana played like Dallas and Dallas played like Indiana—the result being that with 1:12 remaining in the game, the Pacers trailed by a single point, 69–68.

Dallas stayed close, but Indiana led by three with 17.1 ticks on the clock. Then McKey fouled Michael Finley as he attempted a three-pointer, and Finley canned the first foul shot, missing the second. With his team trailing by two, he intentionally missed the third, and, to Bird's dismay, towering 7'6" center Shawn Bradley tapped the missed shot back in to tie the game.

Reggie Miller tried to find his late-game heroic touch in the final seconds of both the game and the first overtime, but both of his shot attempts went awry. Dallas stayed tough, and with the score tied 82–82 with time running out in the second overtime, Michael Finley took a pass at the top of the key, whirled around, leaped off his feet, and swished a game-winning three. The Pacers shuffled off the court, embarrassed.

Continuing to amaze those who chronicled the Pacers season, Bird appeared nonchalant about the loss. Other coaches might have ranted and raved, screamed at the players, ordered a midnight practice, or chastised the lackluster effort in the morning newspaper. Instead, Bird took the loss in stride. While his stomach was likely churning, he told those who listened, "We didn't shoot well. The ball simply wouldn't go in. We couldn't hit a shot." Bird pointed to the third-quarter play by this squad as the reason for the downfall. "We were manhandled," he stated, aware that rebounding had been less than stellar. Writer Mark Montieth perhaps put it best: "It was an improbable loss in an improbable year," he wrote.

Lower than a dog caught tearing up his master's rose garden, the Pacers boarded their charter to Atlanta on Valentine's Day wondering whether their magic was beginning to wear off. Losing to Dallas was devastating, and now Indiana faced two road games—one with the Hawks, and then one with the Bulls three days later. Was a three-game losing streak a possibility?

It was, especially since Atlanta had something to prove. After an 11–0 start, the Hawks foundered, and now stood only 30–21, six games behind the Pacers. Indiana University's Alan Henderson had replaced inconsistent Christian Laettner at forward; and with Steve Smith scoring at will and Mookie Blaylock running the offense, the Hawks were confident they could handle Indiana.

So much for confidence. The Pacers came out in the second half with fire in their eyes, a tribute to the Larry Bird school of coaching—and by the 6:13 mark of the fourth quarter, they led 78–77. Derrick McKey hit a sweet hook and two free throws, and the lead was four with 1:25 to play.

Atlanta stayed close the rest of the way. But Mark Jackson, posting up against his smaller defender, and Reggie Miller, who scored 31 points and shook himself free when it counted, were picture-perfect at the free-throw line. By game's end, Indiana had a much-needed 96–92 win over the Hawks.

Lenny Wilkens wasn't reticent to size up the Pacers. "Indiana has great depth," he said. "Miller and Smits are playing well, and the bench is coming through. Larry has done a hell of a job. They truly reflect the way he used to play. As for Chicago, well, they have Michael." After the game, Bird was pleased. "When we look back on the season," he explained, "this game will mean a lot. We go into Chicago next week, and I wanted a win to get us ready."

Ready they were. As usual, Chicago's season had been a tumultuous one, though the distractions came from new sources. Dennis Rodman, whose television film, *Bad As I Wanna Be* (based on his bestselling book) premiered to less than stellar reviews, was actually behaving himself. No headbutting, no stepping on photographers, no technical fouls or foul language to speak of. Despite that, he'd been unceremoniously left off the All-Star team, which made no sense, considering that he was one of the league's all-time great rebounders.

To replace Dennis the Menace's propensity to keep things lively, the Bulls brought forth (1) Scottie Pippen's annual crybaby stance about his lame salary and desire to be traded to any team in North America, (2) general manager Jerry Krause's displeasure with coach Phil Jackson, who had given Krause five world titles, (3) Krause's intention not to rehire Jackson at the end of the year whether he won number six or not, and (4) Based on (3), Michael Jordan's announcement that he would be retiring since he would play for no other coach than Jackson. Larry Bird told NBC's Bob Costas, "Letting Phil go, breaking up the championship team, there's something wrong there. If Michael were playing on my team, I'd bow out and let him have what he wanted. Championships are too hard to get."

Despite the turmoil, the Bulls had settled down after a rocky start, and their 37–15 record equaled the Pacers' 36–14. "Indiana's playing well," Michael Jordan stated. "Larry's got them hustling and they really believe in themselves." Bulls coach Phil Jackson added, "Larry's getting his message across in a subtle way. He's not like Calipari or Rick Pitino, who like to be more vocal. Larry's instilled confidence, and it's paying off." According to NBC's Peter Vecsey, Bird's attitude was having the desired effect. "There's an air of confidence about him," he said. "Treats everybody the same. And his honesty, that's what the Pacers respect. Against Cleveland, he grabbed Rik Smits after Smits had an open shot and didn't shoot. 'You pass an open shot one more time and I'm going to choke you,' Larry said. That's something the players like."

The Bulls, in what Reggie Miller dubbed "the ultimate game," sought to avenge an earlier loss to the Pacers—and from the opening tip, they were primed. That despite the absence in the starting lineup of Dennis Rodman, banished to the bench for missing the shootaround and the practice. "I lost my car keys," he explained. "What can I say?"

Rodman's antics turned out to be a blessing in disguise for the Bulls. Toni Kukoc replaced him, and his matchup against strongman Dale Davis was a mismatch from the opening whistle. Bird's failure to alter his starting five and put McKey or Rose on Kukoc was a blatant coaching error, especially when the left-handed Croatian began hitting threes from everywhere and driving to the basket uncontested. Unable or unwilling to adjust, Bird had simply been outcoached.

Kukoc's scoring spurted the Bulls into the lead, and Jordan's sharpshooting propelled the Bulls even farther ahead. Phil Jackson stifled Indiana's offense by having Jordan guard the Pacers' Mark Jackson. He was never a factor, joining Rik Smits (clearly outplayed by Luc Longley), Chris Mullin, Jalen Rose, and Antonio Davis, all of whom produced subpar performances.

On the night when Michael Jordan's mother presented him with a 60-pound cake for his 35th birthday, and the Bulls celebrated their 516th consecutive sellout at home, Chicago was truly the superior team. Bird's first trip to the Bulls' lair was anything but enjoyable, and he sat on the bench pressing his tongue against his cheek, shaking his head. When he did rise for a timeout, his familiar habit of sticking his finger in his left ear preceded a deadpan look that clearly showed displeasure with his team.

Before the game, Bird had said beating the Bulls would "build up our confidence; help us keep improving," but in the Pacers' 51st game of the year, his team was outclassed. By halftime, the margin was 14, and much of the suspense of the ballyhooed matchup was gone. The Bulls lead stayed in double digits most of the second half, although the Pacers had a 9–2 run and cut it to six with 42 seconds remaining.

After Jordan hit a 10-footer with 36 seconds left to seal the victory, Bird may have been calm on the outside, but inside he was fuming. Rebounding, or lack thereof—the Pacers' bugaboo the entire season—once again proved the difference. Chicago pulled down 42 rebounds to Indiana's 26. Rodman's 13 illustrated why Phil Jackson put pragmatism ahead of principle in letting him play rather than suspending him for a game. "They outquicked us from the beginning," Bird stated, not realizing his faux pas with the Kukoc-Dale Davis matchup. "We did not play that well tonight, but rebounding was the difference. We've got to learn to hit the boards against a team like this."

Jordan, who scored 27 points but lost his personal battle with Reggie Miller, who totaled 34, relished the victory but saw it as no big deal. "It was a good battle," he told reporters. "But I don't know if you can call it a statement game. We defended our home court. Plain and simple."

As the Pacers slumped their shoulders and limped out of the United Center, one thing was perfectly clear. In order to beat the Bulls, improvement was necessary. Bird had been outcoached, Smits and several of the others outplayed, and the rebounding . . . well, it needed a complete overhaul. Losing the first-place battle with Chicago was more than just a defeat, it hurt the Pacers' pride.

Nevertheless, Larry Legend was philosophical, trying to motivate his players instead of berate them. "We have to get better in every area. I think it's coming, and there's plenty of time, but we have to get better. If they start believing in themselves like I believe in them, they have a good opportunity to win." Bird kept his sense of humor. Told that Rodman had badmouthed the Pacers, the coach told reporters, "I don't listen to Dennis. Never did. I always tried to knock him on his ass when I played against him. If I ever get a chance outside somewhere and it's just me and him, I'll probably do it again."

Despite the rhetoric, practice the next day was lively. Bird remained his calm and cool self, but several players knew they had disappointed their boss. Bird had relished games like the one against the Bulls when he was a Celtic, and to watch his team break down was tough to take. He knew the defeat could haunt the club. It was important to continue on course, to correct defects, and begin a winning streak that would guarantee home court advantage against the Bulls when the playoffs began.

The sting of the defeat in Chicago could have lingered on, but the schedule was kind to the Pacers. Next up at Market Square Arena were Larry Brown's 76ers, but a memorable battle it wasn't. The 76ers played like they didn't know one another, which they didn't, and the Pacers played like the 76ers. The result was a rag-tag, duller than dull, why-did-I-pay-for-this-ticket NBA game that should have been cancelled. The 82–77 win was the Pacers' 37th of the year against 15 defeats, keeping them one game behind the Bulls, who won their sixth straight. It came on a night when one of the franchise's worst nightmares became reality: Rik Smits didn't dress for the game.

All year long, the Dutchman's physical condition had been questionable. If he went down, so did the team's chances for a championship. His feet had behaved themselves for 51 games, but now this new problem forced him to the sidelines.

Mark West, a.k.a "The Hammer," who doubled as an investment counselor to the players, started for Smits but was never a factor. Balanced scoring, with six players in double figures, saved the day, but Bird cringed just thinking about playing without Smits. Overall, he just wanted to go home and put the game behind him. "It's one of those games where you forget it, and move on . . . ," Bird said. "We made a lot of bad decisions, but we got the win, we're happy with it, and we'll move on."

To Orlando and Philadelphia, Bird knew, before home games with the Lakers and Portland. All the while he wondered whether the big fellow in the middle would be available to play, since his status was day-to-day.

At Orlando, Smits did play and was effective, scoring 27 points. Reggie Miller added 21 more, but a last-second three-point attempt bounced off the rim, and the Pacers lost, 93–91. "We underestimated them," Mark Jackson said. "They were short-handed and dangerous." Bird tried to downplay the loss, saying, "If Reggie hits that last shot, we win by one and everybody is happy. But Orlando beat us to the punch today."

The win for the Magic, which coach Chuck Daly called "the most inspirational of the year," was devastating for the Pacers, who played their fifth consecutive subpar game. Though Miller and Smits had been living up to their All-Star billing, Chris Mullin was playing like an inconsistent rookie instead of a veteran, and Mark Jackson hadn't been himself since Michael Jordan shut him down in the Bulls game. Dale Davis still couldn't hit a six-foot jumper, and his rebounding was AWOL.

Based on the dismal performances, skeptics wondered whether the Pacers' bubble had burst. Defensive intensity, team depth, an ability to win the close games, and finding a way to win even when the team did not play well—earlier hallmarks of the squad—had disappeared.

Bird continued to point to rebounding as the key missing ingredient. While Smits was expected to do his share, it was the Davises who were in Bird's doghouse, even though he didn't want to acknowledge that he had one. "Teams know we can't rebound, especially on the defensive end," the coach stated. "So they send as many players as possible to the offensive end. . . . If we don't rebound, we really don't have a chance."

As usual, Bird's comments to the press revealed an inner frustration that he didn't share with the players. Instead, Bird used the media to get across his points. Some Pacers players were tiring of the method, but Bird didn't care. "I couldn't jump two inches off the floor, and I averaged 10 [rebounds] for my career," the coach said. "Sometimes it's just boxing out, getting your man behind you and pursuing the ball. You can't just outjump people anymore. You have to box out and go to the boards aggressively like you really want the basketball."

Discussing it and imprinting his thoughts on the Pacers boardmen's brains were two different things. Bird worked in practice, as did the assistant coaches, showing the Davises how it worked, but the results had been spotty at best. With the trading deadline past, no help from elsewhere was likely. Indiana would live or die with its frontline, ever hopeful that things would get better.

More than anything, the team's play produced self-doubt. Fortunately, the Pacers' next opponents were the good ol' Philadelphia 76ers, who proved to be good for a win as usual. Though pleased with the victory, Bird wasn't saying much. "We played so-so," the coach explained, though the smirk on his face made those interviewing him suspicious. "We turned the ball over a few times, but we had lost a tough game at Orlando, and we came back tonight, which shows a lot of character." Reggie Miller, whose three-pointer late in the game iced the 97–93 victory, said he would trade it for the one he missed to lose the Orlando game two nights earlier. "You always remember the ones you miss more than the ones you make," he said. "I've gotten into the habit of making most of them, and I expect to make them."

This was one he made with a taunt from Larry Brown ringing in his ears. With Eric Snow all over him, Reggie heard someone yell from the Sixers' bench, "Eric, you don't need help. You can take him alone." Turning to confirm that it was Brown, Miller in an instant shucked and jived, arched his long arms out with the ball, faked his defender off-balance, dribbled once, and then launched the ball from 22 feet. It swished as Miller ran up the court in ecstasy, glaring at his former coach. "Just a look," Miller told reporters. "I couldn't play this game if I couldn't talk, couldn't look. I need that verbal warfare to get me going, especially on the road, because I'm guy they usually pick on . . . I thrive on it."

Despite Miller's antics, which threatened to overshadow his reputation as a clutch player, Chris Mullin was impressed. ". . . When it comes to crunch time, he takes over."

The Pacers win, their 38th against 16 losses, wasn't without incident—one that provided a glimpse into the Larry Bird persona. On a night when the same Orlando team that had beaten Indiana two nights earlier nipped the Lakers 96–94 to spoil Shaquille O'Neal's return to the sunshine state (O'Neal took the defeat in stride, telling reporters, "I'm not going to go home and jump in a lake full of alligators or drink a bottle of Clorox"), Bird showed his disdain for stupid play.

Jalen Rose was the culprit. After Rik Smits made an ill-advised pass that cost an over-and-back violation, Rose lackadaisically let the ball go out of bounds at the other end instead of catching it. That meant the 76ers could inbound the ball under their own basket instead of at halfcourt. Seething at the lackadaisical play, Bird called Reggie Miller's name, and Rose became a benchwarmer the remainder of the game. Larry Bird excused mistakes as long as a player hustled, but giving less than a 100 percent effort didn't cut it with the coach.

PART

IV

THE STRETCH DRIVE

*"To play good, sound defense takes five guys playing and
thinking together. But you can't do that all the time.
Sometimes the big stand is taken in the first quarter.
Or the third. The crucial times are the key."*
LARRY BIRD

With 28 games left, the Pacers
remained a step behind Michael and the Bulls, and Bird still wasn't
convinced the team was out of its nosedive (sportcaster Clark Kellogg called it "speed bumps"). He figured he'd find out the last
week in February, when two of the Western Conference elite teams
came to town. First up were Shaquille, Kobe, and the Lakers, followed by Portland, featuring new guard Damon Stoudamire.

When showtime came to Market Square Arena on the 25th of
February, the arena was packed with fans anxious to watch Shaq
and Kobe face Reggie and the boys. Even the Del Harris versus
Bird coaching matchup was intriguing.

Los Angeles had been vying for respect the entire season, but
each time they produced a mini-winning streak, the players fell flat
against less talented opponents. *USA Today* rated them the fifth
best team in the league ("Can't hang with the good teams in the
big games"), behind Chicago ("Only matter of time before Bulls
got back on top"), Utah, Seattle, and Phoenix. Indiana was sixth
("Still figuring out what to do with Derrick McKey").

The battle of the boards was again the key to victory as the Lakers triumphed 96–89. Bird was still trying to find the right combination at power forward, but perhaps he had himself to blame. The minutes Dale and Antonio Davis spent on the court had diminished greatly; and even though Mullin and McKey were strong scorers, they were weak rebounders. Critics said McKey, a small forward, was being asked to fill the rebounding role even though past history proved he couldn't. "Bird still doesn't get it," a courtside reporter commented. "The game is all about matchups, and Derrick has trouble with the big guys. That means rebounding can only come from the center position, and Smits can't handle it alone."

TBS's marquee game of the week, packed with reporters seeking a big story, turned out to be a big dud because the game really wasn't as close as the final score indicated. Reggie Miller forgot his shooting touch (4 for 17 from the field in a dismal performance), and heralded Kobe Bryant played like a 19-year-old kid who should have been at a college game. TBS's Bob Hill, a former Pacers coach, had to bite his tongue to keep from saying Indiana played a bit like they used to play for him before he was fired.

With the loss, the Pacers remained two and one-half games behind the Chicago Bulls, who suffered only their third home loss of the season, this time to the Damon Stoudamire-led Trail Blazers—who then headed south to face Indiana on the 27th.

Indiana once again tried to win their 39th game, matching the victory total for the previous season. They were 13 games ahead of that year's pace, but somehow the electricity that had catapulted the Pacers into prominence was dimming.

Bird decided some changes were in order. He had given up on both Fred Hoiberg and Rose as backups for Miller at the two-guard position, and determined to try Mullin there. The backup shooting guard was critical—when Sir Reginald was on the bench, the Pacers' scoring punch was severely diminished. Travis Best had the ability to score from the point guard position, but he was tentative at times and inconsistent. When Antonio Davis replaced Rik Smits and Reggie was on the bench, there was no one to take up the slack. Bird decided Mullin could tandem with Derrick

McKey, whose offensive tools were slowly coming around after his bout with injury. "Jalen hasn't done what we thought he could do there," Bird announced. "Reggie has to play more, and I don't want to do that. From here on out, we'll play Jalen at the three forward [small forward] most of the time."

If Pacers fans were expecting to see how the new substitution system worked, they were disappointed. Either the Trail Blazers, rich in NBA tradition from the championship days of Bill Walton, partied too long after their victory in Chicago, or they just decided to go through the motions in anticipation of a weekend party in Indianapolis. From the opening tip, they were a step slow, showed little enthusiasm, and played defense as if they wanted to help the Pacers challenge the NBA's all-time scoring record.

A few ticks on the clock after Bird walked on the court with his customary "aw-shucks" grin, scratched his head, and received his IBM Coach of the Month Award for January, the Pacers—mirroring Bird's game-face attitude—exploded out of the gate. At the 8:22 mark it was 8–2. Two minutes and twenty-two seconds later, it was 16–2; then 18–4, then 23–4, and finally 29–6 with 2:47 left in the first quarter. Game, set, and match. Indiana was as good against Portland as they had been bad against the Lakers.

Dale Davis rebounded, Chris Mullin shot the lights out, Reggie was on target, Smits dominated the 7'4" Lithuanian Arvydas Sabonis, and Mark Jackson pulled the trigger from the point guard position and held Damon Stoudamire in check. Coming off the bench, Antonio Davis played with the enthusiasm of a kid trying to gain the last spot on his high school team. Travis Best passed the ball with the zing of Larry Bird in his prime, Derrick McKey shot well and played superb defense, and best of all, Jalen Rose was a factor for the first time in memory, garnering 13 points, 8 assists, and 7 rebounds.

In the Pacers locker room, the 124–59, 65-point win produced embarrassed smiles everywhere. The second most decisive victory in NBA history gave the blue and gold an aura of invincibility, if only for one evening. Travis Best gave the credit to his coach. "We haven't been playing well lately, but Larry doesn't panic," he said. "Coach just tells us we have to work harder, and it helps that he doesn't scream and yell and give us hell. He believes in us and that's a big deal."

Larry Legend preferred to praise his players. "Defense made the difference," he said. "I don't think we can play defense any better than that. Tonight we played about as well as we could. It wouldn't have mattered who we played, we would have won."

The Pacers' lopsided win over a Western Conference contender returned them to the spotlight. Those who thought the magic may have worn off shrugged their shoulders. "People have to understand, it's tough when you get to the top," media relations director David Benner said. "Every team is laying for you. That means we have to play better every time we get out on the court."

Benner's words were true, though it was tough to be serious when the opponent was the dastardly Denver Nuggets, owners of the worst record in the NBA (5–51). Bill Hanzlik's crew came calling on the first day of March with a road record of 1–27. Sealing a victory was important, as a three-game West-Coast swing (Lakers, Grizzlies, and Warriors) was next.

On the night Bird's coaching idol, Pat Riley, earned his 900th career win, the Pacers blasted the Nuggets (said by Dennis Rodman to be "like playing a high school team") in the third quarter on the way to a blowout 90–63 victory. Rik Smits led the scoring with 23 points, and Mark Jackson had 12 assists against his old teammates.

Indianapolis Star reporter Robin Miller echoed Rodman's words about Denver, writing, "In the second half, the Nuggets looked like a bad YMCA team playing outdoors on a windy day. Airballs, glass balls, and balls that barely grazed the rim were the norm. . . ." Regardless, the Pacers' easy win, coupled with the overwhelming victory over Portland two nights earlier, restored self-confidence to a team on the brink. "Our outlook is very positive now," Smits said. "We all know what we are capable of doing as a team, and these last two games reminded us of that." Denver's rookie forward Danny Fortson was impressed, saying, "The Pacers acted like a hyena going after their prey."

In this game, Coach wasn't concerned when his players freelanced. As the second half began, Reggie, Chris, Mark, Rik, and Dale decided to fullcourt trap. The result was a prevent defense that stymied the Nuggets, forcing them into several ballhandling errors. "We're not afraid to go out and do what we feel, because Coach trusts us," Mark Jackson remarked, a clear indication of the closeness between Bird and his players.

Bird suddenly found himself making news off the court as well. In Ann Landers's syndicated column, he was criticized by a writer for leaving Travis Best and Dale Davis behind after they showed up late for a flight to Nashville in October. "How could he be so mean to his players?" the letter, signed by "a former Larry Bird fan," read. Bird laughed when he read it, and told reporters, "And if they're late again, we'll leave them behind again." Before the Pacers' departure, Birdwatching reporters were treated to one of Bird's off-the-wall comments: "But I'm all right," Bird quipped, "Ann and I used to date in college."

Sporting a record of 40–17, fourth-best in the league, the Pacers traveled west with renewed determination to catch the Bulls, who remained two and one-half games ahead. "They're still the team to beat," Portland coach Mike Dunleavy said.

Vancouver coach Brian Hill disagreed. After watching Indiana defeat his team on March 3rd, 111–103, Hill praised them, saying, "The Pacers are deep, and they have the scorers and rebounders to play with Chicago." In the ho-hum win over the Grizzlies, Smits became Indiana's all-time rebounding leader with 4,497. Bird laughed as he told reporters, "The rebounding is mind-boggling to me. He must have been in the league 30 years to get that." The remark didn't sit too well with Smits, but he understood the coach's wry sense of humor.

Armed with a 41–17 record, the Pacers trekked down the Pacific coast to the City of Angels, where the Lakers were coming off a 3–3 eastern road trip. Their mediocre record had fueled rumors that coach Del Harris would be replaced by assistant Larry Drew. Lakers general manager Jerry West put those rumors to rest with a strongly worded statement backing Harris, the scholarly one who at times seemed an odd choice for the fast-break, Hollywood-style basketball Los Angeles played. Especially at the celebrity-studded fabulous Forum, where fans paid $500 just to sit in the cheap seats.

Bird's memories of the Forum brought mixed emotions. He and his Celtics teammates had played many monumental games in the arena, often with Bird matched up with Magic Johnson. "We had some great games here," the coach recalled. "Playing against Magic and the Lakers was very special."

On March 4th, Bird was hoping something special would happen to his Pacers to avenge the home loss to L. A. seven days earlier. It didn't. Shaquille had 18 points by halftime, and the Lakers held a 59–46 lead due to bad defense on the part of the Pacers, who gave up way too many open shots.

Once again, Bird's substitution patterns were questioned. Smits obviously wasn't himself, his feet unable to keep up with his 7'4" frame. Bird stayed with him, but silly fouls by the big fella caused by being too tired haunted him. He was never a factor, and finally fouled out with more than eight minutes to go. Though Reggie Miller scored 24 points, and Antonio Davis, Dale Davis, and Mark Jackson contributed, Chris Mullin, Jalen Rose, Travis Best, and Derrick McKey disappointed. Bird made no excuses, telling reporters, "We had a tough game last night, but that's no excuse, this is the NBA. . . . It seemed like we were a step behind all night long."

Saddled with their 18th defeat, the Pacers headed back up the Pacific coast to play the Warriors, who had surprised San Antonio the night before. That on the day when Golden State received shocking news involving none other than Latrell Sprewell, its bad boy who had tried to choke the life out of coach P. J. Carlesimo and threatened to kill him.

The Warriors had dealt with the incident like any upstanding corporation, firing Sprewell and canceling his $24 million-plus contract. The NBA tagged a one-year suspension onto the penalty, triggering Sprewell's right to appeal the decision to an arbitrator. To the Warriors' dismay, John Feerick ruled that the Warriors were stuck with Sprewell's $18 million, two-year contract; and perhaps worse, that Latrell would be a Warrior again after July 1st. Strangling your boss and then threatening his life didn't get you fired from your job, if you happened to be a player in the NBA. Go figure! Orlando coach Chuck Daly said he knew what the ruling meant. "Coaches," he said, "now had better spend time in the weight room."

Larry Bird just shook his head at the ruling, more concerned about readying his Pacers for the game against the Warriors, still a ragtag team trying to find itself. On the same night the Hornets served notice that they would be a playoff contender by winning their seventh straight over Seattle, 104–98, Golden State finally succumbed to a Pacers third-quarter flourish led by Smits, who finished with 21 points. Able assistance in the 101–87 victory was provided by Jalen Rose, who dazzled the crowd with a left-handed dunk, and Fred Hoiberg, who showed signs of breaking out of his 20-plus game drought by adding not only eight points, but also a steal that resulted in a layup and a foul shot. "It was my turn in the rotation," The Mayor proclaimed with a huge smile on his face. "I took the shots and they went in."

Though the big news of the day had been the return of Chris Mullin, a 12-year veteran of the Warriors, to the Bay Area ("The reception was more than I expected," he told reporters. "It was touching, emotional. I really appreciated it."), Bird was nonchalant about the victory. "The Warriors played better, we had a good run and got lucky and won," the legend explained. Golden State coach P. J. Carlesimo praised the Pacers, saying, "They're a great defensive team, great quickness, and the blend of the team is solid."

Moving within two games of the idle Bulls, whom the Pacers would play March 17th, Indiana had gone 2–1 on a road trip. "Through 60 games, we've had our ups and downs," Coach Bird said. "Twenty-two more to go and then the real season starts." He was referring to the season in which Larry Legend had been a superstar during his days with the Celtics; playoff time meant Bird stepped up his game a notch, providing opponents with even more of a challenge.

16

LARRY: PAST AND PRESENT

*"I told our players the first day, if they think they are
going to be shooting three-pointers through the year and not
working on them, they are crazy. I told them I wanted them to
make 60 to 70 threes every day, and they have been doing it."*
LARRY BIRD

"Larry Bird is like Elvis," Kevin McHale said as Larry Bird approached his ninth season in the NBA. "He's got to get out while's he's the King . . . I don't want him to be like the Everly Brothers, just hanging around after his time."

McHale's comments were his reply to questions about when Larry Bird might decide to hang up his sneakers. As Bird readied himself for the 1987–88 season, he told reporters, "I feel that I could play six more years at this level. . . . But it will probably be four."

The Boston Celtics probably wished it could have been 10. The team had fallen from its perch and was struggling to find the championship form that had made them the dominant team in the NBA. More and more, Bird was shouldering the entire scoring burden—and though he played well, the team was slipping.

After winning his third straight three-point shooting title at the All-Star Game, Bird took off on a streak that saw him average nearly 40 points in six straight games. Against Portland, he threw up 16 in the final nine minutes, despite a fractured eye socket and broken nose. The eye injury came from the elbow of Dell Curry of Cleveland. "I knew there was something seriously wrong with my eye," Bird recalled. ". . . I just couldn't see. When I looked up, I saw two baskets. One was just a little higher than the other. . . . The pain was intense, and when I looked into the mirror there was an egg-sized bump on the outside of my eye and my eye was swollen shut." Despite protests, Bird became a goggles man for several games.

The Portland game made Red Auerbach, who had dodged questions about whether Bird or Bill Russell was the best player he ever saw, finally concede, "Bird, by far." Later, he added, "If I had to start a team and could pick just one player, it would be Bird."

Though Bird was humbled by Auerbach's comment, he was less than pleased with his own game. At age 31, his body hurting after nine seasons of banging with the heavyweights of the NBA, he was worn out. When asked if he was a little tired after a season-ending playoff series with the Detroit Pistons, Bird replied, "No, I'm a lot tired."

The loss to the Pistons came after one of Bird's bright moments in the playoffs. Against Atlanta in the seventh game of their series, the Hawks battled the Celtics through the fourth quarter, hitting on a remarkable 17 of 22 shots. But Bird was better, hitting 10 of 11 as Boston prevailed 118–116. "I never saw a fourth quarter like his in all my years in basketball," Detroit coach Chuck Daly expounded. Larry's explanation was simple. "One of the keys was footwork," he said. "That started to come to me in the fourth quarter. I was coming off the picks and I was in rhythm, and I was getting squared off and in good balance . . . I had the touch today."

"God may not have granted him an all-world body. But from his shoulders to the top of his head, and from his wrists to his fingertips, he played the game better than anyone who ever played it. And he played it with a heart five times bigger than anyone I ever saw." The "he" former Celtics executive Dave Gavitt referred to was Larry Bird. His gifted play continued into the 1988–89 preseason, but then the Good Lord threw Larry a curveball.

Hopes were high for the Celtics that year. Frizzy-haired long-time assistant Jimmy Rodgers took over the reins of the club, but any hopes for a championship were extinguished when Bird went down with bone spurs that pressed on his Achilles tendons, most likely caused when he attempted a behind-the-back dribble against Cleveland. The injuries required surgery, and Bird's season was over after he had played only eight exhibition and six regular-season games. "That was a year I wish I could have started over," Bird said. "It reminded me of when I was hurt in high school. I could barely manage to watch the games. I missed playing so much it made my stomach hurt."

Bird came back to play 75 games the following year, but he and Rodgers—who later joined Phil Jackson's coaching staff at Chicago for the 1990s championship seasons—were at loggerheads most of the season. Believing Bird had lost much of the spring in his legs, which he had, Rodgers devised a diversified offense for the Celtics. Bird became merely a cog in the wheel, not the focus, and his shot total diminished considerably. Rodgers's plan was a failure, and the Celtics lost to the Knicks in the first round of the play-offs. Chris Ford, a hard-nosed former Celtics guard, took over when Rodgers was canned.

During the 1990–91 season, Bird's ability to continue his high level of play was questioned. *Sports Illustrated* ran a cover story, "What's Wrong, Larry?" and Celtics players expressed doubt about whether Bird was helping or hurting the team. Celtics executive Dave Gavitt even considered trading Bird, but told one reporter, "If you trade Bird, you end up facedown in Boston Harbor."

Before naming Chris Ford, Auerbach considered making Bird player-coach, but Larry had no interest. Ever the optimist, he believed he still possessed the skills to lead his club deep into the playoffs. He didn't, mainly due to a major back pain that limited his play to 60 games, and Boston fell to Detroit in the second round.

Off-season surgery for a compressed nerve root was pronounced successful, but it really wasn't. "My back hurt me so bad I could barely move," he said later. "I became a day-to-day player, something I hated."

Bird only played 45 games during his final season, and when his teammates finally realized he wouldn't be able to save them, they produced a late-season rush without him and raced into the playoffs. By the time they faced Cleveland in the semifinals, Bird was back, though he often was forced to lay prone on the court to ease the excruciating pain that bolted through his body like an electric current.

Bird did show a final flash. In a 152–148 double-overtime win against Portland, he racked up 49 points, 14 rebounds, and 12 assists. "Anytime you have Bird on the floor, anything can happen," Clyde Drexler commented. Bird's last game at the Garden was a winning effort over Cleveland. He played, bad back and all, scoring 16 points and dishing out 14 assists.

Larry Legend flirted with the idea of retirement (wife Dinah was insistent, especially after the bad back caused him to eat his meals stretched out on the floor), but decided to try one more year. By August of 1992, Bird knew it was impossible; so at a hastily arranged news conference on the 18th, the Hick from French Lick called it quits.

The timing illustrated a great Larry Bird characteristic: integrity. He had made over $30 million in his 13-year career, including $7.07 million for the 1991–92 season. He was scheduled to make $8 million for the next season, with the first payment of $3.75 million due the 15th of August. By deliberately retiring before the 15th, Bird sacrificed the money, not wanting to be paid when he knew he couldn't play.

The end came a month after Bird had joined other legends of the game on the Dream Team in the Olympics in Barcelona. He and his teammates were unstoppable and easily won the Gold Medal, while Bird discovered he was truly an international star. At a nearby shopping mall, Spalding had set up an autograph signing for Bird. ESPN producer Bill Fairweather recalled, "The line stretched for what seemed like five miles. Twenty people wide. I walked down there, and there's Larry signing his name. He looked like he was shocked. They loved him."

No more than Magic Johnson did. Of all the players Bird competed against, it was the Magic Man with whom he was most identified. In his book *My Life*, Johnson noted similarities between the two. "The truth is that we're both a couple of small-town boys. We're still close to our families, our teachers, former coaches, and the people we grew up with. It's no accident that Larry went back to French Lick every summer and I returned to Lansing [Michigan]."

Johnson's memories of Bird were special ones. "One time I was out with an injury, and we're playing at the Forum," Johnson recalled. "Larry says, 'I'm going to put on a show for you. Sit back and enjoy the Larry Bird Show.'" Bird did just that, scoring 36 points, hauling down 20 rebounds, and handing out 15 assists. "And every time he scored, he looked over at me and smiled," Johnson said.

Number 32 had enormous admiration for Bird's work ethic. "The amazing thing about Larry is that he achieved his success without some of the natural talents that other people take for granted," Magic said. "My own physical gifts are limited, but compared to this guy I'm one of the Flying Walenda Brothers. . . . And he did it the old-fashioned way. He worked, and worked, and then worked some more. To most players, basketball is a job. To Larry, it was his life. . . . He was always the yardstick I measured myself against."

Realizing Bird had laced up his sneakers for the last time, sportswriters and fans began to recall images from the storied career. There was the string-bean kid who made the big free throws to win games in high school and the lanky youngster who propelled Indiana State to an NCAA runner-up finish. Celtics fans remembered him diving for loose balls, scraping a rebound off the glass, amazing teammates and opponents alike with unbelievable passes—while scoring at will against defenders who shook their heads in disbelief as the white guy who couldn't jump sliced toward the basket for an easy hoop or spotted up for the patented Bird jumper.

Red Auerbach put it best when he said, "Nobody has ever been more self-motivated, and nobody I've ever seen played the way this guy did. It was for the love of the game." Agent Bob Woolf believed he knew why, telling reporters, "Larry brought the values he had in seventh grade and made them work in the NBA." Most of all, fans and basketball aficionados alike knew Larry Bird played basketball for all the right reasons. "When I came into the league, Artis Gilmore told me, 'You won't stay very long if you keep moppin' up the floor.' I didn't agree, and besides, that's the only way I knew how to play."

Bird also had his priorities in order. During one summer, he was busy working at the Boys Club in French Lick. Agent Bob Woolf recalled, "I told Larry that the president of Harvard wanted him to give a speech. He said no. I told him, '*Sports Illustrated* wants to do a cover story on you.' He said no. I said '*Life* will do a 10-page spread, complete with photos.' He said no. And then he said, 'Mr. Woolf, I thought you said this call was important.'"

Bird was arguably the most popular player ever to wear the Celtics green. His faithful fans even combed his trash looking for any souvenir that would link them with number 33. "One time I threw out some old basketballs," Bird recalled. "And there were cars of people out there going through the stuff."

Fans around the globe worshipped Bird and his fiery spirit. Babies were named after him, coaches pointed to the Birdman as a role model for their youngsters, and kids idolized the overachiever who never gave up by saying, "You be Magic Johnson, I want to be Larry Bird" in pickup games. "He was my favorite player when I was growing up," Zach Wray, who had number 33 emblazoned on his Honda motorbike, said. "I loved to watch him play."

To his credit, the Birdman knew when to quit. In a day and age when many superstars played after their skills had deteriorated, or retired and then came back for an ill-fated last hurrah, Bird knew the 1992 season had to be his final one. At the news conference announcing the decision, Bird, holding back tears, said, "It's tough for me because I'm giving up something I love. . . . But I have to give it up. I don't want to go out this way, but I have to."

When he walked off the court in an emotional ceremony at Boston Garden, Larry Legend had logged 34,443 minutes in 897 games, totaled 21,791 points, confiscated 8,974 rebounds, handed out 5,695 assists, and stolen the ball a record 1,556 times during 13 seasons. Three championship rings were his prized possessions, along with 3 MVP seasons and 10 as an All-Star. When basketball experts picked their top five all-time players in NBA league history, Bird's name was a solid choice.

More than the stats, Bird had left an image filled with wondrous play: towering court-length passes that floated into teammates' hands as they sped for the basket; a spin-and-shoot move that left defenders bedazzled; the bank shot that arched off the glass with perfect grace; a behind-the-back pass that hit a driving teammate in stride; the batted ball from out of bounds that saved a Celtics possession as Larry tumbled into a row of photographers; and the underhand, reverse lay-in that hit nothing but net. Larry Legend's other trademarks included the touch, or "bat" pass; the reverse, two-handed Bird dunk; the behind-the-back dribble; the off-balance, falling out of bounds shot over the backboard that found the bottom of the net; the corner jumper with a defender inside his uniform; the give-and-go sequence he perfected like no one before or since; the no-look passes; and the uncanny ability to hit half-court or last-second shots that won ballgames that had been lost. Against the Mavs one year, with his team trailing by two and with five seconds left on the clock, Bird was so arrogantly confident that he pulled up for a three (and swished it, of course), when he could have had an easy two closer to the basket.

Bird also had an uncanny ability to draw defenders to him—and just when he seemed to be bottled up, a deft pass set up a teammate for an easy basket. Coach Bill Fitch said Bird utilized "Come into my web, said the spider to the fly" deceptive tactics to hoodwink opponents. Longtime Celtics announcer Johnny Most believed Bird confounded defenders because he had "eyes all around his head."

On defense, Bird left his mark as well. He took the charge, often sitting on the floor with a grin on his face after an offensive foul was called on a startled opponent. He dived for loose balls, his knees pockmarked with floor burns, and was always the one slinging his body out of bounds into the scorer's table trying to save an errant pass.

Donnie Walsh, when told of Bird's decision to hang up his sneakers and green-and-white uniform, said, "It's kind of like when Alexander the Great decided he wasn't going to conquer any more countries."

Retirement meant Bird could rest his sore back, play golf, and live the life of a family man. But it didn't take long for him to get edgy and realize that taking it easy wasn't his bit. "I'd go to bed at 8:00 at night and get up at 5:00 in the morning and just lie there for two or three hours," Bird said. "Just wasn't enough to keep my mind working." Basically, Bird was bored, and his job as "special assistant to the senior executive vice-president for the Celtics" produced little satisfaction. Competitive juices still flowed in his veins, but there was no outlet for his energies. Caught in no-man's land—too old to play professionally and too young to retire—Bird was an unhappy camper until word reached him that Pacers coach Larry Brown might resign. "The moment I heard that," Larry admitted, "a smile came to my face. I knew something might be coming around." A short time later, Bird was introduced as the new coach of the Indiana Pacers. Destiny had blessed Larry Legend, and he was determined to prove that he could mold the Indiana Pacers into an NBA championship team.

Through the first 60 games of his rookie coaching season, Bird's words of wisdom had propelled the Pacers to new heights—but another legend was on target to reclaim the league MVP award he had lost to Karl Malone in 1997.

On the 8th of March, the day the NCAA field of 64 was named as March Madness in college basketball took center stage, Michael Jordan proved to a national television audience and the New York Knicks that Father Time hadn't caught up with him. In a 102–89 victory, Jordan scored 42 points during the most spectacular display of his talents all year. He hit the jumpers, many of them fadeaways that gave the defender no chance. He sliced through the lane and dunked the ball with authority. He stole the ball, flipped it back inbounds, and watched as his teammates waltzed down the court for an easy basket. If Jordan really was going to retire from the game, he bid New York adieu with style.

Playing in his original red-and-black Air Jordans that he had scooped from the closet before leaving Chicago for New York ("You wouldn't believe the blisters I have on my feet right now. I paid the price for going back to 1984"), Jordan also added one more image of greatness to his photo album. As NBC's Bob Costas said, "You will watch this, not believe it, and then want to watch it again."

"The Shot," as it would be known on the New York streets the next day, came of necessity. Jordan attempted to hit a scoop shot from just to the left of the basket, but got tangled up with a Knicks defender. Instead of dishing the ball off, or resigning himself to defeat, he somehow turned his back to the basket, stuck out his tongue, arched his body in the air, and as he fell away, cupped the basketball in his right hand and flung it dipsy-doodle-like back-handed toward the glass. The ball rolled through the net. Charles Oakley was so amazed that he stood transfixed as if to say, "Did that really happen?"

Jordan had a simple explanation. "Those were 1984 moves," His Airness revealed.

The Bulls bench went nuts, and Jordan sported that smirky smile of his that let everyone know he thought the shot was quite special too, thank you. Then he galloped on down the court, ready for more heroics.

When Jordan retired for the evening—the victory assured thanks to his efforts, Scottie Pippen's 25 points, and Dennis Rodman's 20 rebounds—the capacity crowd provided Mr. Jordan with a standing ovation. Knicks coach Jeff Van Gundy believed Michael and his pals were still the best team in the league, telling reporters, "We need everybody on our team to play well. They need only three, Jordan, Pippen, and Rodman."

At home in Indianapolis, Bird watched the Jordan Show with admiration. Every once in awhile he thought his Pacers might win the NBA championship, but seeing Michael in action let him know the challenge would be formidable. Twenty-two games remained in the regular season, and Bird knew Indiana had a few potholes to fix, though the recent good play by his team gave him cause for hope.

As the season wound down, Donnie Walsh continued to marvel at Bird's ability to inspire the team. "Coach Bird coaches like he played, all-out, give it 100 percent," Walsh explained. "He looks at the game from more of a coach's mind than a player's mind. That's what our guys have sparked to, and I think we can continue to stay at the top. We've got so much confidence now."

Walsh hoped that observation proved true as the team began its drive to the playoffs. With Chicago in front by two and one-half games, and the Heat lurking just a half-game behind in the Eastern Conference standings, the Pacers faced the Celtics again on the 8th of March.

Rick Pitino still hopped up and down the court like a college coach, but his Celtics had improved considerably—especially after the wily Pitino had stolen point guard Kenny Anderson in a trade before the deadline.

Attempting to win their 43rd of the season, the Pacers played the first half as if they had just stepped off a plane from the West Coast and were suffering from jet lag—which they were. While the contest with the Celtics was a 12:30 Sunday matinee, the players felt like it was 9:30.

Though the Celtics played the Pacers tough, experience and the neverending will to win instilled by Bird prevailed. Fred Hoiberg's three-pointer tied the game at 88 with 8:09 remaining, and the Pacers went ahead and stayed there the remainder of the way. More important, when the game was close again in the final two minutes, Indiana kept getting the ball inside to Smits, who delivered from the field and at the foul line.

The 104–100 win was spearheaded by Reggie's 25 points and a season-high 22 from Dale Davis. His effort was simply the latest achievement inspired by Larry Legend. Mark Jackson didn't choke in the clutch, remaining cool when the game was on the line. Rik Smits was playing with confidence, unafraid of any of the other

NBA big men. Reggie Miller still wanted the ball at crunch time, and Bird's confidence in him elevated Reggie to new heights as he came through time and time again. Chris Mullin was everything Bird thought he would be, providing stability, leadership, and a hard-work ethic that had caused Donnie Walsh to say, "I've never seen a guy work out as much as Mully, ever."

Pacers reserve Jalen Rose had returned to top form after a short-lived slump as Bird continued to believe in him like no other coach Rose had experienced. Travis Best had nights when it appeared as if he could start at the point for any NBA team, and Fred Hoiberg had regained his confidence by employing the Bird ethic of hard work and practice, practice, practice. And Antonio Davis, who sported a heart-and-rose tattoo on his arm that bore the names of wife Kendra and twins Kaela and A.J., was playing the best basketball of his career, battling for the ball on the backboards and diving for loose ones all over the court.

Bird's biggest enigma, Dale Davis, had struggled, but Larry continued to believe there were parts to Dale's game he didn't even know existed. The coach with the magic touch urged Davis on, trying to motivate him with harsh words to the press. Sometimes Dale sulked—but he kept trying to improve not only his rebound positioning, but also his offensive game and his foul shooting.

Against Boston, Davis had put it all together. He rebounded well, hit the short jumpers he should hit, and, most impressively, came through when the Pacers needed two foul shots with 10.1 seconds to play. His ability to do so was a direct result of Bird's promise to obtain improvement from each player as the season progressed.

To that end, Double D had shot thousands of free throws in practice, normally 100 each session, trying to find a comfort zone. Though his percentage (44) was still dismal, Davis had started to believe in himself, waiting for the chance to show that the practice had paid off.

Davis's mind-set was a simple one. "In the game, I try to remember what Coach Bird has taught me in practice," he said. "He said to visualize the shot when I'm shooting in a game." Of course, Bird knew of what he spoke. After an incident in 1985 in Boston when Bird had injured his shooting hand in a bar brawl, he had to tape the hand for playoff games against Philadelphia. *Boston Globe* sportswriter Dan Shaughnessy kidded him about his effectiveness, and Larry challenged him to shoot 100 free throws at $5 a shot. The scribe had to peel off $160 when the wounded Bird hit 87 of 100 to Dan's 55.

Against Boston, the baldheaded Davis toed the line, realizing Bird had confidence in him. Reggie Miller tried to rev up the crowd as they held their breath, expecting a brick—or worse, an airball. But calmly, as if he had somehow been transformed into Miller for an instant, Dale elevated the ball over his head, pushed it with his huge hands toward the basket, and not once, but twice, swished it through.

On the sidelines, Larry Bird smiled that smile of his, and looked at Rick Carlisle, who had spent much of his time working with Dale on his shot. Bird patted his assistant on the back, and sat down and enjoyed the moment. Later, he told reporters, "I guess that free-throw practice paid off," and then added, "Dale played a huge game, played with fire out there."

The Pacers win impressed Rick Pitino on the day when his beloved Kentucky Wildcats won the SEC tournament en route to the NCAA championship. "Indiana is the deepest team in the NBA," he explained. "They are so difficult to wear out." Larry Bird saw it another way—as a milestone of sorts, telling reporters, "Our guys showed a lot of character today. . . . Down the stretch, we made the plays we had to."

The night after the Chicago Bulls trampled the Miami Heat 106–91, ending Pat Riley's team's 11-game road win streak, the Pacers traveled to Detroit to play the Pistons, whose season had been a nightmare. If Indiana had been the surprise team in the NBA, Detroit had been the most disappointing. Coach Doug Collins had not survived a player coup led by Grant Hill, who was proving to be a superb player, but perhaps not the heir apparent to Michael Jordan everyone had been predicting.

On paper, it looked like a mismatch—with the Pacers headed for their best record in years and a chance at the NBA title; and the

Pistons, coached by Alvin Gentry, apparently going on vacation immediately after the regular season. True to form, the game was a mismatch, but in the opposite direction—the Pistons came out charging and mauled the Pacers by 31 points, 122–91.

The result was not based on anything fancy, since Detroit simply played Indiana man-to-man with a defense Bobby Knight (fresh off a $10,000 fine from the Big Ten Conference for his three-technical antics in a game his Hoosiers played against Illinois) would have been proud of. Led by Grant Hill, Jerry Stackhouse, and Brian Williams, Detroit blitzed to a 21–3 run in the second quarter and never looked back.

While Bird looked on in disbelief, the Pacers played defense as if they wanted the Pistons to score 200 points. They were beaten on the fast break, rebounded like a bunch of weaklings, and argued calls with officials so that they looked like frustrated prima donnas. During the second quarter of the horror story, Miller, displeased that Stackhouse kept bumping him, decided to show up the ref by banging the ball against the court surface so hard it catapulted 15 feet in the air. The resulting T provided a free throw for the Pistons and a disgruntled look from Bird that could have burned through Miller's chest.

Bird's coaching tactics also contributed to the loss. When the second quarter began, Bird, upset with Mark Jackson, replaced him with Travis Best, who was then assigned to guard Joe Dumars. Enjoying a four-inch height advantage, Dumars overwhelmed Best to the point of scoring the Pistons' first 11 points of the quarter. Per his manner, Bird sat silently and watched the onslaught, but leaving Best on Dumars had created a nightmare matchup as the Pistons quickly went up by 13.

"Obviously, we didn't come to play tonight," the Indiana coach lamented to reporters after the team had sustained its 19th loss in the 62nd game of the year. "Tonight the Pistons played by themselves, we weren't out there. . . . When a team hits some shots and the other team doesn't come to play, it's easy to get a lead. Guys are just not anticipating like they were."

Attempting to rid themselves of the bitter taste of defeat, Bird decided a change of scenery was in order. Instead of practicing at

Market Square Arena on the day after the Detroit debacle, the Pacers traipsed across town to historic Hinkle Fieldhouse, built in 1928. It became famous when the final game in the motion picture *Hoosiers*, which was based on tiny Milan High School's miracle championship in 1954, was filmed there.

Wherever Bird went, there were memories galore. He had a fondness for the storied fieldhouse, having scored 47 points while a Sycamore at Indiana State against the Butler Bulldogs, who called Hinkle their home. "I'd practice in a parking lot," Bird told reporters, "but Hinkle is a special place with a great tradition." Mark Jackson felt the ambiance of the arena, saying, "You can see how this building speaks to you."

Having suffered their worst loss of the season, and given up a season-high 122 points, the Pacers returned to Market Square Arena to face the Bucks of Milwaukee, weakened by the absence of former Purdue University star Glenn Robinson, who was out with an injury. After a stiff practice the day following the Pistons defeat that reminded the players of training camp, Indiana spurted out to a 9–2 run to begin the third quarter and crushed the Bucks, 96–76. Without Robinson and Terrell Brandon, also sidelined with injuries, Milwaukee was a pushover. "Defense was the key," Bird explained. "It hasn't been that good, but tonight it was. We struggle when we give up a lot of points."

Indiana, still blessed with few injuries throughout the season, was without Fred Hoiberg, who was hurt badly during practice when he was knocked to the floor first by Rik Smits and then by Mark West. (Having 511 pounds slam into one's frame would do that.)

A highlight of the win against Milwaukee was the play of the Pacers bench, even without Hoiberg. Thirty-six of the 96 points came from the reserves, a sign the second unit was contributing after inconsistency had marked their performance over the past few games.

Now 44–19 and still two games behind the Bulls, who had recovered from a startling loss to Dallas to beat San Antonio, the Pacers ventured to the Big Apple to play the Patrick Ewing-less Knicks at Madison Square Garden. On the day that featured shocking upsets in the NCAA tournament by Rhode Island, which knocked out Kansas, and Valparaiso, a winner over Florida State, Indiana was hoping to win in New York for the first time since April 4, 1995.

Though it wasn't advertised as such, the game turned out to be the Mark Jackson Show. In the Garden, which Bird called the "mecca of basketball," Jackson took over a close game and made it one to remember for the player who grew up in nearby Brooklyn. Time and again, as the seconds ticked off toward the end of the game, Jackson—the conductor of the Pacers symphony—canned the big shot. Each was of a different variety. He hit the jumpers, the scoop shots, the shotput efforts, and, most importantly, all of his attempts from the foul line. When the game was over, Mr. Mark had a season-high 28 points to go with 11 assists. Significantly, 27 of his points came in the second half.

Jackson's heroics caused him to grandstand in front of the crowd, which included his parents, wife, kids, and dozens of friends. The animated Pacer, who had ridden the subway to play Bird's Celtics in a 1988 playoff game, blew on his fingers, danced his patented shimmy, and waved at the Garden's sellout crowd, who were asking themselves why they ever traded him. When the game was over, there were fans—even one carrying a "Kill Reggie" poster—who actually cheered for Jackson, something unheard of in New York.

Though he was the man of the hour, Jackson shared the stage with Derrick McKey, who sealed the Pacers' 91–86 win with a three-pointer from the right side with just 36.1 seconds to play. Held scoreless until then, and having made only one previous three before the Knicks game, McKey had come through in the clutch. "McKey hit the big shot," Bird extolled. "And I also thought he did an excellent job on Allan Houston. Derrick showed me a lot tonight."

Despite McKey's efforts, the night still belonged to Mark Jackson. The mustachioed one had not only scalded the Knicks with a dazzling array of ability, but capped off his stop in the Big Apple by being a part of a touching scene after the game. While the fans headed for the exits and the streets of New York, Jackson stood at centercourt holding hands with several Knicks players, including Terry Cummings, a minister off the court, and Charlie Ward. The spent warriors, who had just battled one another for supremacy for 48 tense minutes, bowed their heads and took a few minutes to pray. "We might play hard on the court, but we're all brethren under God's eyes," said Jackson, who wore his wedding ring tied to a shoelace out of gratitude for his good fortune in marriage and in life.

Armed with a 45–19 record with just 18 games remaining in the season, Jackson and his teammates flew back to Indianapolis a happy bunch. Winning in New York had rekindled the spirit of the club, still wavering after inconsistent play in recent weeks. Next up was a most important opponent, for the Bulls were coming to town determined to show the Pacers that Indiana was a second-place club.

For Chicago, the season was rounding into form as the playoffs loomed closer. Despite the setback in Dallas, coach Phil Jackson was pleased with the progress of a team looking for a third straight world championship. Scottie Pippen was back, telling reporters his fresh legs felt like it was December instead of March; and sharpshooter Steve Kerr had also returned, his deadeye shooting touch in tow.

Having split the first two meetings between the clubs, with a later game scheduled in Chicago, the Pacers realized they needed to win to keep the potential for the home court advantage in the playoffs if the two teams met. Carve out a victory on St. Patrick's Day, and the pressure would be on the Bulls to even the season series when they faced each other in the Windy City.

In many ways, the fate of the Pacers as a team to be reckoned with was on the line. If they beat the defending world champions, they pulled to within a game of Chicago in the Central Division. A loss, and they were three back with only 17 to play. Pacers guard Mark Jackson believed the Bulls were on the spot. "We come up with a win, and we're right there with them," he proclaimed. "There's so much pressure on those guys, believe me, they can be caught."

Bird was brimming with confidence, especially after the team effort against New York. "It was a hard-fought game against the Knicks," he said. "And the guys didn't quit. They battled and they scrapped. I knew it was going to be a low-scoring game, so every loose ball, every rebound meant something. The guys really fought hard."

Chicago's Johnny "Red" Kerr, the first coach of the Bulls and their veteran broadcaster, agreed that the Pacers were a playoff contender. "Larry's got them playing well," he said. "It's pretty much the same team as last year, but they have more confidence. The key is that Bird is a Hall-of-Famer sitting on the bench. He's been through everything and the players have to respect that. It's hard for them to bitch and moan when they know he knows what he's doing."

Bird appreciated Kerr's words, but he suddenly had concerns about his players' behavior. On the morning of the Chicago game, three of them showed up late for the shootaround. "We didn't have a good shootaround, and that set a bad tone," Bird lamented. "I am very disappointed, because I know what this game means."

Despite Bird's reservations, his Pacers battled the Bulls in a matchup that had all the earmarks of a playoff contest. With scalpers having gotten more than $500 for a courtside seat, and media from outlets like *Sports Illustrated* and *USA Today* looking on, the two teams proved why they were the elite in the Central Division. As NBC's Bob Costas, merely a spectator, having flown in from his home in St. Louis, said, "The Bulls are the team to beat, but the Pacers are the only one who can unseat them in the East."

After Dale Davis opened the game with a dunk, Bird watched as his charges fell behind for most of the game. With Smits enjoying a huge height advantage over all of the Bulls, the obvious strategy was to get the ball to him in the low post. But the Pacers failed to exploit this advantage, as was too often the case during the season. Instead of Bird having Smits down low, he allowed him to play on the perimeter, relying on 10- and 15-foot jump shots over the outstretched hands of Toni Kukoc and Dennis Rodman. Most were unsuccessful; and Bird didn't object to Rik's play, seemingly more interested in watching the game than coaching it.

Bird's counterpart, Phil Jackson, knew what was at stake—that this was truly a "statement" game. His strategy was simple: have Rodman battle on the boards (he pulled down 19 rebounds); provide scoring supplements from Pippen, Kukoc, and Harper; and then let Michael Jordan take over when the game was on the line. Help from the bench would be a plus, but not critical, and that proved to be the case when Steve Kerr, Scott Burrell, and company failed to produce a single point toward the Bulls scoring total.

Images abounded in the game televised by TNT. There was Rodman, his hair weaved in golden curls, prancing down the court after number 91 had banged the boards and snatched a rebound away from the muscular Dale Davis. During timeouts, while the rest of the Bulls hovered around coach Phil Jackson, Dennis sat on the floor down the way from the team and wiped the sweat off his body with a towel. Just before the Bulls broke for center court, Rodman swayed past Jackson, who whispered brief instructions to the proverbial lone wolf, who seemed more interested in watching the scantily clad Pace Mates than in playing the game.

Scottie Pippen, though held to 15 points, provided other images. The Central Arkansas graduate, who played all five positions in college, moved with the grace of a fawn, his sleight-of-hand fakes a pleasure to witness. In the second quarter, he dipped a shoulder, pump-faked, bobbed his head, and then ducked down and around the arm of Chris Mullin (who played his heart out for the Pacers) to bank a ball in off the glass. Teammates on the Chicago bench leaped to their feet as Pippen sprinted down the court.

Meanwhile, the remaining member of the Bulls Big Three, Michael Jordan, dazzled the sellout crowd (many dressed in the bright-green color of the holiday) with a series of moves that showed once again why he is the greatest basketball player who ever lived. With Miller hounding him and doing everything to stop the scoring champ but grab his jock, Jordan still managed to slip away for shots that others only dreamed about. Early in the first quarter, Jordan had backed his way from the right corner toward the basket. Miller's sticky hands kept trying to slap the ball away—but Michael backed in, backed in, ever so slowly. At just the right instant, he sprang back, faded away from Miller, and canned a 10-footer that had the crowd oohing and aahing. In fact, when Jordan scored, the crowd provided thunderous applause that normally was reserved for the hometown boys. Realizing that number 23 might be making his final appearance at Market Square Arena, the fans serenaded him as if he was their own, wanting to make sure that Michael knew how much they admired his play.

Jordan provided another unforgettable moment just before halftime. Larry Bird didn't like to double-team, even against Shaquille O'Neal, and had taken flack from the experts—especially Slick Leonard, who believed that his reluctance to do so had cost the Pacers on occasion. But Bird had stuck to his guns, and winning 45 of 64 games proved him right. The Jordan magical play came when, for one of the few times, there *was* a double-team. Driving from the left perimeter, Sir Michael found himself confronted by not only Derrick McKey, who had found success against Jordan on occasion, but Chris Mullin. No matter—Jordan simply gave the two of them a head fake toward the basket, then recoiled, and faded away for a soft 15-footer that hit nothing but net. On the Pacers bench, Larry Bird's eyes drooped to the floor in disbelief.

As the game moved into the fourth quarter, it was clear that the Pacers were a step short of being able to play with the Bulls. Rik Smits became more active, and Chris Mullin continued to contribute with three three-pointers—but there seemed to be a cog missing in the Pacers machine. There was, and his name was Reggie Miller.

Coming off a poor shooting performance at Madison Square Garden, Miller hoped he'd find his touch on the home court. He didn't. Hoping to be known as a big-game player, Miller was anything but—and 4 for 14 shooting from the field put Reggie in a bad mood. His failure to contribute played a huge part in deciding the game; Michael scored 35 points, Miller had but 14. One unruly fan who had paid his $62 to sit behind the Pacers bench was especially unhappy, calling out to Reggie, "You're a f...... choker, Miller, I'm glad they burned your house down." How Reggie kept from going after the jerk, no one knew.

Larry Bird had some stern postgame words for his superstar. "Reggie gets down on himself when he doesn't shoot well early," the coach, his brow furrowed, said. "At times, I think that's selfish on his part."

Despite Miller's failure to show up, the Pacers fought hard to stay close as the game moved to the final two minutes. Images of Bird and Bulls coach Phil Jackson differed; Bird sat serenely on his seat, while Jackson was more animated, looking down at the floor in his customary manner when things didn't please him. Both realized the game would revert to one thing: either Michael would take over at crunch time or he wouldn't.

Unfortunately for Bird and the Pacers, Jordan did. As the clock wound down, Michael hit a key jumper, and then sank two free throws to trigger an 8–2 run that left the Pacers gasping for air. Then he compounded Indiana's frustration with a superb defensive play, stealing the ball so that the Bulls led with 76 seconds to play.

The Pacers tried to catch up, but still trailed by four with 11.1 seconds left. After a timeout, Reggie Miller inbounded to Rik Smits on what turned out to be an ill-conceived play. After a toss back and forth between the two players, Smits threw up a three-point brick that had no prayer. Chicago rebounded the miss and left the court savoring a 90–84 win that said, "Hey Indiana, you may be good, but we're still the king—long live the king."

After the game, Bird's dour facial expression reflected the final score. He knew his team had folded in the fourth quarter, something he couldn't tolerate. The final play was embarrassing, and left a sour taste in his mouth. Instead of finding fault with his players, Bird pounded out at the officials, saying, "One was so-so and the other two weren't out there." The comment, uncharacteristic for Bird, made him appear to be a whiner on a night when the officiating had little to do with the outcome of the game.

More than anything, Bird knew the difference had been that Phil Jackson had Michael Jordan in his lineup and Larry didn't. "Anytime you have Jordan on your team," the coach lamented, "it makes it easier on the other guys. It's awesome to watch. He hits the touch shots and creates opportunities for the other guys to score."

And what did Michael think of the Pacers, who absorbed their 20th loss of the season on the day when Houston star Clyde Drexler, set to retire after the season, was named coach of the University of Houston? Asked in the crowded locker room what his assessment of the team was, he used an interesting choice of words. "They're capable," Michael, who had scored in double figures for the 824th game, proclaimed, refusing to elaborate.

Being "capable" wasn't exactly what Larry Bird had in mind. His ride home from downtown Indianapolis wasn't a pleasant one. The Pacers had lost an important game, perhaps the most important one of the season. His team would have one more shot at the Bulls; but from what he had seen on St. Paddy's Day, they had a long way to go to play at a level where they would be considered to be a true contender for the world championship.

The next day's practice for the Pacers was filled with long faces. Finger-pointing might have been justified, but Bird did his best to rally the troops. A bout with Washington in the nation's capital, still swirling with the latest scandal in the White House, was next—and Bird hoped his Pacers could rebound from the devastating loss to Chicago.

In the MCI Center in Washington, Indiana faced a team dotted with so-called superstars, including Juwan Howard and Chris Webber. Bird had his own theory about the new breed of player, and his comments weren't especially kind. "One thing is, a lot of stars want to play with superstars," he told the *Chicago Tribune*. "When I first came into the league, we wanted to try to win championships with the team we were with. Now, it seems like all the players want to go play with Michael Jordan or Shaq instead of staying where they are and trying to do something there. Everyone wants to be on a championship team, but they don't want to pay the price to do it."

Whether Howard or Webber, alumni of Michigan's "Fab Five" along with Pacer Jalen Rose, were hoping to escape Washington wasn't clear—but against the Pacers, they and pepper-pot guard Rod Strickland played well enough to keep the game close throughout. Close enough that Bird had a chiseled look on his face from the tipoff until the final buzzer; close enough that he displayed enough nervous habits (finger in the cheek, finger browsing the nose, fingers rubbing his chin, fingers ringing out his ears, and fingers fluffing up his hair) to last a lifetime; close enough that he had to wonder whether fishing on his boat in the Gulf off the shore of Naples didn't seem like a great idea.

As the seconds wound down, Indiana desperately needed to win to keep any momentum going into the final games of the season—and Bird looked like a man who could use a good night's sleep. His face was near ashen in color, and he appeared to have aged 10 years in the previous two weeks. The Bulls debacle still irked him, and he could only hope that during the fourth quarter his starters would play better than they had when the Bulls had eaten them alive.

Bird also hoped Miller would recover from his surprisingly poor play against the Bulls—and when the gum-chewing Reggie hit his first jumper, Larry relaxed a bit. But his mouth puckered up when on successive plays in the last three minutes, Miller missed a five-footer a grade schooler could have canned and then shuffled his feet, resulting in a traveling call. Bird gazed down at the floor and rubbed his eyes in disbelief, wondering what could happen next.

With the score knotted at 91, the best shot the Pacers could get was a dial-a-prayer three-pointer from Mark Jackson (whose 12 assists moved him into fifth place on the all-time list) at the top of the circle. The shot clunked off the rim, but the gods smiled on Indiana when Rik Smits grabbed the rebound. One of two free throws put the Pacers ahead, and they then got another break when Chris Webber missed an easy lay-in by deciding to try a left-handed scoop that banged around and fell away. The Pacers rebounded, and despite Rik Smits taking an ill-advised shot, Antonio Davis saved the day with a rebound. Reggie was fouled and canned two to provide a cushion—and when the Pacers survived a last-ditch three-point try by Webber, they savored a thank-goodness-we-can-get-out-of-here-with-a-win, 95–91 victory, their 46th against 20 losses.

More important, Larry Bird could relax for a day before the team played New Jersey at home. Observers had seen a change in the coach's demeanor over the past two weeks, a state of urgency

Larry Bird's disdain for referees was captured by his "Who, me?" look.

Copyright © Steve Lipofsky

Kevin and Larry: When Bird set the Celtics single-game scoring mark with 60 points, he broke McHale's record of 56.

Copyright © Steve Lipofsky

Knicks star Patrick Ewing on the receiving end of the trademark Larry Bird grin.

Copyright © Steve Lipofsky

Two legends watch as their East team demolishes the West during the
1990 All-Star Game in Miami.

Copyright © Steve Lipofsky

Red Auerbach called Robert Parish, Larry Bird, and Kevin McHale
"the greatest front line in NBA history." Few would disagree.

Copyright © Steve Lipofsky

Larry Bird enjoys a light moment with former Celtics coach Chris
Ford, who coached the Birdman for two NBA seasons.
Copyright © Steve Lipofsky

Frequently, temporary relief for the back pain that prematurely ended
Bird's playing career could be found only by lying prostrate on the
floor.
Copyright © Steve Lipofsky

Sculptor Armand LaMontagne created this likeness of Larry Bird, which is located in the New England Sports Museum.

Copyright © Steve Lipofsky

Larry Bird congratulates Reggie Miller after replacing him during the Pacers first visit to Boston, January 18, 1998.

Unflappable as always, Larry Bird's demeanor on the sidelines was a steadying influence on the Indiana Pacers during the 1997–1998 season.

Copyright © Steve Lipofsky

Players (left to right) Travis Best, Austin Croshere, and Rik Smits sit alongside the Pacers braintrust: (left to right) trainer David Craig, assistant coach Dick Harter, Larry Bird, and assistant coach Rick Carlisle.

Copyright © Steve Lipofsky

During the news conference following his election to the Naismith
Memorial Basketball Hall of Fame, Larry Bird was all smiles.
James Yee/AP/Wide World Photos

having replaced the easygoing attitude of prior months. With the season winding down, and the teams vying for playoff spots, Bird was feeling the tension. He had discovered that being a player on a team in contention was clearly different than having the responsibility of coaching on his shoulders. Though he tried to downplay his part in the equation, he was the man, the one expected to lead his team to victory.

The current mystery was Reggie Miller, who suddenly couldn't hit his shots. Against Washington, he had scored 20 points—but his confidence was low, his spirit drained by the long season. Bird knew great shooters went through slumps, but he was aware that without Miller's bulls-eye scoring touch, the team was doomed.

As for the victory, Bird was delighted, telling reporters, "This was definitely a big one, we really needed this. It wasn't pretty, because we were sloppy in the fourth . . . but we hung in, and a win is a win. I think we dodged a bullet tonight."

When New Jersey visited Market Square Arena on the 20th of March, former Orlando Magic center Rony Seikaly was their new center—but he wasn't much of a factor, playing sparingly. At least he agreed to play. Late in the game, Nets guard Sam Cassell decided to decline an invitation to return to the fray after an expletive-filled shouting match with John Calipari, New Jersey's explosive coach. "It was nothing major," Cassell said later, not realizing he had let his coach and his team down. "I just took myself out. I was exhausted. When you're chasing Reggie Miller around the court like I was, it's tough, very tough." Right, Sam.

Calipari was mystified by Cassell's actions, but All-Star center Jayson Williams (the free agent who prior to the season had asked a reporter, "Do you know Donnie Walsh? Tell him to make me a Pacer") put things in perspective. "I just know if I was cussing like that, my father, my mother, and my priest would have to come in the next day . . . [Sam and Coach] have a strange relationship."

On the night when the Lakers beat Seattle 93–80 to close to within three games of the Pacific Division leaders, Indiana sought its 47th victory in 67 games. With five straight home games on the horizon after a March 22nd visit to Milwaukee, the Pacers hoped to nip New Jersey and stay in the hunt to catch the Bulls.

Despite 21 points from Rookie of the Year candidate Keith Van Horn, Indiana repeatedly blunted New Jersey comeback efforts—especially in the third quarter, when Mullin singlehandedly kept them at bay with 17 points. He finished with 20, and Reggie Miller chipped in with 21 as the Pacers won 99–92 for their fourth win in five games.

Though reserves Fred Hoiberg and Jalen Rose contributed critical three-pointers, it was Mullin who was most responsible for the victory. Bird had expected Mullin to score at least 15 points a game, but the veteran had nights when lack of aggressiveness caused him to disappear.

Mullin had quick answers for his critics. "It's a flow thing," he said. "I had gotten into a rut where I thought I was doing what I was supposed to do—spot up and make guys play me. But it got to the point where I wasn't involved." Mullin was right, and it took a few chats with Bird, Slick Leonard (who had been helpful to Bird all season long with his savvy words of advice), and Mark Jackson to convince Mullin he needed to become more aggressive.

Against New Jersey, the bony player with the flat-top haircut was on target, diving for loose balls, batting away errant passes, and downing his patented left-hand jumper with regularity. That impressed the Nets' Jayson Williams, who also was impressed with the entire Pacers squad. "This team has everything," Williams told reporters. "The best shooter is Chris, and in my opinion, the second-best center is Rik. They've got one of the best point guards in Mark Jackson. And I'm happy for Larry Bird. He's a good man."

Larry Legend, whose hometown fans still worshiped him, may have strayed from southern Indiana, but he would never be forgotten.

COACH LARRY

*"Red Auerbach once said, 'If I had a broken arm,
I'd play.' I would do the same. I expect players to play hurt
if they possibly can. There's no room for sissies
in professional basketball."*
LARRY BIRD

The 25-foot pole is jet black. Atop it sits a green circular metal sign painted to resemble a basketball. White lettering spells out "Larry Bird Boulevard." Though the tribute to Bird in his hometown of French Lick, Indiana (population 2,164), has been stolen by pranksters on occasion, it remains a symbol of the self-proclaimed Hick from French Lick who made good. Residents are proud of Larry Legend, and many traveled the 110 miles north to Indianapolis during the basketball season when their favorite son haunted the hardwood as coach of the Indiana Pacers.

The "new" Larry Bird was a sporty one, having abandoned basketball shorts and a T-shirt for fancier duds provided by Nordstroms. That didn't mean he was comfortable doing so. "Some [people] like to dress up," he said. "That's the way they were brought up. They had money, I didn't. I always had pants with holes in them . . . I'd rather go out in a coach's pants and shirts. You're a coach. You're not trying to be a fashion designer out there." When Bird ambled onto the court as head man of the Pacers, he was stylish, if not comfortable. He didn't have the flash of Pat Riley or Mike Fratello, but he looked good in coat and tie.

Through 60-plus games, the Pacers looked good, too. Bird's old-school coaching style—being in good shape (before the season, Bird had said, "You won't see any beer bellies on this team"), working hard, and playing smart—had earned the Pacers admiration throughout the NBA. "That's the way I played," Bird had said earlier in the season, "because I loved to compete every night. This really is no different, to get these guys to play to a level and consistently every night."

Except for a few instances of slack play, the Pacers exhibited Bird-like mettle. But with 15 games left in the regular season, Larry Legend wanted them to increase the intensity a level, gearing up for the playoffs just a few weeks away.

Two days after beating New Jersey on March 20th, the Pacers ventured to Milwaukee to play the Bucks, a team still crippled by injuries. While Indiana had avoided the sidelining of any key players for an extended time, the Bucks were without Glenn Robinson, Terrell Brandon, and Tyrone Hill, three frontliners.

Despite the disadvantage, Milwaukee played tough on its home court, which featured the retired uniform banner of number 1— the Big O, Oscar Robertson, the only player from the basketball state of Indiana that many felt greater than Larry Bird. The Bucks, behind Michael Curry, whose basketball travels had taken him to several NBA teams as well as Germany, Turkey, Greece, the CBA, and the USBL, kept pace with Indiana until overtime.

In what could be called at best only a lackadaisical effort against Chris Ford's Bucks, the Pacers finally prevailed 96–94. The game, which saw Bird coupling and uncoupling his hands more times than a nervous groom moments before his wedding, was in doubt until just before the final whistle, when Mullin's sticky hands caused Milwaukee's Jerald Hunnycut to bounce the ball off his knees out of bounds. Prior to that play, Mullin had been the goat, missing several crucial three-point tries. But his gutsy nature prevailed, just after the Pacers had produced the type of last-second clutch play that had escaped them all season long.

Despite their proclivity for winning close games, rarely had Indiana been able to execute late in the game. With 32.2 seconds left and the score tied, Mark Jackson, who played superbly, backed his way toward the basket from the right corner, his defender Ray Allen with him step-for-step. The remaining players were positioned to the left perimeter of the basket for the clearout, with everyone expecting Jackson to throw up a successful scoop shot or get fouled.

Just as Jackson backed to within four feet of the basket, he made eye contact with Smits, who left bewildered defender Ervin Johnson and cut toward the hoop like a wild stallion. Before Johnson or Allen could react, Smits received a perfect pass from Jackson and dunked the ball with the authority of Karl Malone. The basket and ensuing free throw put Indiana in the lead, and they escaped potential last-minute heroics by Ray Allen. The win on the same weekend that Utah, North Carolina, Stanford, and Kentucky earned spots in the NCAA Final Four gave the Pacers their 48th victory and permitted them to keep pace with the Bulls, who won in Toronto on a patented M.J. jumper with 5.4 seconds to play.

More than the victory, the Pacers coaching triumvirate was ecstatic over the Jackson-to-Smits play. With 14 games remaining (9 at home, 5 on the road), the successful execution with the game on the line provided hope that this type of under-pressure play was possible when the playoffs began.

In addition, Reggie Miller regained his shooting touch to score 32 points, adding to the 17,000-plus points he had scored in his 11 seasons as a Pacer. "I felt better today," Miller said. "But I'm still not as sharp as I'd like to be."

Miller and company knew they would all have to be sharp when the Houston Rockets came to town on the 25th of March. Ever since Kevin Willis had replaced Charles Barkley in the Rockets lineup, with Barkley coming off the bench in a sixth-man role, Houston had been tough to deal with.

Realizing they needed 10 wins in their last 14 games to hit the 58 written on the chalkboard at the beginning of the season, Indiana hoped to break out fast and put the Rockets away early. Unfortunately, they didn't—and worse, they couldn't put them away late.

After Bird told reporters, "We have to pick it up a little. . . . We hope to get a higher tempo out of these guys," his Pacers competed as if they had deliberately ignored their coach's instructions.

The same day that newspaper headlines touted President Clinton's trip to Africa and shocked readers with news that five people had been gunned down by students at an Arkansas middle school, the Pacers' dysfunctional play led to an 86–81 defeat. Porous defense, lack of rebounding, and poor shooting made it a long night for the Birdman. During the game, he sat on his haunches, stood with his hands in his pockets, scratched his forehead, licked his fingers, propped his head on one hand while his arm rested on his knee, rubbed his lips, rubbed his chin, and watched in disbelief.

Before a sellout crowd of 16,587, the Pacers fell behind by 10 with 5:50 to play, prompting Slick Leonard to remark, "The hole we're digging is getting deeper." Too deep, Slick—and when Mark Jackson and Reggie Miller couldn't find the range on last-second three-pointers, the Pacers suffered their 21st loss of the season. Live by the three, die by the three.

Hakeem Olajuwon, who had hit a believe-it-or-not, over-the-shoulder four-footer that banked off the backboard during the last minute, thought the Pacers had taken his team for granted. "They knew we didn't have Clyde or Charles," he said. "Maybe they thought we'd lie down, but we didn't." No, Hakeem, the Pacers did. Larry Bird knew the Rockets center had won the battle of the big men, saying, "Rik didn't get anything going. Olajuwon had his number the whole game."

Besides berating the sensitive Smits, Bird challenged his players, telling reporters, "The guys are going to have to decide if they're going to play hard . . . to have momentum going into the playoffs. Or maybe they're happy with 48 victories."

Bird tried to brush off the defeat, but it was a bitter one. The Pacers had already clinched a playoff spot, but the loss dropped them four games behind the Bulls. Worse, Miami whipped Boston in Boston, and the Pacers now had only the third-best record in the Eastern Conference.

The game was played on a day when Pacers president Donnie

Walsh announced he had voted with the majority to reopen collective bargaining talks with the players union. Walsh admitted that his team was one of 15 NBA clubs to lose money during the previous season—to the tune of *$17 million*. "Wonder whose fault that is, Donnie?" one journalist asked. "Who's been giving guys like Kevin Garnett $100 million contracts?"

Before the Pacers played the red-hot Hornets on the 27th of March, Reggie Miller was confronted with some pointed remarks by Michael Jordan in the current issue of ESPN *Magazine*. He wasn't alone—the Heat's Alonzo Mourning and Bulls management took a few jabs to the chin as well.

Jordan on Mourning: "Dennis Rodman gets into Alonzo's head now. Alonzo's weak in the mind. Alonzo's an intimidator, but sometimes an intimidator can be intimidated. The bully can be bullied."

Jordan on Bulls owners: "I won't play for another coach. If [Bulls owner] Reinsdorf and the other owners don't like it, sell the team. The Bulls are worth a couple of hundred million. Reinsdorf put in $13 million, so that's a hell of a profit." He added, "You know what I'd consider, a change in ownership. Change the GM. Let Phil be the general manager and coach."

Jordan on general manager Jerry Krause: "I can operate with or without Krause, but when we walk past each other, we never speak."

Jordan on continuing to play another season: "The question is, who's going to take a step back? Who's going to flinch? Not me . . . I'll tell you this. I'm not coming back as a player-coach. There won't be any coaching for me at all . . . You want odds on me coming back. Okay, 70–30. [Which way?] Whichever way you want."

Jordan on Reggie Miller: "I really don't dislike playing against anybody in the league, but playing Reggie Miller drives me nuts. It's like chicken-fighting with a woman. His game is all this flopping-type thing. He weighs only 185 pounds, so you have to be careful, don't touch him, or it's a foul. On offense I use all my 215 pounds and just move him out. But he has his hands on you all the time, like a woman holding your waist. I just want to beat his hands off because it's illegal. It irritates me."

When told about the remarks, Reggie, though his eyes were sparked with anger, simply said, "I'm not going to talk about it."

What Miller would talk about was the Pacers' chances of winning the NBA championship. Even though Donnie Walsh had admitted that it would take everything to be just right for the team to win, Reggie was upbeat. "We can do it if everyone comes together," he professed. "On a given night, we can beat anybody."

Assured of a winning record and a playoff spot, they still faced the challenge of locking up the second-best record in their conference. Chances of catching the Bulls had all but disappeared, but it remained to be seen whether Indiana or Miami would secure position number two. Heading into the final few games, Chicago, Miami, Indiana, Charlotte, Atlanta, New York, and Cleveland were assured of a playoff berth in the Eastern Conference, with Washington, New Jersey, and Orlando battling for the eighth and final spot. If the standings remained the same, the Pacers would play the Knicks, a dangerous foe with or without Patrick Ewing, while the Heat would tackle Cleveland.

Larry Bird didn't want to speculate on playoff opponents, but playing Cleveland was obviously better than playing the Knicks, especially if Patrick was back. Even though the Pacers would enjoy home court advantage in the best-of-five series, anything could happen.

Assessments of Bird's job as a rookie coach were not hard to come by. Donnie Walsh had joined the Bird bandwagon before the second Bulls game, telling reporters, "The very first thing he said was, 'I've got to have a team well-conditioned, well-prepared, and well-organized, and then let them play. . . . One thing he captures is the essence of the game. He wants the team to get into the flow. He wants the ball to move. There are few isolation plays. Defensively, it's a team concept. He's straightforward and he pushes the team."

Sportscaster Don Hein believed Bird was the perfect coach for the perfect team. "He's a straightshooter," Hein said. "You ask him a question, and you get a straight answer. Players respect that. Larry Brown was a coach 24 hours a day, always in their face. Larry's not like that." Hein's colleague Ed Sorensen added,

"The key is in the credibility Larry has. He was a player who delivered the goods, and they are in awe of what he accomplished. That gave him instant credibility. They play hard because they don't want to disappoint him. Hell, they've got a living legend on the bench."

Slick Leonard's wife Nancy believed Bird's feeling for the players was key. "Larry gets a lot of satisfaction out of them doing well," she explained. "He puts the game in the players' hands and depends on them. Bob was like that, and it helps the players believe in themselves. They're just like Larry's kids; he really loves them."

Former NFL great and NBC commentator Ahmad Rashad said, "Playing for a guy who was a legend himself makes a big difference. It was like that for me with Bud Grant. With the Pacers, Larry has instilled a sense of pride, and they play harder because he doesn't ask them to do anything he didn't do. Plus, he played so recently that they can remember how good he was."

Bill Cartwright, the Chicago Bulls assistant coach who had known Bird since "Tall Bill" was a collegian at San Francisco, thought Bird's chief asset was the ability to inspire. "He's raised the team's expectations," Cartwright said in a gravely voice. "They all want to play. They don't want to be injured. They love playing for Larry because he really believes in them."

Pacers players like Antonio Davis had grown fond of Bird, but it wasn't that way to begin with. "You have to learn that he will call you out in a minute," Davis said. "He'll tell you if you haven't come ready to play. I hated him in the beginning, but he was right. . . . And he never gets personal, that's what I like."

Dale Davis, whose scoring potential had improved under Bird's tutelage, said his coach's ability to motivate came from the heart. "Coach never puts pressure on us," the muscular forward said. "I don't have to look over my shoulder. Just go out and play, that means a lot." Rik Smits believed Bird was just what the team needed, saying, "He has kept everyone together. It's a great collection of guys, and Larry knew how to get the best out of us."

Mark West said, "Bird came in and told us from day one that we could win a championship. Other coaches might say, 'We want to win so many games, or get to the playoffs,' but coach was positive from the start that we could be world champions." Jalen Rose pointed to another Bird asset. "Coach really understands the game, and that's important. And you know he's been there, done that. I have more respect for him than anyone I ever met."

Fan Wesley Jackson of Dayton, Ohio, assessed Bird's first year as Pacers coach another way. "For a superstar, he really surprised me, because he teaches discipline. The Pacers know what he wants, and they do it."

Assistant coach Dick Harter believed Bird's demeanor was the difference. "The key is patience and understanding. Larry's got great tolerance for someone else's mistakes, as long as they're trying hard."

Harter was right. During the long and laborious season, Larry Legend had never made any of his players feel as if they were being measured by an "I did this, so you should" standard. Bird had treated the Pacers as individuals, and his philosophy paid off.

Especially for Reggie Miller, who was enjoying an outstanding season despite Michael Jordan's verbal attack. The day after the ESPN *Magazine* article was published, Reggie and the Pacers faced Dave Cowens's Charlotte Hornets, who had won 14 of their last 15 games. Acting like a man possessed, the Reg pounced on poor Dave's team, which was exactly what he meant to do.

Miller opened the game with a rare four-point play, hitting a 25-foot jumper while Hornets guard Bobby Phills hacked his arm. By the end of the first quarter, Reggie had 14 of his 24 points; and with Chris Mullin contributing 12, the Pacers removed the drama from the game.

On the night an NBA-record Georgia Dome crowd of 62,046 watched Michael Jordan total 34 points in a Bulls 89–74 win over the Hawks, and Chuck Daly recorded his 600th career win as Orlando moved into a tie with Washington and New Jersey for the Eastern Conference's final playoff spot, Indiana put the hurt on a Charlotte team that had been burning up the league. Reggie set the pace, and the rest of the Pacers followed suit in what was one of the finest team efforts of the season.

Miller watched a quarter and a half of the 133–96 romp from the bench, after deciding he would show Serb Vlade Divac that he couldn't come to Market Square Arena and play like a thug. With 5:50 to play in the third quarter, Divac blocked Dale Davis's shot, then backtracked down the court. Standing in his way was Reggie, setting a pick for Rik Smits. Instead of avoiding Miller, the giant Hornet bumped Reggie to the side. No foul was called, but Miller was incensed.

After Reggie resumed his offensive position, he slid off his defensive man and headed for the basket. When he encountered Divac under the basket, Miller raised his forearm and popped the bearded center square in the kisser. Divac glanced backward holding his chin, and fell to the floor as Reggie moved toward the center line. Bye-bye Reggie, said Don Crawford the ref, and Reggie headed for the locker room, having been ejected for a flagrant foul.

Miller believed his actions were justified. "It's unfortunate," Reggie stated, "it looked a lot worse than it was, . . . and was out of character for me. On the other hand, I'm not going to let someone run over me, especially if he's 7 feet, 260."

Pacers official Paul Furimsky believed Reggie should have been more assertive. Asked if he taught Reggie how to use the forearm, Paul answered, "No—if I'd have taught him, Vlade would still be lying there."

Larry Legend, never one to back away from retaliation when he was a player, defended Reggie while chastising the officials, who had ignored his warnings earlier when Matt Geiger smacked Rik Smits. "When Geiger first hit Rik in the lane, Crawford was telling me, 'I missed it. You're right.' I said, 'Just wait, something's going to happen.' Then finally Reggie and Divac get into it. You could see it coming. If you know the game of basketball, you can see those things getting ready to happen."

As for Miller's intentional forearm to Divac's face, Bird surprised many by saying, "I'm just proud of him for finally hitting someone this year." Reporters wondered if the stressful season had finally caught up with Bird, since Miller's actions were sure to bring a suspension, something the Pacers could ill afford as they jockeyed for playoff position.

Reggie's cheap shot notwithstanding, the Pacers, who tied the club record with just four turnovers, savored the victory, their 49th against 21 losses. Bouncing back from the Houston debacle proved their resilience, a trait burned into them by a coach who had never strayed from his belief than Indiana was a championship team. "It's like when a game is over," Mark Jackson explained. "It's over. We don't dwell on losses. Larry has taught us that. Each game is a new challenge. That's why we haven't had any long losing streaks like we did last year. Larry knows more about how to motivate a player than any man I ever knew."

It also helped when the Pacers were at full strength, not only physically but mentally. "Reggie got us off to a great start," Antonio Davis said. "We fed off that. It's fun when everybody comes to play." Smits echoed those thoughts, telling reporters, "It was one of those nights when everything went well. Reggie set the tone, and was phenomenal. We want the home court [for the playoffs], and we played like it tonight."

Having reached the 70-game mark for the season, the Pacers entertained another playoff-bound team, the San Antonio Spurs, on the 29th of March—a day after Utah and Kentucky advanced to the finals of the NCAA championships.

Led by the 7' triple towers—lefty David Robinson and righties Will Perdue and Tim Duncan—the Spurs were imposing. They had defeated the Pacers with ease in December, when Bird's charges couldn't stop their big men.

Before the game, Rod Thorn of the NBA office, after reviewing tapes of Miller's forearm shot, brought down the hammer on Sir Reginald. He was fined $7,500 for his actions—but worse, he was suspended for one game, which meant the Pacers would be without their leading scorer.

Worse yet, the suspension occurred at the same time Smits, the team's second-leading scorer, was sidelined because of sore feet. "It's like I have a needle stuck between my toes and it broke off," the Dutchman proclaimed to Jan van der Nat, a journalist from the Netherlands covering Smits for his home country. "It's a sharp pain." Bird, clearly disappointed, nevertheless praised his big center, saying, "I feel sorry for the guy, because I know he wants to play, and he showed me a lot of heart the other night. But today, he couldn't go and you have to live with that."

Miller's stupidity (one disgruntled fan brought a sign that said, "Hey, Reggie, play with your head, not your elbows") in getting suspended during a critical part of the season, and Smits's injury, meant the Pacers would surely be shorthanded facing the Spurs, coached by Greg Popovich. After considering several combinations, Bird and his assistant coaches decided Fred Hoiberg and Antonio Davis would join the starting five.

Reggie's absence would not only weaken his team's effort on national television, but disappoint fans who came from far away to watch him play—none more so than 11-year-old Jacob Clover, whose family saved their money and made the four-hour journey from St. Louis to Indianapolis once a year to watch the Pacers play. "It's real disappointing," Jacob, proudly wearing the number-31 uniform of his idol, said. "Real disappointing."

To add to Jacob's discomfort, the Pacers played their worst game of the year. On a day when the Bulls won their ninth straight, and Miami clinched the Atlantic Division crown with a win over Atlanta, Bird's bunch were an embarrassment. Tim Duncan and David Robinson, who seemed to be playing volleyball with the shorter Pacers, dominated the boards.

When the final whistle sounded, amidst boos from the crowd, the Spurs finished with only 74 points—which 99 percent of the time guaranteed a loss in the NBA. The only problem was, Indiana scored 55—at that time, the lowest point total ever since the league adopted the 24-second clock. (Later, in the playoffs, Utah proved even more inept than Indiana by scoring 54 points in Game Three of the NBA Finals against the Bulls.)

Larry Bird, who had scored 60 points in one game all by himself, was livid. "I wondered where we were going to get our scoring today," the coach said after watching his team shoot just 27 percent. "I was hoping somebody would step up and score some points, but it didn't happen. I was very disappointed at the offensive end." Jalen Rose spoke for the players, saying, "It's always an embarrassment when you don't play up to your capabilities, maybe more so when the whole country is watching." Rik Smits, resplendent in an expensive multicolored Coogi sweater as he sat behind the bench, added, "I was in pain, and not only in my feet."

Whether the debacle against the Spurs—combined with the day-to-day status of Rik Smits, an important link to potential playoff success—would turn the Pacers season sour remained to be seen. Lost in the shuffle was Reggie Miller's selfishness, which cost the team when they needed him most. Columnist Conrad Brunner hit the nail on the head when he wrote, "This is the time of year when veterans are supposed to take control, not lose it."

Saddled with their 22nd loss of the season to go with 49 victories, the Pacers dropped a game and a half behind the Heat. The national television audience must have wondered why anyone would think the Pacers could be a contender for the NBA championship. "They stunk up the place today" a fan, clearly disappointed that he came from Illinois to watch the Pacers play, said as he left Market Square Arena.

While the loss hurt the pride of the team, the main concern was Smits and his sore feet. Without the big fella, the Pacers might as well pack it in, since his absence had such an impact on the effort the other players put forth. Miller knew the Pacers' mental approach was critical, saying, "When this team puts its mind to it, it can play with anybody. When it doesn't, it's an average team."

The absence of injuries had been a key. Bird's words about the subject were blunt as always. "When you win, guys will play through injuries," he said. "But a team starts losing and a guy sprains an ankle, he'll say, 'To hell with it' for two weeks. That's just the way it is. The way it has always been."

Bird believed that good conditioning prevented injury and his practices reflected that belief. He kept his forces running, resisting the temptation to stop and instruct or point out mistakes. Even the shootarounds were tough, as hard as full-blown practices for other teams.

Bird's work ethic, brought to the team from his days with the Celtics, made them work harder. Most players lifted weights after practice even though it wasn't required, especially the reserves who were trying to impress Bird and get additional playing time. Bird appreciated their efforts, saying, "They've showed me they are true professionals, and that's the way you win championships."

That from a championship player who amazed trainer David Craig with his down-to-earth qualities. "At the end of nearly every practice, there's one of the greatest basketball players who ever lived standing under the basket rebounding and tossing the ball to the players. He encourages them, points out things they might try, and so forth. The players can't get over it. They feel like they should be tossing the ball to him."

While one of those players who had benefited from Bird's tutelage, Rik Smits, rested his feet, the Pacers got another break from the schedule on the night after Kentucky wrapped up their seventh NCAA championship with a 78–69 win over Utah. During a season filled for the most part with the mystical energy of Larry Legend, several times Indiana faced an easy opponent after encountering a disappointing loss. After the Spurs debacle, the team needed a confidence-builder—and who should show up in town but the lowly Clippers, losers of 55 games in 70 tries. That dubious record tied them for the second-worst in the league with Golden State, ahead of the Denver Nuggets, who had recently hired former coach Dan Issel as general manager to help guide the team that still hadn't won its 10th game of the season.

Against the Clippers, the Pacers finished off the month of March with a resounding, quit-making-fun-of us 128 106 victory that propelled them to their third 50-win season in four years. Despite the absence of Smits, who admitted his feet hurt so bad he couldn't sleep unless he kept the sheets and blankets off them, Indiana rebounded from the depths of doom with a team effort led by Mullin's 24 points. That night also saw Seattle beat Utah by two in a matchup of the best in the West, and Chicago move to a league-best record 56–17 by beating Detroit in overtime.

At 50–22, the Pacers, whose team record 14 three-pointers against the Clippers had Slick Leonard yelling "Boom Baby" so often it sounded like a tape recording, got ready for the Timberwolves, who had a winning record despite no punch in the middle. What they did have were Kevin Garnett, a 21 year-old youngster with a $100 million-plus contract, and Stephon Marbury—two of the best young players in the league. They also had two assistant coaches with Indiana ties—Jerry Sichting, a Martinsville native and former Bird teammate, and Randy Wittman of Indiana University.

Still stalking Miami for the second-best record in the East with 10 games to play, Indiana—again without Smits—beat Minnesota 111–108 on the 3rd of April, a night when Shaquille O'Neal hit up the New Jersey Nets for 50 points. More importantly, the Heat, running scared after Alonzo Mourning fractured his cheekbone and was day-to-day, lost to the triple towers of San Antonio by 14—meaning the Pacers had crept to within a half-game of the Heat. Antonio Davis was the catalyst against Minnesota with 23 points, and a last-second block by Derrick McKey preserved the Pacers' 51st victory.

With nine games to play in the regular season, the Pacers ventured to Charlotte to play a Hornets team still seething over Miller's forearm shot to Divac a week earlier. Miller didn't foresee any trouble, telling reporters, "It's all part of the game, the Hornets understand that." The Hornets mascot disagreed, dancing around center court wearing boxing gloves.

After player introductions were made in Charlotte, the Pacers—still Smits-less—hoped to overcome the hype of the Reggie versus Vlade confrontation and produce a solid, get-ready-for-the-playoffs victory. But it wasn't to be.

On the positive side, Travis Best scored a season-high 19 and minimized costly turnovers. Dale Davis also provided hope with his offensive game, hitting 3-, 5-, and 10-foot jumpers. Not bad for a guy making $6 million a year.

Offsetting Best and Davis were the negatives: Miller failing to record a field goal in the second half; Mullin and McKey being pushed around under the basket by Anthony Mason and bald-headed Matt Geiger as if they were rag dolls; and Mark Jackson missing every one of his 11 shots. Bird got caught watching instead of coaching again and left Jackson on the court long past the time it became obvious "Jack" was playing like a raw rookie.

The 96–89 loss, their 23rd against 51 wins, came on an evening when the Bulls won their ninth straight and the Lakers their 14th in 16 games. With the playoffs and likely first-round opponent Cleveland lurking in two weeks, the Pacers knew they had to have the big guy back, and fast, or the team would be an easy target.

Before the Hornets game, Smits loped up and down the court in an effort to see if his tender feet would hold up. Though he reported less discomfort, the Dunking Dutchman sat in street clothes when his teammates sorely needed him.

That didn't mean he wasn't trying to discover a cure for his ills. Over the season, David Craig, one of the most respected trainers in the league, had tried everything: heat, ice, electric stimulus, magnets, rest, you name it. Others offered help as well. Chris Mullin brought in Jussi Lomakka, a Northern California massage guru of Finnish descent. Bird even got in on the act, calling Dan Dyrek, the Boston-based physical therapist who eased his back pain. "I'll try anything," Smits said, perhaps realizing his value in the free-agent market was evaporating unless he could find a cure for his ailing twinkies. "Anything."

Attempting to tie the record for most regular-season wins in Pacers NBA history, Indiana played the Milwaukee Bucks on the afternoon of April 5th. Smits kept his street clothes on, and many of his teammates should have as well. In what could only be called another subpar performance, Indiana eked by the Bucks, 93–92, chalking up a victory they didn't deserve.

The win came only after the Bucks' Michael Curry missed a wide-open-as-you-please 15-footer from the left corner with time running out. So wide-open, in fact, that he could have eaten lunch before anyone could defend him. But miss he did, prompting Mullin, lying on the floor, to say, "I was hoping he saw the rim like I did." Apparently Curry had, providing coach Chris Ford with yet another disappointing loss in an already disappointing season.

Once again, the magic of Larry Legend had saved the Pacers—though he didn't see it, commenting, "Curry was probably *too* wide open. You don't like to have that, when you're one up and he gets a wide-open shot." Upon hearing that, one player commented, "Larry is one of the great rationalizers of all time. Talk about the glass being half-full."

Assistant coach Dick Harter had another explanation, saying, "This is the year of the Bird." More to the point, he believed the team's success was based on three factors. "One, it's due to Larry's composure down the stretch in games; two, we have veteran ballplayers like Reggie who can hit a last-second shot; and three, we have prepared the team well."

The Pacers' lethargic effort came on a night when the Bulls, led by M.J.'s 40 points, routed Houston for their 10th straight win. They were a remarkable 24–2 since the All-Star break. Perhaps the league should just call a halt to the season, crowning Chicago with their sixth NBA championship in the 1990s so that Michael could retire and get ready for the Senior PGA Tour.

At 52 and 23 for the season, Indiana readied themselves for an important game against Cleveland, their projected first-round opponent in the playoffs. Fiery Mike Fratello's Cavs had been hot, winning 9 of 10.

Prior to the matchup, Bird was so intense that he looked as if it was Game Seven of the championship series. He knew his team was stuck in idle, playing just well enough to beat the bad teams while losing to most of the good ones. "I told the guys . . . it's a big game for them," Larry Legend, who admitted he hadn't been able to work off the 12 pounds he had gained since becoming a coach, professed. "They can do something that's never been done [break the Pacers' NBA franchise club record with 53 victories in a season]. Plus they're playing the team they'll probably see in the playoffs. They need to be prepared to play. Play for 48 minutes."

In their 76th game of the year, the Pacers, ranked seventh-best in the NBA by *USA Today* ("Pacers are mediocre without Rik Smits"), kept Bird pensive throughout the game. Several times the cameras caught him with that faraway look in his eyes, index finger securely positioned on his left cheek, watching intently to determine the performance level of his players. For all the world to see, Bird was calm and collected—but inside, his stomach was churning. He wanted to beat Cleveland and beat them soundly, showing the upstart team that they had no chance against Indiana in the playoffs.

Inspiration for the Pacers, cheered on by two boisterous fans who painted their upper torsos Pacers blue and gold, came from the homefront. Writer Bill Benner decided to show Bird he wasn't "soft" on the Pacers by producing a column entitled, "Maybe This Team's Best Games Already Have Come and Gone." When Pacers players read it, they set out to prove the bearded journalist was mistaken.

For three and a half quarters, they did so. With Antonio Davis, Rose, and McKey leading the way, Indiana—still without Smits—hammered at the taller Cavs at such a pace that coach Mike Fratello simply shook his head. Then the Pacers hit the skids, and didn't score a single point for more than five minutes of the fourth quarter.

Bird sat and watched his team self-destruct, and forgot to take a timeout when his team needed it most. Before he could do so, Cleveland knocked down their second straight three-pointer and the Pacers fell behind by two with 3:08 to play.

With tornado warnings swirling around Market Square Arena, prompting announcer Reb Porter to order 16,000-plus fans to stay inside, Indiana tried to win a game they were desperately trying to give away. Two plays down the stretch made the difference, one unexpected and one predictable.

The unexpected came from Dale Davis, chastised so often for his inability to hit a five-foot jump shot or can a free throw. The 6'11", 230-pound muscleman, who had battled his counterpart Shawn Kemp (6'10", 256 pounds) to a draw on the boards, faced two from the charity stripe with less than a minute to go. With the sellout crowd, drawn to the game to celebrate mascot Boomer's birthday (Wacker, Sly, Clutch, and Gee Whiz, mascots from other teams, joined the fun), holding their breath, Double D calmly swished both of his attempts.

For Davis, it was redemption. For his fellow players, it meant he was doing something he often did after practice when he fleeced his teammates out of a few bucks in free-throw contests. "Dale beats us all," Fred Hoiberg said. "He just has trouble in games."

The second play came with the game tied at 80, and Reggie Miller was the designated hero. Roaming the baseline, he suddenly darted to the left perimeter, and launched over the out-stretched hands of his defender a picture-perfect shot that cuddled in the net. When the Cavs' Carl Thomas missed a 20-footer at the buzzer, the Pacers recorded their 53rd victory of the season.

Bird, who had glared at officials during the game with what was known as the "Bird Stare" (standing at halfcourt, one hand in his pants pocket, and one scratching his ear as he stared down the offending ref), clearly enjoyed the moment. "I'm very proud of these guys," he said. "We were 2–5, fought back, and this is kind of a milestone. . . . They really wanted this one, and I'm glad they got it."

Mark Jackson had some words for journalist Bill Benner, who had questioned the Pacers' future, in the locker room on the night when Karl Malone scored an NBA season-high 56 points for Utah. "We ain't that bad now, are we Bill?" he roared. "Give us a little credit, as bad as we are." Jackson also complimented Larry Bird. "He's the coach of the year," Mark extolled. "What we did might not be done again. And he's the reason."

Larry Brown agreed, despite the team's recent inconsistent play. "They're an old, experienced team," Brown explained. "Larry Bird has done an amazing job. They're a team that can win it all. They're like Utah now. They just know how to play. There are no egos involved."

Sportscaster Mark Patrick saw Bird's contribution in a differ-ent way. "The team accepts everything he says," Patrick remarked, "because Larry's a contemporary. The players not only have heard of him, but many of them played against him. When he shares his experiences with them, they take his direction. Larry Brown wore them out; Larry [Bird] doesn't do that."

Slick Leonard also commented on Bird. "He has an unbeliev-able perception of the game," he said. "But what I like most is that he's got a heart as big as a house. These guys, he really cares about them."

Standing 53–23, the Pacers moved into a tie with Miami for the second-best record in the Eastern Conference. Though the Heat would automatically receive the number-two seed at playoff time for winning the Atlantic Division, home court advantage was still up for grabs. With six games remaining, four on the road, the Pacers hoped they might cap off the regular season by finishing second to Chicago, which had seized their 13th straight victory despite the absence of Luc Longley and Toni Kukoc.

The first of three consecutive road games came in Atlanta against the Hawks, who also were playoff-bound. On April 9th in the Georgia Dome, Lenny Wilkens, the NBA's all-time winningest coach, faced a revamped Pacers starting lineup in which Antonio Davis—substituting for Smits—had joined Dale Davis, Chris Mullin, Mark Jackson, and Sir Reginald. First off the bench was normally Derrick McKey to replace Double D and play power forward, an awkward position for him. Travis Best replaced Jackson, and Jalen replaced Mullin as before, but in recent games rookie Austin Croshere was relieving Reggie Miller. That meant Fred Hoiberg, who had lost his shooting touch, was the odd man out.

Croshere, a rawboned first-year player from Providence with milky-white skin whose favorite book was Anne Rice's *The Vampire Chronicles*, had worked hard to gain Bird's favor. His relationship with Bird through the season had been a paradoxical one that left him unsure of his status. When he returned from the injured list and played a game before sitting out the next several, a reporter asked what Bird had said to him. "I don't know," Croshere, who along with fellow rookies Pope and Etdrick Bohannon had continued a Pacers tradition by bringing Krispy Kreme donuts to practice for the players, remarked. "He hasn't talked to me since training camp."

Croshere's words surprised many who believed communication with the players was one of Coach Bird's strong points. "Unless he has something to say, something important he thinks the player needs to hear, he doesn't talk to him," a Pacers official explained. "With Larry, it's kind of the Bob Knight way of thinking, without the yelling of course. Larry believes you practice hard, and then play the game. He just expects everyone to do their jobs."

Columnist Conrad Brunner's comment was apropos: "When the game starts, Larry's job is over," he wrote. That work ethic had produced a winning season and the buzz of possible postseason honors for Bird. John Smallwood of Knight-Ridder newspapers predicted he would be Coach of the Year, writing, "Last season, with Larry Brown, Indiana went 39–43 and missed the playoffs. This season under Larry Legend, the Pacers will post their highest victory total since entering the NBA in 1976." Bird, a man of true humility, played down the accolades, telling the *Chicago Tribune*, "I think it's a joke. I'm not big on that stuff. . . . There are a lot of great coaches in this league who have been around a long time who are very deserving."

Against Atlanta amidst "Bird Is the Word" signs in the crowd, the Pacers posted a nerve-wracking 105–102 overtime win featuring several sides of their superstar Reggie Miller. Those included a disappearing act for most of the game (he had hit only 3 of 10 shots with five minutes to play); a desperate last-second three-point bomb from the right perimeter, where he somehow squared his body while suspended in midair to tie the game and send it into overtime; a picture-perfect three from the left side (the 1,584th of his career, the most in NBA history) to open the overtime period; an off-balance, ill-advised three that was an embarrassing airball; and then two clutch free throws to seal the victory.

With a one-game lead over Miami and five games to go, the next stop was Boston—where Celtics officials had to be wondering if they had selected the right coach to mold their young team into a contender. Pitino's efforts had led to a sub-.500 team with potential, while Bird was heading for Coach of the Year honors.

The day after Sandra Day-Del Valle won a $7.85 million suit against the NBA for being passed over as the first female official, the Pacers charged into Beantown aware that they were close to completing a regular season filled with great memories. "This has been a great experience, playing with these guys," Fred Hoiberg said. "A real honor. There's not another team in the league like this one."

Hoiberg was right. Everything had fallen together for the Pacers. The season had been one of those meant-to-be, serendipity situations, one for the ages. The perfect coach, who was laid-back but straightforward, had corralled two ideal assistant coaches—Dick Harter, who knew defenses as well as anybody in the league, and Rick Carlisle, who was an offensive wizard. The three coaches had guided 12 spirited players, all with question marks about their pasts and futures, with an even-keeled hand that had produced few games where the team didn't have a chance to win in the final quarter of play.

More than that, the coaching staff had created an atmosphere in which playing the game was fun. In a day and age when most multimillion-dollar NBA athletes grudgingly competed, Indiana had a bunch of guys who actually hated to leave once the workday ended. They enjoyed the camaraderie (Etdrick Bohannon said it was "like having 14 big brothers"), the banter, and the teasing— and sincerely cared about one another, leaving any inflated egos outside the workplace. There was no division among the players, no hints of jealousy or backbiting, and few complaints. The Pacers were more like a high school or college team that hated it when practice was over, often lingering on the court practicing shooting, playing one-on-one, or wagering a few bucks on a free-throw contest. Indicative of that spirit was the configuration of the Pacers' dressing spaces in the locker room. Great pains had been taken to integrate the veterans and rookies so no one felt isolated. Along the south wall, Mark Pope and Etdrick Bohannon were positioned on either side of Derrick McKey, with Reggie Miller, whose esteem for Bird increased every day, next to Bohannon. Smits and Jackson (a poem by his mother Maria taped to his locker) surrounded Fred Hoiberg in the corner.

Along the north wall, Austin Croshere was squeezed between Chris Mullin and Antonio Davis. Jalen Rose (a smiling picture of the "Ice Man" George Gervin pasted above his locker) was next to Dale Davis, with Mark West beside Travis Best. True to their spiritual beliefs, royal-blue Bibles were evident in front of the dressing spaces of several Pacers, including Mark Jackson, Dale Davis, and Bohannon, all of whom attended a pregame chapel service regularly.

Bird loved what he saw, and knew that the team chemistry was perfect, just as it had been when the Celtics won their NBA championships in the 1980s. "This team has a lot of pride," he explained. "That's better than having big egos, and even ability."

Pride was evident once again when the Pacers met the Celtics on Easter Sunday, the day after Michael Jordan astounded fans at the Bulls-Orlando game by airballing a left-handed free-throw attempt. "I was missing right-handed, so I decided to try left," Jordan explained. "It didn't seem to work."

Boston's crowd should have been hostile toward an opposing team, and especially their coach, but the love affair Celtics fans had with their former hero was in full view once again. Bird had said earlier in the season, "I haven't seen a tough crowd yet. I like it the way it used to be when you had to fight tooth and nail to get out of a place. People are too nice anymore. The league has softened up." Boston fans did nothing to change Larry's mind. Posters lauding Bird were everywhere, and from the moment he walked on the floor, he was the story and not the game.

Attempting to sweep the four-game series with the Celtics and log their 55th victory, the Pacers broke out early, fell back, broke out again, and fell back in each of the four quarters. The topsy-turvy contest against Rick Pitino's collegelike team, which pressed for 48 minutes, turned on the play of two Indiana stalwarts— Antonio Davis and Jalen Rose.

In effect, it was the A.D. and Jalen Show, with Davis producing a 28-point, 10-rebound performance and Jalen adding 18 points, 12 in the fourth quarter. Antonio's performance overshadowed the return of a rusty Rik Smits, who played 11 minutes of basketball like he had never seen one before. Testing his tender feet, he stumbled around like a clumsy bird, was two steps slow on defense, and had several passes slip through his hands.

Clearly Smits's mind was focused on the pain in his feet and not on the game, but his courageous reappearance after seven games gave Bird, attired in a dark checked sportcoat, gold tie, and blue shirt, hope that the big fella was on the mend and would be available for the playoffs. He was encouraged because the physical therapy Dan Dyrek had prescribed was reducing scar tissue that had built up after surgery on Smits's feet. "The whole structure of my foot is changed, and I'm walking more normally again," the Dutchman said with obvious relief.

Working through Smits's injury presented a glimpse of Bird's management technique at its best. Several times during the season, the Pacers coach had mentioned that he was more of a manager than a coach, and those close to the team saw what he meant. Having been injured himself as a player, he knew teammates could get down on an athlete if they felt he was dogging it. Bird made certain to point out Smits's discomfort to the team, preventing doubts about his injuries.

Despite the big fellow's presence at Boston, the Celtics' ball-hawking defense had Bird rubbing his lips, his forehead, his ear, his chin, and the side of his head as the Pacers nearly squandered a 10-point lead in the final minutes. "I don't believe our players think they can win it all," Bird said, trying to motivate his team. "Right now that's something we have to acquire down the stretch."

Nevertheless, when the final buzzer sounded, a 93–87 victory was Indiana's on the day golfer Mark O'Meara won the coveted Masters title. Diehard Celtics fans showed their love and respect by chanting "Lar-ry, Lar-ry, Lar-ry," as the game wound down. Wonder how Rick Pitino felt?

Outside the Pacers locker room, reporters heard unusual noises. As they awaited entry after the customary 10 minutes (which normally stretched to 20), they heard the players whooping and hollering. Later the media found out that happened because Bird had actually praised the win, something he wasn't prone to do. As Derrick McKey said, "Coach doesn't pass out much in the way of 'nice goings,' but this win he really appreciated."

The next day in Chicago, the Pacers met Michael Jordan's Bulls in their 79th game of the year. Though strapped by injuries to Luc Longley and Toni Kukoc, da Bulls were sailing toward the playoffs, believing they could repeat the three-peat before the makeup of the team changed drastically.

Attempting to even the season series against the world champions, stay ahead of Miami, creep within two victories of their preseason goal of 58, and—more importantly—bust the Bulls on their home court to make a statement heading into the playoffs, Indiana came roaring out of the gate with the vengeance of a Midwest tornado.

From the opening tip, all nine players Bird employed played all-out, fast-paced, in-your-face basketball that left the packed United Center crowd gasping for air. The effort caused Wayne Larrivee and his Bulls broadcasting partner Johnny "Red" Kerr to use such words and phrases as *determined, relentless, attacking the basket,* and *physical presence* to describe the super effort by Larry and his warriors, who wore black bands on their uniforms in memory of longtime equipment manager Bill Hart, who had died of cancer.

By game's end, there were enough highlights to fill 10 reels of film. Mark Jackson and Travis Best ran the offense and moved the ball upcourt at such a lightning pace that the Bulls defenders were stunned. Both players also hit key shots: Jackson his patented floaters close to the hoop, and Best soft left-handed jumpers, especially at critical times when the Bulls threatened to inch back into the game that Indiana dominated from quarter one.

Forwards Mullin, McKey, and Dale Davis played as if this were their last game, hustling—especially on defense, where time after time they made Jordan and company pay for every trip into the lane. The Bulls' reward was a clean but hard foul and a trip to the line instead of a dunk or lay-in. Dale Davis kept Rodman at bay. At one point, he tore the ball out of the Worm's hands with such brute strength that Dennis shook his blonde curls in amazement.

In the post, A.D. shined, maneuvering his way around and through Bulls players as if they were standing still. He also canned his short jumpers, as did Double D, providing offense when it counted. When Antonio rested, Rik Smits contributed with key rebounds and a deft touch. Late in the game, he leaped high over Rodman to snare a rebound, showing that he was rounding back into form.

If there were two stars who narrowly outshone their brethren, they were Reggie Miller, whose mysticism was symbolized by a tattoo in the small of his back that had "Boss" emblazoned above it, and Jalen Rose. Miller used the Bird "don't get mad, get even" approach to Jordan's ESPN *Magazine* remarks, slicing around the court like it was his first game of the season. His scoring matched Rose's (22 points, including a critical three-pointer from the left corner off a pick of Dennis Rodman late in the fourth quarter); but even more, it was his tenacious defense on Michael in the first quarter that set the tone for the entire game. Twice in the first few minutes, Jordan was stymied by Reggie's long arms—one time resulting in a block, and the other time in a stuff from Antonio Davis, who came over to help after Reggie had Jordan bottled up.

Though Michael scored 27 points, he was a nonfactor, never elevating his game to superstar status. He was sluggish, out of sync, never able to hit a rhythm that was comfortable. In the third quarter, he became so frustrated with his shooting (7 for 19) that he tarnished his all-world image by losing his temper after a hard foul from Mark Jackson on the right wing. Instead of walking to the foul line, Michael heaved the ball and hit Jackson squarely in the head, a cheap move that was uncalled for. One fan, Kent Harvey, put it into context, saying, "That was a Reggie move!" a reference to Miller's tendency for such antics.

Michael drew a T for his effort, which he didn't protest. Later, Jackson and company laughed about the incident, but it wouldn't be forgotten when the teams met in the playoffs. Especially when Jordan, who won his 10th NBA scoring championship, sloughed it off, remarking, "Normally I try to keep my head in that situation . . . I lost my head for a split-second, but it didn't cost us the game. It didn't detract from my game—if anything, it picked it up."

Though Reggie clearly outplayed Jordan, it was Jalen Rose who made the difference. Every time the Bulls (after the loss, one pundit called them the "Vulnera Bulls") made a charge against the Pacers, Rose hit a big shot, captured a crucial rebound, stole the ball, or found a way to propel his team back to a safe lead. Whether he was scoring with rainbow jumpers or slicing around defenders on the baseline for an easy layup, Jalen had that determined look in his eyes that said he was unstoppable. Red Kerr said he knew the reason why, saying, "Rose was a shattered ballplayer last year, but Larry Bird has given him the confidence and he's proven himself all year long."

More importantly, while Rose was making magical plays, Chris Mullin, whom he had replaced, sat on the bench watching, a smile on his face. Instead of sulking about lack of playing time, or worrying about his ego, Mullin turned cheerleader, providing another example of the true team spirit the Pacers enjoyed that turned them into a contender instead of a pretender in just one year.

When the 114–105 victory that the *Chicago Tribune* dubbed "Pitiful Playoff Preview" was recorded, Dale Davis and Mullin were high-fiving and laughing by the Pacers bench. Mark Jackson stood nearby bear-hugging Jalen Rose. Bird, hands in pockets, even managed a smile, so proud was he of his team.

As the players and their three true-believer coaches walked off the floor, each had a warm feeling in his heart for a performance that was not one scintilla short of outstanding. Especially Reggie Miller, who knew he'd shown his nemesis Jordan a thing or two.

Reggie thought he knew the reason for the win. "We made the Bulls do things they aren't used to doing by setting the tempo for play, keeping them defensively on their heels, and beating them off the dribble." But Michael Jordan told reporters, "We simply got outhustled." Larry Bird summed up the victory succinctly in a way that sounded strangely familiar to his days as a player with the Celtics. "We came out and played hard and took it to them," he explained with the emphasis on the "them."

That Bird credo, play hard, had worked as well in Chicago in April of 1998 as it had when Bird was learning to dribble in French Lick at age 10. Somehow Larry Legend, though never having coached basketball in grade school, junior high, high school, college, or the pros, had in one season imprinted his work ethic on a bunch of million-dollar athletes. Now the Pacers were a true championship contender, ready to play the best the NBA had to offer, led by a coach who had inspired them to be better team players than they had ever thought possible.

PART

V

CAVS AND KNICKS

"Boxing out is the key. How to get good position.
Use the body correctly. There are certain tricks that can be used.
You can't win without rebounding well. We will rebound."
LARRY BIRD

The play was called 52-Up, and it was designed to free Reggie Miller up for a three-point shot. The Pacers had used it wisely during the regular season when a three was needed either during the final seconds of a game or to bring the club back from a double-digit deficit.

While many of Dick Harter's defensive schemes had earned headlines, the stability Larry Bird and Rick Carlisle brought to the Pacers offense had helped make the team a contender. They emphasized running crisp patterns, setting no-holds-barred picks, and fighting through defenders to find the open shot. 52-Up epitomized the teaching. All five players on the court had assignments—and if carried out correctly, the play provided the open jumper for three points. With Reggie lingering in the low post to the left of the hoop, Mark Jackson controlled the ball high to the right of the circle. Mullin was positioned to the right of the basket, keeping his defender out of action. Dale Davis stood outside the three-point line on the right perimeter, ready to cut for the basket as the play developed.

The key to 52-Up was Rik Smits. The big fellow dragged his man to the high post corner of the free-throw line, and when

Jackson gave the signal, Smits set a pick on Miller's defender. Reggie squeezed around the pick beyond the three-point line, where Jackson hit him with a darting pass. If all went well, Miller canned the three, and the team celebrated; but if Mullin's man left him to cover Reggie, that meant Chris was open for a pass. Miller also had three other options: feed Smits in the post, swing the ball back to Jackson, or put the ball on the floor and drive for the basket.

Simple basketball to be sure—but during the 82-game regular season, the Pacers had fed off that play. Now they hoped it and the others in their arsenal would be successful as they took on the young and spirited Cleveland Cavaliers in a best-of-five series in Game One of the NBA playoffs.

Of the Pacers players, only Mark West—the rugged 15-year veteran described by Mark Pope as being so strong "it's hilarious," had ever tasted the glory of playing in a championship final, and none of the Pacers had a championship ring adorning his finger. Larry Legend had three rings (he once said, "I live for them things"), and he hoped his leadership could inspire Indiana toward a championship the franchise hadn't experienced since the team won three ABA titles.

In Game One, the Pacers tried to focus on their mentor's words regarding what it took to be champions. "If you want to be a great team, . . . win a championship," Bird said, "you've got to fight through everything. You've got to keep hammerin' and focusing yourself . . . I wouldn't be telling these guys they're great, because they're not great. But they can be. If they listen, they can be a great basketball team—if they really put their heart and soul into it."

Throughout the season, the Pacers lived up to Bird's expectations. Earlier in the year, Chris Mullin had said, "Larry never thought he would lose, and he doesn't now." Indiana had adopted that mind-set and believed they could run the table on the Cavs.

Returning to Cleveland had symbolism for Bird. The final game of his professional career during the 1991–92 season had been played there, and the result was a 122–104 loss. Bird, playing amidst signs that read, "Larry's Last Game," scored 12 points and hauled down 5 rebounds. Months later, he announced his retirement.

Six years later, in the opening game against Mike Fratello's Cavs, Bird, labeled by sportscaster Joe Smith as "a player's coach, in capital letters," performed with the same style players and fans had become accustomed to during the regular season. If butterflies filled his stomach, he didn't show it. His nervous habits (stretching his arms, picking at his right ear, brushing his hand alongside his lips or over his nose) continued, but Bird remained calm and composed with no expressions of emotion. When timeouts came, he huddled with his assistant coaches a few steps in front of the Pacers bench, and then slowly sank his 6'9" frame into a chair, where he provided words of wisdom that caused Mark Pope to say, "Some coaches talk all the time in the huddle. Larry only says three or four things, but they're three or four really important things."

Starting out well was vastly important to the Pacers, who sported a surface confidence that was easily swayed. Every team member, along with their coach, still questioned whether the team could step up in the big games and advance toward the ultimate goal. Veteran players such as Miller, Mullin, West, Smits, and McKey, and even seasoned professionals like the Davises, Travis Best, and Jalen Rose knew their opportunities to gain a championship ring were limited. "Win now, worry about later later" was their battle cry, for who knew what tomorrow would bring.

Chris Mullin saw advantages to having Bird cruising the sidelines for his team. "No matter what sport you're in, you want him on your side," Mully said. "He's always got something up his sleeve to beat you."

The main advantage Bird provided was motivation. During his playing days, he forced his teammates to step up their performance by challenging them to play harder. After the devastating 34-point loss to the Lakers in Game Three of the 1984 playoffs, Bird had not only called his comrades "sissies," but added "If there's not blood on the floor, we aren't doing our job." His words worked, and the Celtics prevailed in seven games.

Besides motivating the Pacers to play hard with the same take-no-prisoners intensity that had beaten the Bulls in Chicago during the final days of the regular season, Bird's biggest dilemma heading into the playoffs was whether to continue starting Antonio Davis in the pivot or bring back Rik Smits. When the big guy sat on the sidelines with excruciating pain in his feet, Bird and Pacers fans had gasped in disbelief, but A.D. had stepped into the Pacers lineup and played like gangbusters. Down the stretch, he provided more fluidity to the team—both on defense, where he battled the bigger centers with streetfighting capability, and on offense, where Tony, the soft-spoken man with the clear brown eyes, proved he could be a 20-points-a-night scorer.

True to the team credo of unselfishness, Smits said he understood his coach's dilemma. "I can't lie," the Dunking Dutchman said. "I'd rather start. . . . But Antonio's been playing well. I don't want to mess things up. Whatever we have to do to win, that's what it comes down to."

Against Cleveland, which featured its own giant, 7'3" Zydrunas Ilgauskas, Bird's decision would be critical. The 22-year-old Cav from Kaunas, Lithuania, one of three rookies in Fratello's lineup, was a force to be reckoned with. Smits certainly had the size to match up with him; but A.D. was much quicker than the Cleveland center, and provided more offensive potential.

Bird tried to play down his decision, saying, "Antonio's been playing well enough to deserve to start, there's no question about that. He's done an excellent job filling in for Rik. Rik might be filling in for Tony, you never know. We'll play whoever's playing best."

Bird's decision was complicated when a development occurred far across the Atlantic Ocean in Holland. Rik Smits's uncle died, and the Pacers gave their All-Star center permission to attend the funeral. ". . . I'm a firm believer if you've got somebody who's close to you in your family and they pass, you should be there," Bird said. "The timing is unfortunate, but I understand."

Smits returned to Indiana on the Tuesday before the Thursday game with Cleveland, chipper and ready to go despite experiencing jet lag from his flight halfway around the world. On the night

Houston upset Utah in their Western Conference best-of-five series, Rik answered the opening tip at center. For the time being, A.D. was a reserve once again.

At game time, Rik sported a new look that made him look like a 7′4″ 12-year-old kid. He and the other Pacers who didn't choose to play with shaved heads during the regular season all adhered to the Pacers playoff tradition of baldness and presented themselves to the sellout crowd as the "Bald Bunch." Injured guard Haywoode Workman characterized two of his teammates, calling Fred Hoiberg "Norman Bates," and suggesting that Dale Davis "be given a serial number since he looks like a criminal." Bulls coach Phil Jackson took one look at the Pacers and Charlotte, which also went the bald route, and told ESPN *Magazine*, "I wish the white guys would use that instant tanning stuff for their heads. Smits, Divac, Mullin—they look like turned-on light bulbs on the court."

In the spirit of a college team, the players also donned black sneakers in a true "all for one and one for all, kind of like going to Catholic School," as Jalen Rosen put it, credo. Reporters kept wondering what the Birdman would look like without his fluffy blonde hair, but Larry would have nothing to do with the regimen.

Ever since the Tuesday practice, Bird knew the Pacers were raring to go—and from the moment Reggie bounded onto the court and bounced the game ball around before tipoff, they were. Chris Mullin and Reggie fired away like Old West sharpshooters, and within minutes the Pacers had a double-digit lead they never relinquished.

By the fourth quarter, the game with the rookie-laden Cavs was a joke. Mullin led the way with 20 points; Dale Davis, whom Donnie Walsh never gave up on despite the advice of others, added 12 points; and Mark Jackson produced three no-look, behind-the-back passes for baskets that had the crowd in a frenzy. He also had several lay-ins with his back-the-smaller-guard (Brevin Knight)-toward-the-basket offense that he learned from Earl "The Pearl" Monroe; and perhaps most critically, Reggie Miller stifled the Cavs' high-scoring guard Wesley Person, former Pacer Chuck's little brother, with in-your-face defense that held him scoreless.

The final tab was a 29-point win, 106–77, that marked the first playoff victory for Larry Bird as a coach in the NBA. Typically, he was modest with his remarks, telling reporters, "Our team was ready. They were focused. They took care of business the way they had to." Especially on the defensive end, where Bird was pleased with the hard-nosed effort. "We were very physical," the coach said. "We've been trying to get them to do that for 83 games."

Bird's emotionless expression didn't mean he wasn't concerned about the game. After ambling onto the court, dressed impeccably in a blue shirt with white collar, gold print tie, and gray pinstripe suit, he continued his nervous demeanor until the final buzzer sounded. Whether he meant to or not, Bird developed a new nervous energy release by constantly staring at his fingernails, or pressing them together as if they were going to fall off his hands. Only twice during the game did he leave the bench to contest an official's call, one of them resulting in his shouting "Bullshit!" twice toward his foil.

In Game Two of the series, played one week after the Indianapolis Colts had electrified the city by choosing quarterback Peyton Manning as their top draft pick, and one night after Chicago squeaked by a spirited New Jersey team that Michael Jordan said couldn't win unless "the Bulls fell asleep," Cleveland came out of the chute with fire in their eyes. They hit 9 of their first 10 shots, frustrated the Pacers with tenacious defense, and took a double-digit lead late into the second quarter.

Larry Bird contributed to the debacle, leaving Reggie Miller and Chris Mullin on the bench too long as the Cavs assumed a 17-point lead. Not to worry, since Jalen Rose, the sleepy-eyed number 5 from the University of Michigan, was in the lineup. In the second quarter, he led a comeback that saw them inch toward the nervous Cavs until they finally took the lead with 2:37 left in the third on a sweet-as-you-please Mullin three-pointer from the top of the key. That shot brought a bear hug from teammate Mark Jackson as the Pacers continued to exhibit team spirit like a college team heading toward the Final Four.

Rose's saviorlike role later brought words of praise from Antonio Davis, who said, "Jalen likes the show. He likes things to go down to the wire. . . . That's why I think he's going to step up and play his best basketball now." Mark Jackson added, "The guy was a whipping boy in the past. People questioned his ability, his character. He deserves everything he gets now because he's making the plays."

The play of the game came with 4:58 to go, when Shawn Kemp, the Hoosier man-child with a step-lightly gait that belied his ferociousness, tried to dunk the ball over Dale Davis and Rik Smits. The "Reign Man's" effort was stuffed, and Smits, after dribbling out of trouble, fired a court-length baseball pass to Jalen, who dunked the roundball to give the Pacers an eight-point lead. Despite some poor judgment down the stretch, when the final buzzer sounded, the Pacers had won 92–86 to draw within a game of sweeping the distraught young Cavs.

While Bird praised his team for having won on "pure hustle and guts," his afternoon had not been pleasant. The Pacers' poor play caused him to chew gum so intensely that his jaw must have hurt, scamper up and down the sidelines shouting instructions like a first-year college coach, and scratch his forehead so often that it looked like his hand was attached to his eyebrow.

Bird's nervous demeanor (many times he stood near the scorer's bench, his hands in his pockets and head cocked upward, making it appear that he was poised for flight) made reporters wonder whether the Birdman was a mental wreck for the playoffs. Travis Best said it wasn't so. "No way," Best explained. "Even at halftime, when we were down, there's Larry, solid as a rock. Didn't seem like there was a nervous bone in his body. That gives us confidence, makes us just want to work harder."

Mark Jackson, whom NBC's Isiah Thomas said would be the "perfect point guard" if his mind was put into Travis Best's body, had a different take. "Coach is like a Rottweiler at the gate," the St. John's grad who teamed with Chris Mullin to take his team to the Final Four in 1985 said. "I thought I saw him get a little excited today, especially in the first half." Regarding Bird's demeanor during the halftime locker room chat, Jackson remarked, "Coach Bird being a man of few words, there were no Knute Rockne speeches."

Jackson and company's comeback win brought comparisons with another great Pacers team from longtime team official Paul

Furimsky. "Their never-say-die attitude reminds me of the '73 Pacers who beat Kentucky to win the ABA title," Furimsky, who had spent 31 years with the club, remarked in the locker room. "This team is just oozing with confidence. And they really like each other. The camaraderie is special."

When the series moved to Cleveland, Shawn Kemp—whom Bird had eaten alive when they competed during Kemp's first years in the league (Bird used to score on Kemp, then yell out, "I'm the baddest guy who ever came from Indiana" as he ambled down the floor with a smile on his face)—and the Cavs were determined to beat Larry Legend and his players.

Prior to the game, Rick Carlisle put the Pacers through their pregame practice, a ritual no other team in the NBA scheduled. While Bird watched from the bench (he wanted to lead the practice, but the assistant coaches talked him out of it), Indiana players worked through maneuvers they employed later against the Cavs.

A sweep of the Cavs would produce two significant results. Since the Heat and Knicks, one of whom the Pacers would face in the second round, were deadlocked at a game apiece, the team had been promised at least two days off—something they had not enjoyed during the regular season. Second, trainer David Craig had promised to join the bald brigade. Rumor circulated that even Larry Bird might shave his head if the team moved deep into the playoffs, something that frightened even the most avid Birdwatcher.

Unfortunately, the young Cavs and their superman Shawn Kemp had other ideas. On April 27th, Mike Fratello's players raced past Indiana on the way to an 86–77 victory, denying the Pacers their 61st win of the year.

Three factors caused the defeat. Chris Mullin disappeared for the second straight game; Antonio Davis was ineffective, showing signs that coming off the bench wasn't producing the high level of play he showed as a starter; and Larry Bird left offensive stars Mullin, Miller, and Smits (playing with shoes dyed black, which trainer Craig called "Air Craigs") on the bench during a Cavs blitz when they went from four down to eight up, a lead they never relinquished.

Down the stretch, the Pacers were stymied, causing Bird to lower his head and stare at the floor for answers as he swept his hand through a fluff of hair, sucked his lips, and stuck his tongue in his cheek so that it appeared he had a jawbreaker stuck next to this teeth. By game's end, Larry Legend was disgusted with the overall play of the Pacers—though he did compliment Smits, who led the team with a superb effort that resulted in 26 points.

Several times during the game, Bird stood, hands in pockets, on the sidelines, giving his team the "Larry Look," the look Chris Mullin said "could turn you to stone." Later, Bird told reporters, "For some reason we had too many guys that didn't play."

As Game Four approached, two days after San Antonio's Tim Duncan was a near-unanimous pick for NBA Rookie of the Year, Bird knew that all nine Pacers had better be ready, for the Cavs' young team was bent on returning the series to Indiana for a deciding fifth game. Fortunately, Antonio Davis, Travis Best, Derrick McKey, and Chris Mullin were.

While the latter three contributed heavily to the Pacers effort on both ends of the court, from the outset it was apparent that A.D. was producing his best game of the series. After replacing Smits, he excited the Pacers fans with aggressive play that caused Cavs coach Mike Fratello to remark, "I have visions of Antonio Davis flying through, keeping balls alive, and coming out with the ball and knocking it out again."

Though Davis's play was outstanding, the fate of the game rested in Reggie's hands. A day after being chastised in reporter Bill Benner's column (Benner asked when the "trash-talking, imaginary-gun-totin', moonwalkin', takin'-a-bow, takin'-on-the-crowd, in-Spike-Lee's-face Reggie" was going to show up in the playoffs), Sir Reginald displayed why his tombstone might one day read, "Reggie Miller might have been a lot of things, but he was never dull."

In Game Four, Miller reappeared with his pinpoint shooting, garnering 19 points—the final four coming on free throws that were critical to his team's fate. But Reggie also played like a nervous rookie in the final few minutes just after cutting through the Cavs' defense for a reverse layup that gave the Pacers a 75–69 lead with 2:30 to go. On successive plays on the Pacers end of the court, he picked up a stupid offensive foul when he used a forearm to ward off a defender, stepped on the sideline marker during an ill-fated three-point attempt, and lost the ball while driving down the lane. Thankfully, Fratello's Cavs couldn't take advantage, and when the final buzzer sounded in Gund Arena, the Pacers had waltzed into the Eastern Conference semifinals with a hard-earned, total team effort (even the two Marks, Pope and West, played), 80–74 win. "The guys played very well," Bird commented. "Antonio, Travis, and Derrick were just awesome. They played hard and aggressive."

The Pacers were touched when they returned to the airport in Indianapolis to discover diehard fans waiting in the rain cheering. "We've got the best fans in the world," Mark Jackson said. "Talk about loyalty."

While the Pacers were handling the Cavs, Michael Jordan and his band of Bulls taught New Jersey a few lessons about playing in the NBA. Although Seattle's coach George Karl, later to be fired from that post, had said, "I honestly think that the Bulls got a year older and not a year better," M.J. and his buddies swept the Nets in three games. If these playoffs were to be Jordan's last, he was closing in style. In Game Three, he hit 9 of his first 10 shots and totaled 39 points for the game, causing New Jersey coach John Calipari to exclaim, "It's like playing blackjack against the dealer. He ain't losing and he takes all ties and pushes."

Also contributing to the Bulls' success was Dennis Rodman. In need of a boost of energy, he invited Eddie Vedder and Jeff Ament, singer and bassist from his favorite band, Pearl Jam, to Game Three. Armed with their support and his new multicolored hairdo (black leopard-like striped knots of hair woven around red and putrid knots), the Worm contributed 17 rebounds and a 26-foot three-pointer late in the game.

Also escaping first-round play was the Bulls' next opponent, Charlotte, which beat Atlanta and the NBA's Most Improved

Player, former IU star Alan Henderson, in five games. In the Western Division, San Antonio, the Lakers, Seattle, and Utah advanced, though the Jazz were nearly derailed by Houston, whose Charles Barkley once again was left lacking a championship ring.

Indiana's semifinal opponent was New York, though they had won more because of the stupidity of Alonzo Mourning than because of their own play. Their series with the Heat went five games, although the final seconds of Game Four resembled a back-alley gang fight more than a basketball game. With 1.4 seconds to play, the Knicks' Larry Johnson and Miami's Alonzo Mourning locked arms, wrestled briefly, and then put on a 30-second fight so futile that any referee would have stopped the bout and asked to see their boxing licenses. One fan, David Neal, said the strapping warriors "fought like two girls."

Knicks coach Jeff Van Gundy added to the embarrassment by racing onto the court and trying to tackle Mourning, only to fall to the floor grabbing Zo's leg like one of the passengers trying to survive the sinking of the Titanic. "He looked like a jockey that fell off a horse," guard Chris Childs said.

When the melee was over, Game Five in Miami was played without Mourning and Johnson, who were heavily fined and suspended for two games. Reggie Miller didn't care who won, telling reporters, "They play the same way. They both hold, hit, smell, look ugly . . . it's the same team. We're just hoping they beat one another down and come in here limping."

In a winner-take-all matchup, the Knicks prevailed against the Mourning-less Heat by what Chris Sheridan of the Associated Press labeled "Knicks by a Knockout." That set up a confrontation at Market Square Arena in Indianapolis on the 5th of May, the day Indiana voted in the 1998 primary elections. It pointed to the good fortune Larry Bird had enjoyed throughout his rookie season coaching in the NBA. All season long, the Pacers had been a team of serendipity, as if leading a charmed life. If they suffered a devastating loss, or faced the prospect of a lengthy losing streak, the next opponent was a patsy. Except for Smits's absence late in the season, Indiana had stayed basically injury-free while most other teams suffered losses that decimated their chances.

In addition, last-second heroics to win games had been the rule, not the exception. If the Pacers needed to make a buzzer-beater, they did. If the opponent had the same opportunity, they missed, even when the shot was a wide-open 15-footer, as it had been for Milwaukee.

True to that pattern, Larry Johnson, the Knicks' top rebounder and a prolific scorer, sat in street clothes for Game One. Though this gave the Pacers an edge, the Knicks were a team experienced in playing shorthanded since Patrick Ewing was still sidelined with his hand injury.

Whether Ewing would play remained to be seen (Jalen Rose called it the series' "X-Factor"), but the Pacers-Knicks matchup was an NBA beat writer's dream. Contrasts appeared everywhere, beginning with the coaches. On New York's sideline was the redoubtable, dour-faced, balding former assistant coach to Pat Riley, Jeff Van Gundy, who ranted and raved each night like a high school coach playing his chief rival. Larry Bird was his opposite—cool and calm, no rah-rah, go-get-'em pep talks in his coaching scheme.

Intrigue with the series also centered on Mark Jackson, whose heart was still fond of his New York roots; Chris Mullin, the St. John's grad who craved a championship ring; and Reggie Miller, who would step into the spotlight he loved so much, especially when the series hit Madison Square Garden where his nemesis, film director Spike Lee, awaited. The Pacers' counterparts were John Starks, the proverbial bad boy with the hurt look plastered on his face; Charles Oakley, the tree of a man who was the guts of the team; and Allan Houston, the Knicks sharpshooter whose inconsistency was a constant irritant to the diehard New York faithful.

Preseries hype centered on how the Pacers' four-day layoff would affect their play. Bird, ever the simplistic one, saw it both ways, telling reporters, "It might be the worst thing that ever happened, or it might be the best thing that ever happened."

The matchups between the Knicks, whose Patrick Ewing would don a brown gentleman's suit for Game One instead of a uniform, and the Pacers, especially regarding size, appeared to favor Indiana. Smits towered over the Knicks centers Chris Dudley and

Terry Cummings, and the Dutchman was expected to have a big series. New York, however, had what 38-year-old Buck Williams called "a ton of forwards," in contrast to the Pacers' three or four. "It's not about size, it's about heart," Williams explained.

His comments proved true, but the team with the heart in Game One of the series was the Pacers, who needed all the heart they could muster after falling behind the Knicks 28–9 in the first quarter. Smits, Jackson, and Mullin were the culprits. Smits missed 9 of his first 10 shots; Jackson, sporting his Fu Manchu mustache, was so pumped up that he embarrassed himself with terrible, show-off-type passes and lackadaisical defense; and Mullin simply disappeared again, never taking a shot until late in the second quarter.

So who saved the Pacers? The Davises? Reggie? No, the men in the Superman uniforms most responsible were numbers 5 and 4, Jalen Rose and Travis Best.

In the second quarter, the two left handers outscored the entire Knicks team 21–14. With a little help from McKey and Miller, and some stingy defense that saw the team scrapping on every play, Indiana fought back to actually lead by two by halftime. It was, as Bird later said, "quite remarkable."

He was right. Without superb play from the bench, the team would have been in the hole, one game down. But Rose and Best continued their fine play in the second half, and the Pacers roared down the stretch to garner a 10-point victory, 93–83. All while the Indiana crowd, who had booed nearly every Knicks player during the game, serenaded them with "New York sucks" in retaliation for the New York newspaper headline, "It's Knicks Versus Hicks" that hyped the series.

Knicks coach Jeff Van Gundy (whose bug-eyed, puffy face was reminiscent of Vincent Schiavelli, the subway specter in *Ghost*) summed up the Pacers performance by saying, "We got our heads handed to us by their second unit. Rose hurt us in the post, McKey's defense disrupted us, Best hurt us with his penetration, and Davis killed us with his effort."

Jeff was right, especially regarding Rose and Best. With Jalen towering over defensive opponents with his 6'8" frame, darting down the lane, or setting up for soft jumpers, and Travis, furiously dribbling the ball between his legs before faking Charlie Ward or Chris Childs out of position so he could drive to the hoop, or let fly a split-second jumper, Indiana simply was not to be denied. "Travis and Jalen were great off the bench," A.D., whose strong rebounding contributed to the victory, said. "They knew what had to be done and they did it."

When Game Two began two nights later, the Knicks welcomed back Larry Johnson, whose ability to goad Miami's Alonzo Mourning into a fight cost the Heat their playoff chances. The day after Shaquille O'Neal said Seattle coach George Karl "looks like a woman coach sometimes, one who cries all the time," provoking Karl to retort, "There are some great women coaches in the game. I'm thinking about wearing an apron tomorrow," and the Hornets upset the Bulls in the second game of their semifinal playoff series when Michael Jordan actually played like a mortal, the Pacers and Knicks locked up in a no-holds-barred battle that left coaches, players, and fans feeling like they just witnessed a war.

The drama of Game Two was heightened when Patrick Ewing, wearing number 33, jogged onto the Indiana court at 6:49 P.M. The 7', 255-pound, square-jawed behemoth loped through warm-ups with nonchalance, attempting to ignore the fact that he was donning his uniform for the first time since December 20th.

Sporting a bright blue cast covering the dislocated bone in his right shooting hand, Ewing hoped his presence might ignite the other returnee, Grand-mama Larry Johnson. Bird said he knew how to tell if Ewing was ready for the rigors of play, deadpanning to reporters, "We'll test him right away. One good slap on that wrist and we'll see if he can play."

Adding Ewing and L.J. to Charles Oakley, Buck Williams, and Terry Cummings beefed up the Knicks. If the Pacers were to be successful, the team had to play aggressive basketball, something Bird had been preaching all season. Rookie Etdrick Bohannon believed the team was ready, quipping, "Even the shootarounds are rough."

True to form, Game Two, which featured an appearance by Hoosier astronaut David Wolfe as honorary ballboy, was not a basketball purist's delight. In what could only be called ugly, the norm for a Pacers-Knicks contest, the teams pushed and shoved each other around like brothers vying for their mother's attention. Players dove for loose balls on the court, catapulted into the crowd chasing errant passes, and attacked each other on defense like they were mortal enemies. "It was a defensive war out there," Double D surmised in his whisper-like voice.

Though he was troubled with early fouls, and clearly less than 100 percent physically, Patrick Ewing gave a good account of himself. He was a tiger on the backboards and exhibited enough mobility to remind defenders that he was one of the NBA's 50 all-time greatest players, who could still score with ease. By game's end, he totaled 10 points and 6 boards. Based on Ewing's play, Bird knew what lay ahead, telling reporters, "He's going to get better every game."

The outcome of Game Two was decided by several factors, one of them a mistake by Bird that the Knicks failed to take advantage of. To his delight, disheveled New York coach Jeff Van Gundy saw that Chris Mullin was guarding Grand-mama. Larry Johnson proceeded to bury Mully, using his strength and savvy, and singlehandedly took a Knicks deficit on the scoreboard and turned it into a lead. But then Van Gundy erred by not going to Johnson on every play, and Bird was spared further embarrassment when he finally substituted Derrick McKey, a more capable defender, for Mullin.

Rik Smits, the day after a reporter ruffled his feathers by calling him "the Kerplunking Dutchman" and "Brick Mits," regained his shooting form to score 22 points, and two others also stood up to be counted as the game wound down. Reggie Miller, hounded on defense by John Starks, who was super-glued to Reggie's jersey, contributed his full repertoire of shots—including perfect-form threes from the perimeter, floating one-handers from the baseline, and, most importantly, an off-balance jumper from 10 feet in front of the basket that gave the Pacers a 77–71 lead with 2:13 to play.

Aiding Miller's efforts was the redoubtable Antonio, who produced two key plays that decided the game. With 45.9 seconds on the clock and Indiana up by two with the ball, the team faced its most critical possession of the playoffs. Coming off a screen, Reggie had a good look—but his jumper was off-kilter, the ball ricocheting off the rim to the left of the basket. Just as it began to tumble into the hands of an opponent, the huge hand of A.D. stretched up and pulled the ball down with powerful force. As he cradled the Spalding sphere, he was fouled, setting up two critical free throws. Utilizing his line drive approach at the line, he calmly canned both, and the Pacers led by four with 28.1 seconds to play.

But Antonio wasn't through. John Starks decided to drive for the Knicks basket, and when he darted by A.D., it looked like a sure two. Recovering, Davis cut quickly toward the hoop, and then used that huge hand of his once again to block the shot. When the ball tumbled into Pacers hands, the game was history, and Larry Bird could quit licking his lips. All the while, colored confetti rained on the frenzied Pacers fans, whose team racked up a victory and moved closer to a highly anticipated battle in the Eastern Conference finals against Michael and the Bulls.

Antonio Davis said he simply did what his coach asked. "If Coach Bird puts you on the floor at crunch time, he expects you to have your head screwed on right," Davis explained. "And to make the plays. When Starks went by, I panicked, but I remembered what coach says about patience—take every possession as if it is the last, and so I just stayed with the play."

The 85–77 victory meant Indiana led two games to none as they headed to the Big Apple, where Spike Lee and the outrageous New York fans awaited. Though he swore he had nothing to do with it, Lee's name had been signed to a delivery of four black roses to Reggie Miller before Game One, indicating a Knicks sweep. Sorry, Spike.

Game Three was played a few days after the NBA announced its All-Defensive team. Among the 42 players listed on the first team, second team, and even "other vote-getters," only Reggie Miller had been mentioned, and that with the latter group. The snub of Pacers players was amazing in light of their tremendous effort on defense all season, but it was a tribute to Dick Harter's help defense that had proven so successful.

When the Pacers and Knicks squared off in Game Three on the 9th of May, the day after Michael Jordan had so much fun drilling the Hornets to tie their series that he laughed even when hit with a technical foul from veteran referee Dick Bavetta, the story was the second coming of Patrick Ewing. The New York press, which has had a love-hate relationship with the big fellow during his career, welcomed him back like the prodigal son. Coach Jeff Van Gundy lauded his big guy, saying, "He's got the heart of a champion." That prompted Bird to tell reporters, "The way Jeff talked about Patrick, it almost made tears come to my eyes."

For the Pacers, the outcome of the game wasn't so much determined by Ewing scoring 19 points, but by the sudden departure of one of their main weapons: bench play. Travis Best was tentative and not a factor; Derrick McKey, clearly hampered by a hamstring injury, was a step slow; Antonio Davis was inconsistent; and worst of all, Jalen Rose played as if he had completely forgotten every lesson he'd learned during the year.

Combined with an inability to hit free throws (the Pacers were 19 for 32, Dale Davis 2 for 10), and the Knicks' propensity to can the critical shots in the final minutes, the Knicks prevailed 83–76. Larry Bird, whose latest McDonald's french fries commercial with Grant Hill aired during the NBC telecast, wasn't happy after the game, fuming about the lack of effort from his reserves. "Our bench played like they were on vacation," Bird lamented. . . . We had them on the ropes and we let them off. We got careless and the guys got lackadaisical."

The loss came despite 23 points from Reggie, whose every appearance reminded fans of his superhuman effort in Game Five of the 1994 Eastern Conference finals against the Knicks, when he scored an NBA playoff record 25 points in the final quarter—and of the hard-to-believe-it-happened eight points he scored in 8.9 seconds in Game One of the Eastern Conference semifinals against New York in 1995. In both games, diminutive, bespectacled film director and Knicks fan Spike Lee was Miller's foil, the two egging each other on like bratty brothers. Lee was present for the Knicks' first semifinal win of 1998, joining other celebrities like Woody Allen, Matthew Modine, Billy Crystal, Itzhak Perlman, and hockey great Wayne Gretzky.

Game Four of the Pacers-Knicks matchup was a doozy of a game—played after Bird had psyched up his players with words of wisdom during a bagel-and-juice session prior to tipoff. "He talked about keeping emotions in check and how the crowd could rattle you, and to just go out and play basketball," assistant coach Rick Carlisle said. "That really enhanced our focus."

Indiana was the team shorthanded this time, since Derrick McKey's hamstring injury put him on the sidelines in street clothes. That factor and the immense importance of the game caused Bird to chew gum at a racehorse pace while tugging at a too-tight shirtcollar for most of the game.

When the game had ended, four Pacers veterans (Bird earned the praise of assistant coach Dick Harter by yanking his reserve players early in the fourth quarter) had stolen the show at historic Madison Square Garden. In the first quarter, Chris Mullin's pinpoint shooting kept the Pacers in the game. Then Mark Jackson took over with razor-sharp passes and three-pointers that repaid Knicks fans, who consistently booed him.

In the fourth quarter, Rik Smits showed his mettle. Despite poor shooting for the first three quarters (Smits admitted that the early 11:30 A.M. start time was a problem, saying, "I'm not a morning person"), he kept firing, and suddenly everything he threw up went in. Outside, inside, it didn't matter, since the Dunking Dutchman swished nearly every shot. By game's end, he totaled 23 points to go along with an outstanding defensive effort against Ewing, who wasn't a factor in the outcome. An ESPN sportscaster correctly assessed Rik's performance, proclaiming, "Smits happens." Throughout the battle, Reggie Miller, who had said of Madison Square Garden's fans, "They hate me, but I love to play there," answered the call. Sensing the moment, his chance at the spotlight, Sir Reginald raced around the court like a madman, sliding off picks and darting around defenders. By halftime, he had 20 points, and not a Knick in sight could stop him, despite the fans' chant of "Cheryl, Cheryl."

When the game was on the line, it was Miller Time. Despite having taken a full-force elbow in the face from John Starks, Miller kept the pressure on New York's offense. Along with Smits, Reggie canned critical jumpers to keep the Pacers close, even though they had trailed by eight points with five-plus minutes to go. During a timeout, Bird had been his calm self, telling his players to "take it one play at a time," a reminder of Mullin's comment that when "the game gets tight, [Larry] gets more comfortable."

The game, and perhaps the Knicks' season, came down to one play. With 19.3 seconds on the clock, the Pacers trailed by three. During a timeout, Carlisle took his green magic marker and diagrammed a play. It was designed to favor Reggie Miller, but when he was covered, Miller found Smits inside with a crisp pass that resulted in a close-in attempt. His shot bounded off the glass, but then was batted to the perimeter, where John Starks tried to grasp it. Chris Mullin, hustling as always, stuck his left paw in, and batted it to Mark Jackson, whose bullet pass found Reggie Miller outside the three-point line in front of Spike Lee, aptly clad in his number 33 dark blue Knicks jersey.

As Knicks fans held their breath, Miller's high-arching shot was perfect, and it tied the game at 102 with just 5.1 seconds on the clock. When the Knicks failed to score, the game went into overtime, which was dominated by the play of Jackson. He hit a three to open the extra period, and then a patented floating fling shot that propelled the Pacers to a seven-point lead. Smits, who continued to dominate inside, and Miller, who hit a three-pointer and two critical free throws on the way to 38 points, made sure of things to end the Mother's Day afternoon. The result of their efforts was a 118-107 win that saw Knicks fair-weather fans heading for the exits as Mark Jackson sang "Silent Night" on the way to the locker room.

Though NBC's Jim Gray dubbed Miller "The Knick Killer," the *New York Times* sported the headline, "Miller's Three Sends Knicks to Edge of Abyss," *Times* columnist Harvey Araton called Reggie a "rooftop terrorist who stalks the Knicks," and ESPN opened its Sportscenter broadcast by referring to "the curse of Reggie," Miller was prophetic with regard to his heroics, saying, "I'm a shooter, and I'm not going to leave any bullets in the gun." Mark Jackson was pleased he hadn't, saying, "If I'm red hot and Reggie's ice cold, I'd still rather have him take the shot."

The Knicks and their fans were stunned by the sudden turn of events, especially since the culprits were two hometown boys and a longtime nemesis. The *Times*'s Araton wrote, "Chris Mullin of

Flatbush, Brooklyn, tapped a fatal rebound to the former Knick Mark Jackson of St. Albans, Queens, who rerouted the ball to Reggie Miller, who now, more than ever, believes he owns the expensive real estate in front of Spike Lee's front-row seat."

True to the spirit of the day, Smits celebrated the Pacers victory by finding the nearest pay phone to call his mother, Margie Van Der Welde, in the Netherlands. She was not home, but Rik reached his dad, Ad Smits, who had watched the game. The grin on Smits's face reflected his father's words of praise.

Joining the Pacers with three victories in the playoffs were the Bulls, the Jazz, and the Lakers, whose 7'1" and 315-pound Shaquille O'Neal was dominating Seattle so much that coach George Karl, who had chastised Shaq for his Hollywood connection, admitted that "he's playing much closer to Kareem than Kazaam," a reference to the genie O'Neal played in the film of the same name.

All four teams had moved within one win of the "final four" of professional basketball, ready to earn a spot in the conference finals, one step from a chance at a championship ring. Players from New York, Charlotte, San Antonio, and Seattle were beginning to make plans for summer vacation.

The day before Game Five, Indiana and the NBA held a joint news conference to announce Larry Bird as Coach of the Year. True to his nature, Bird gave the credit to everybody but himself.

Earlier in the year, Dick Harter said he knew the moment when he saw success ahead for his boss. "The day I knew he was going to be good at this job was the day he walked in after a rough game and said he couldn't sleep at all," Harter recalled. "I jumped up and started laughing. 'You can't sleep? Now you're a coach.'"

Team leader Mark Jackson said, "The first time I talked to Coach, he told me coaching was overrated. I knew he was going to be a great coach. I can say to him, 'Hey, this is the way they're playing, I think I can do this.' And he'll say 'Okay.' That means a lot to a player." Later, Jackson added, "People questioned whether a great basketball player could coach a team whose talent didn't measure up to his. This award says he can."

Their comments all rang true. Larry Bird *was* the NBA Coach of the Year because of one main factor, which had also made him a great player: he couldn't stand to lose. The sum total of his dedicated players (Mullin was a near carbon copy of Bird, Jackson passed like Bird, Miller shot like Bird, Dale Davis rebounded like Bird, Pope worked hard like Bird, and so forth), Larry Legend had used his work ethic to mold a team into a powerhouse that was one victory away from the Eastern Conference finals. The success brought to mind Rick Carlisle's comment in late January, when he told reporters, "A lot of this is Larry having the right pressure on the reins, loose enough and yet tight enough. He's smart enough to stay out of these guys' way and let them play the way they can play."

Bird, the first league MVP ever to win Coach of the Year, was his ever-humble self, saying he was "very embarrassed." About the Pacers, he said, "I'm no dummy. I knew we had a pretty good team here. We've hung together—when one player is down, the others pick him up. I have a great deal of faith in my players, and they've carried me through." Bird then added, "I love it. I love to watch these guys compete. That's what it's all about."

The Birdman showed his embarrassment at the honor when his players left the news conference. A few hooted and howled, amidst clapping for the coach they saw as a surrogate father, a buddy to get a beer with. Bird was clearly touched by the affection, but his face reddened as he continued to answer questions from the media.

Despite the NBA accolades for Bird, the Knicks weren't about to let the Pacers waltz through Game Five without fierce resistance. After an intense practice the morning of May 13th, one in which the quotation on the back of Pacers aide Joe Qatato's shirt (Hustle, Sweat, Desire, Heart) set the tone, Bird's players took the court trying to close out the Knicks.

On the night after the Lakers and the Jazz eliminated Seattle and the Spurs to reach the finals of the Western Conference playoffs, Indiana blasted out of the gate like they had a tee time at Augusta National, slid back as they rounded into the second and third quarters, and then mounted a charge that led them to the brink of victory as the clock ticked toward the four-minute mark. That surge was led by the spiritual one, Mark Jackson, who later said that the last time he'd performed so well was when he was playing Sega Genesis with his son.

All Jackson did was record the first triple-double in Pacers playoff history, a 22-point, 14-rebound, 13-assist night that hit the Knicks like a tornado. Jackson was everywhere—chasing loose balls, diving out of bounds to save errant passes, setting up teammates with on-the-mark passes, craning his body upward to snare rebounds, and providing the boisterous Market Square Arena crowd with a shot variety that included enough "teardrop," inclose underhanded buckets to provide Knicks guards Charlie Ward and Chris Childs a year full of nightmares.

Most critical to the Pacers effort was Jackson's ability to hit all 10 of his free-throw chances in the final minutes. Utilizing his regimen (right arm thrust into the air, followed by two bounces of the ball, then the shot), Jack closed the door on the Knicks, providing the final dagger in the Knicks heart with two free tosses at the 19.1 mark. It came after a superb defensive effort by the Pacers, which resulted in a stop after New York had crept to within nine.

Jackson's supercharged game, along with ample support on the offensive end from Miller, who totaled 24 points, and Smits, who finished with 22 (most came from his "flip" shot, a soft one-hander where his right hand remained in the air until the ball swished), catapulted the Pacers to a 99–88 victory that had Ewing and the Knicks packing for the off-season. Credit also went to stickyfingered Chris Mullin; Dale Davis, who battled the boards as if he were possessed; and Antonio Davis, a defensive force who swatted away Knicks attempts like he was Spiderman.

Indiana's raucous sixth-man crowd also had a hand in the victory. They provided a standing ovation and resounding applause for Bird when he received his NBA Coach of the Year award prior to the game, and then proceeded to cheer at a deafening level, all the while being prodded on by Pacervision videos, especially one depicting actor Gene Hackman firing up his players in the locker room for their championship game in the film *Hoosiers*.

Inspired by that memorable moment and Bird's leadership, Indiana had come through, especially since Mark Jackson had played like Bob Cousy and Magic Johnson rolled into one. "M.J. was fantastic," Reggie said. "He played the game of his life, a game for the ages. He takes it personally every time he plays the Knicks."

Bird saw it another way, providing Jackson, who avoided his famous "shimmy shake," though the temptation was there, with the ultimate compliment: "He played a magnificent game and kept his composure," the Birdman explained. "Jackson reminds me of myself. Not great foot speed, but he competes and he competes hard."

Enough so that the Pacers, whose fans partied outside the arena like it was Mardi Gras in the Heartland, had advanced to the Eastern Conference finals, where their very own Larry Legend would match up against Michael Legend, whose Bulls had defeated Charlotte on Dennis Rodman's 37th birthday. Talk about one for the ages.

TALE OF TWO LEGENDS

*"I try not to get caught up in worrying about officials
the ways some other people do. You have to know their habits.
And know when to argue. If a referee has been in the league
for 30 years, you're not going to bullshit him."*
LARRY BIRD

"Our team is playing like a finely
tuned orchestra," the 6'7", 228-pound owner of two Rottweilers,
Chichio and Zowie, said. "Everything is in sync." So proclaimed
gifted number 33, Scottie Pippen, of the five-time world champion
Chicago Bulls on the eve of the Eastern Conference finals. After a
season of chaos brought on by Pippen's threat to never return to
the Bulls once his foot injury had healed, the nightly potential that
bad boy Dennis Rodman might be banished from the game,
hoopla over whether Michael Jordan was playing his last season,
and constant bickering between coach Phil Jackson and general
manager Jerry Krause, da Bulls were ready to sweep aside the
Pacers to qualify for a chance to add to the five championship
rings displayed on four fingers and a thumb on the cover of the
Bulls media guide.

Coach Larry Bird and his roustabouts believed the Bulls would
hit a dead end. "Beating a team like Chicago four games will
be tough; they are the best team in the world," The Birdman
stated. "But we have some guys over here who really believe in
themselves."

Matchups would be the key to victory, and pundits wondered whether Bird would learn from past mistakes. Earlier in the season, he tried Dale Davis on Toni Kukoc, and the former Croatian national table-tennis champion had burned him. On another occasion, Bird watched in agony as Derrick McKey battled with Dennis the Worm, only to be shoved aside by the Tattooed One.

While the anticipated Jordan-Miller, Longley-Smits, Jackson-Harper, Mullin-Pippen, and Rodman-Davis confrontations took center stage for the best-of-seven series, comparisons between the coaches were inevitable, and perhaps appropriate for study by a learned psychiatrist. On the Bulls bench was Phil Jackson, the bearded Svengali and former role player in the NBA who had led his team to five world titles, and yet wondered whether he had a job coaching Chicago next year.

Jackson's counterpart was Larry Joe Bird, the three-time NBA Most Valuable Player who downplayed his ability as a coach. Sam Smith of the *Chicago Tribune* said of Bird, "What coaching he does is undetectable to the naked eye. Bird is from the taxidermy school of emotion. His pulse is taken by seismography. The Celtics retired Bird's number; the Pacers now may retire Bird's Barcalounger."

The coaching matchup was an official's dream. Jackson had spent so much of his time meditating, he appeared to be in a continual trance. Bird, who got so excited during the final seconds of the Pacers win over the Knicks that he actually clapped his hands, rarely uttered a word over a disputed call. Thank goodness emotional players like Reggie Miller and Michael Jordan were around to provide excitement.

Speaking of Michael, was this his last appearance in a Bulls uniform if Chicago lost, or just a cruel hoax designed to save Phil Jackson's job? The Almighty One was noncommittal, though Bulls fans hoped Jordan would play until he was 90 years old.

Prior to the series, Bulls assistant coach Tex Winter provided advice on how to defend The Great One if he were an opponent. "Double-traps can give Michael a little problem," the wily coach explained. "He has a little problem getting out of those. I think mainly because he wants to see if he can beat them. It's sort of a challenge to him, and there are times when he shouldn't attempt to beat it."

Bird knew all about Jordan's propensity to shine in the playoffs, recalling his 63-point effort against the Celtics in 1986. "You have to challenge him," Bird said. "You can't back down." Assistant coach Dick Harter added, "We once held him to 13 points in the fourth quarter in New York. Then he went back to Chicago and hit us with 50. I don't think anybody's got the answer."

When the tip for Game One was held at 2:33 on the 17th of May at the United Center, Chicago and Indiana faced off with contrasting agendas. The Bulls saw the Pacers as a stepping stone to their legacy as one of the great teams of all time, while Indiana craved a spot in the NBA Finals, where they knew they could beat Utah or Los Angeles.

While various newspaper headlines described Game One—played the day after Utah had smashed the Lakers, 112–77, their worst playoff defeat in 526 games—the logical banner should have been "Bulls Outsnooker Pacers." Or, more to the point, "Bulls Triumph as Pippen Smothers Mark Jackson."

The Pacers loss was due to a matchup Chicago coach Phil Jackson approved. Aware that the Pacers' 6′3″ Jackson was the key to their motion offense, the coach planted 6′7″ Scottie Pippen on him, and the Central Arkansas gazelle with the sleepy eyes, dead pan facial expressions, and arms as long as the Snake River hounded Mark as if he were the Fugitive.

The idea wasn't originally Phil Jackson's, but had been hatched during a workout at Michael Jordan's house. Ron Harper (who had been studying tapes of Reggie Miller prior to the series), Jordan, and Pippen discussed the matchup and then sprung it on their coach. Jackson was convinced the idea had merit—and when Game One began, there was Pippen shadowing Mark Jackson.

Besides preventing Jack from posting up, which removed a potent Pacers offensive weapon, Pippen's intense pressure defense made him eat up the shot clock. By the time the Pacers guard was ready to gear up the offense, there was little time left to run a play. Jackson's rhythm was interrupted, and he committed seven of Indiana's inexcusable 26 turnovers. Pacers broadcaster Mark Boyle summed up the debacle, saying, "Pippen is simply suffocating Mark Jackson." NBC announcer Doug Collins put it another way, quipping, "Pippen is eating him alive."

Besides the Pippen-Jackson matchup, Phil Jackson had two additional surprises for the Pacers. Harper, sporting a tattoo of a shark on his lower left leg and the Batman insignia on his right, battled Reggie at every turn; and, more importantly, Jordan played Chris Mullin so tight that he was ineffective. With Rik Smits a nonfactor, the Pacers had little offense. *Chicago Tribune* columnist Steve Rosenbloom summed up the Pacers' plight, writing, "Indiana's Big Three of Reggie Miller, Rik Smits, and Chris Mullin appeared to have gotten a volume discount on embalming fluid."

When the final buzzer sounded, Indiana was saddled with an 85–79 loss that had Bulls fans singing as they left the arena to the tune of "Another One Bites the Dust." Thirty-one of Chicago's points came from the gum-chewing Jordan (Watermelon Bubblicious, if you please), who maneuvered in and around Pacers defenders, his bald head sparkling with beads of sweat. The best of the best of Jordan's baskets came with 7:25 remaining to play, when His Airness lost defender Jalen Rose with a backcut, took a bounce pass from Luc Longley, was bumped by Dale Davis, and then soared to the other side of the basket, where he delicately laid the ball off the glass with a reverse layup.

Whether it was Bird's stubborn streak that kept him from replacing Mark Jackson with Travis Best, or at least inserting Jalen Rose into the lineup, was anyone's guess. But Phil Jackson, the grown-up hippie, had clearly won the battle of the coaches; and it remained to be seen whether Bird—who had never been defeated by the Bulls in the playoffs during his playing days with the Celtics—and his cohorts Dick and Rick could make the necessary adjustments for Game Two.

Bird's coaching effort was hit hard by critics who felt he should have anticipated Jackson's strategy or at least been able to adapt during the game. The banner line for *Tribune* writer Bernie Lincicome's column read, "Coach of the Year Could Use a Little Coaching." Lincicome not only chastised Bird for not adjusting to the Bulls' matchups as the game progressed, but was extremely critical of him and the Pacers for their inability to challenge Chicago as the game wound down.

What Lincicome and other pundits noticed was that with 39.2 seconds to play, and Indiana trailing by six points, Pacers players failed to foul and instead simply stood transfixed as Jordan palmed the ball while precious seconds drained off the scoreboard. He finally fired up a prayer, and when Luc Longley rebounded, the game was history.

Lincicome was shocked at Bird's unwillingness to call a timeout, or to tell his players to scramble for the ball. After spelling out the various alternatives open to the Pacers, the columnist wrote, "Send the answer to the Indiana Pacers bench. To the attention of a Mr. Larry Legend. He's the fellow leaning on his elbow. . . ."

After much deliberation and intense videotape review, the Pacers braintrust of Bird, Harter, and Carlisle reorganized their game plan against Chicago. Convinced Jackson had made all the changes possible with his lineup, Indiana intended to counterattack and attempt to discover weaknesses they could exploit.

One question remained unanswered for the Bulls, and that was the status of Dennis Rodman. Disregarding the importance of playing in the Eastern Conference finals, The Worm had celebrated his 37th birthday with a Rodmanfest. The Monday night before the Tuesday game, Dennis and his buddies livened up Illusions, a nightclub he co-owned, until the sun came up. On Wednesday evening, the party continued—first at Illusions, then at the Crazy Horse stripper bar, and finally at Crobar, a dance club. Two nights later, Rodman and his friends partied at a watering hole (appropriately called Drink) until 7:00 A.M.

When the Bulls practice began on Saturday, "the crazy man," as Luc Longley described him, was a wee bit late. He was banished by teammates from running plays, ordered to the weight room, fined, and yanked from the starting lineup in favor of Toni Kukoc. Nevertheless, when it came time for Jackson (who said of his tattooed one, "Dennis has his own measurement of what's important") to call on Rodman's considerable talents as a ballplayer, he responded with exuberant, helter-skelter play that made Larry Bird comment, "He causes havoc out there."

Containing Rodman, who contributed 11 points, 10 rebounds, and his usual stingy defense, plus Jordan, Pippen, and the rest of the Bulls in Game Two meant the Pacers would have to return to the type of play that had earned them a victory at the United Center late in the regular season. In that game, Indiana had been as physical as a heavyweight boxer, fouling with vengeance anyone who dared streak for the basket. "We've got to scrap and fight with the Bulls," Bird said. "That's the key." Miller echoed his coach's thoughts. "We have to quit waiting for things to happen," Sir Reginald professed. "We have to take the game to them."

Miller's words were a reminder of how important winning was to him. The mark of a great player was an NBA championship ring, and Reggie still hadn't earned one. At 32, Reggie knew time was running out in his quest for a championship. His highlight film featured many memorable moments, including a 50-point regular-season performance and two 39-point playoff gems as well as enough last-second game heroics to fill 10 scrapbooks. Miller was also known as a tough player who rarely missed a start, and his work ethic was unquestioned. All that was missing was the championship ring, and Reggie was determined to lead his team to victory against the Bulls. "I know the window is there," he lamented. "And it won't be open much longer. We need to win now."

In Game Two, played the night after Utah beat the Lakers, 99–95, behind Karl Malone's 33 points to take a two-to-zip lead in the West, Reggie tried his best to lead Indiana to victory. From the opening tip, he zigzagged across the floor, hustling on every play, attempting to find a rhythm that could propel him to a super-human effort that could overshadow that of Michael Jordan.

Reggie should have known better. Though Miller tried everything to defend the Great One but tie his shoelaces together, Michael proved why he was awarded his *fifth* Maurice Podoloff Trophy as the NBA's Most Valuable Player before the game. Utilizing his catlike quickness and a court sense second to none, Jordan was unstoppable—and only his inability to shoot well (13 for 22) kept him from scoring 60 points.

Jordan was especially effective at three critical points in the game. With 2.7 seconds left in the second quarter, and the Bulls trailing by nine, Michael streaked down the floor, Reggie trailing him like a cop chasing a bank robber. After a series of stop-and-go moves, Jordan meandered into the far right corner in front of the Bulls bench. Waiting for him was a perfect court-length pass from Scottie Pippen. After stretching high in the air to grab it, Michael took two dribbles, and then rotated his body 180 degrees so as to face the basket. Extending his hands in the air away from a frantic, arm-waving Reggie Miller, he let fly a high-arching jumper that swished through the net. Bird simply shook his head as he strode toward the locker room while the United Center crowd stood and cheered their hero.

But Michael wasn't through. As the buzzer ending the third quarter sounded, the kid who was cut from his 10th-grade team hit a fadeaway, impossible-to-defend jumper from the right perimeter to provide the Bulls with a four-point lead instead of two. Larry Legend, who knew a thing or two about last-second shots, rubbed his forehead with his right hand, tugged at his shirt-collar, and puckered his lips as he rose to huddle with his assistant coaches in front of the Pacers bench.

If there was any doubt about Jordan's ability to take charge of a game, it disappeared as the final seconds ticked away in the fourth quarter. Every time Indiana made a run, there was Michael. When the Pacers closed the Bulls' lead to five at 96–91 with 2:30 remaining, Jordan hit a turnaround jumper. When Chris Mullin, whose hustling play was a bright spot for Indiana, scored and Miller hit a perimeter shot to bring the Pacers within three, Jordan spun his way to the top of the key, lost his balance and nearly fell, recovered, kept dribbling, sliced his way into the lane, and then canned a 10-footer. When Indiana tried a last-second effort to score, Jordan kept Mullin from getting the ball, and then raced down the court, took a pass from Harper, pulled up along the right baseline, and hit nothing but net with a fadeaway 15-footer. No wonder former NBA player and coach Doug Collins said of Jordan, "It's nice to have a nuclear weapon on your team."

By game's end, Michael had totaled 41 points and added to his legendary persona by stating, "I kind of started calling my own plays in the third quarter."

Scottie Pippen, the youngest of 12 children who played school-yard ball and dreamed of being Dr. J, added 21 points to the Bulls effort, reiterating why he and Michael were the finest one-two punch in the NBA. Pippen also hogtied Pacer Mark Jackson, forcing him to play a loosey-goosey game filled with errant passes and turnovers.

Larry Bird once again shouldered part of the blame for the loss. Whether it was inexperience or simply a refusal to comprehend the importance of having the right players on the floor at the proper time, Bird started the all-important fourth quarter with a lineup that included Antonio Davis, Travis Best, Chris Mullin, Jalen Rose, and rookie Mark Pope. Before Bird realized that he had little offensive punch on the floor, especially since Rose and Best had been ineffective, the Bulls exploded for five straight points, including a three-pointer from Steve Kerr, upping their lead to 9. From that deficit, Indiana never recovered, losing 104–98.

When the final buzzer sounded, Phil Jackson, suspenders and all, sat on the sidelines sipping bottled water, while Bird, shoulders slumped, headed toward the Pacers locker room to confront his least favorite task—being interviewed by the media. He managed to praise the Bulls, and Jordan in particular, but he wasn't pleased with the officiating, telling reporters, "I'd like to see Pippen guard Michael Jordan full court the way he does Mark Jackson. We'd see how long he'd last. He got away with a lot of bumping and chest contact."

The forgotten man in Game Two was Reggie, whose high expectations had been quashed by Ron Harper. Miller was only 4 for 13 from the field, and never got into the flow of the game. "They've got a big guy hitting me to force me off-balance," Miller said. "But we just have to play better. You've got to knock out the champ. You can't just decision the champ. Right now we're the only ones taking the punches." Asked if he was spent from being roughed around by the Knicks, Miller refused to make excuses, saying, "Coming off the New York series, c'mon, this is a cakewalk."

The Bulls had demonstrated why they had won back-to-back NBA championships, and five in the 1990s. Indiana, hustling all the way, had not played that badly, and their effort would have beaten 99 percent of the teams in the league. But Chicago was special, an odd collection of role players who complemented future Hall-of-Famers Jordan, whose will to win was second to none, and Pippen, a superb defender with outstanding offensive capabilities and explosive speed whose best asset was a Cheshire cat grin. Ron Harper, a popular player who provided a bridge between the superstars and the role players, added leadership and poise to the team. Toni Kukoc, who had suffered a dismal shooting night in Game One, remained a potent offensive weapon. And Steve Kerr, the crew-cut veteran, was still a threat, especially behind the three-point line, cutting out the hearts of teams who double-teamed Jordan and Pippen and left him free. Along the frontline, Luc Longley provided muscle and solid defense on centers like Rik Smits. Luc's replacement, Bill Wennington, still possessed a soft jumper, and two of them in Game Two stoked the Bulls fire. And then there was Dennis, troubled Dennis, his hair afire, his manner demonstrative whether he was toweling off his tattooed body or arguing a call with an official. His defense, superb passing ability, and court smarts meshed perfectly with his teammates—especially Jordan, who recognized Rodman's importance to the team.

Molding the cast of characters together was another future Hall-of-Famer, Phil Jackson, and his assistants Tex Winter—author of the Bulls' famed "triangle offense"—and Jimmy Rodgers, the former Celtics coach. Somehow they kept the peace, dealt with the egos, and created the strategies that wreaked havoc against league opponents.

Larry Bird had seen that firsthand in Games One and Two. Instead of sticking it to the Bulls in Chicago, his team had fallen short. Now the Pacers returned to Indianapolis, hoping to sweep Phil Jackson and his boys and square the series at two games apiece.

Despite being aware that only seven NBA teams had ever come back from a two-game deficit, and that the Bulls were 20–0 in playoff series when holding such a lead, Indiana still believed they could beat Chicago. The day before the Indianapolis 500, they were determined to do that before a sellout crowd.

Before the game, Bird gained two supporters in defense of his coaching tactics. Boston legend Bill Russell, on hand to congratulate Michael Jordan for his MVP award, said Bird "was really a bright man" and that he "knew what he was doing." Former UCLA legend John Wooden told the *New York Times*, "Bird's fresh approach to coaching and to leadership should be welcome. . . . All too many coaches, at the pro and collegiate level, rant and rave. Bird stays on an even keel. In my view, quiet confidence gets the best results. As Lincoln said, 'There's nothing stronger than gentleness.' "

Whether Bird was questioning his capabilities, no one knew—but in Game Three he expected total effort from his players for 48 minutes. And he got it. Three days after former UCLA star Larry Farmer was named head coach at Loyola University Chicago ("He can be for us what Larry Bird has been for the Pacers," athletic director Chuck Schwartz said), Indiana scrapped and fought like a team on the brink, which it was. To aid the effort, Pacers management enlisted "Back Home in Indiana" crooner and former Andy Griffith Show star Jim Nabors to sing the national anthem; Hoosier-born television comedian David Letterman to tape a pep talk shown on the Pacervision screens; and legendary Indianapolis 500 driver A.J. Foyt to toss the game ball to the referees.

For three quarters, the Pacers and Bulls produced a highlight film. Reggie Miller came out of the gate firing away, and his early baskets matched those of Jordan, booed by the Pacers crowd at every turn, and Scottie Pippen. When the reserves (NBC's Peter Vecsey dubbed them "nuclear subs") took over, Travis Best played his best game of the season (11 points, 4 assists), and proved the Bulls had no match for his quickness. Antonio Davis, a tower of strength on the offensive backboard and contributor of 10 points, was outstanding—as were Derrick McKey, who played Jordan tough, and Jalen Rose, whose fiery play (15 points) and never-give-up spirit ignited the Pacers as the game wound down. Every player on both teams—except Rik Smits, suffering through a subpar game that incurred Bird's wrath, and Dennis Rodman, who seemed bored with all the hoopla—abounded with energy, diving for loose balls, battling for rebounds, and playing defense like they were glued to the chest of the opposition.

With more than 16,000 fans roaring, Indiana readied themselves for the final quarter, the most important 12 minutes of the season. To stress the importance, and provide inspiration, Mark Jackson gathered his teammates in a circle after the third quarter timeout. The message was simple: stay focused and beat the Bulls.

With Bird clasping and unclasping his fingers like he was trying to rub the skin off them, and Phil Jackson (whose need for a hip replacement made him walk like a 90-year-old) pulling at the suspenders under his suitcoat as if they were going to pop off, the two teams traded hoops until the five-minute mark. Pacers hopefuls held their breath, for not only did their team trail the Bulls, but redoubtable Reggie Miller, Indiana's best hope down the stretch, was limping badly.

Disregarding a sprained ankle ("I stepped on Michael's foot," Reggie explained, "and heard something pop"), Miller stayed on the court. Bird, a man who knew something about playing hurt, would say later, "You go with your best. Reggie wanted to play. He said he could go. Everything was on the line. Like all great players, even when they're hurt they want to be out there. I almost took him out because he couldn't do anything on the defensive end, but he wanted to gut it out."

Yes he did, and in a remarkable display of courage, Miller simply took over a game in which every possession was played like it was the last. At a critical point when it was either going to be Miller Time or Michael Time, it was Reggie who added to his legend and Michael, though he scored 30 points in the game, who proved mortal.

Perhaps Jordan needed his wife's presence to provide inspiration like Miller's did. Prior to the start of the fourth quarter, sexy fashion model Marita Miller, sporting spray-on blue pants, stood by her seat in the front row dancing to the music while waving a sign that read, "We Love You Reggie." When Reggie left the huddle, he noticed Marita, and the grin on his face portended great things to come.

Three never-to-be-forgotten plays during which Miller scored eight points in 95 seconds proved Reggie's mettle. Chastised by Jordan for "playing defense like a woman" and by pundits for being a crybaby, Miller began his run with a three-point jumper with 4:11 left on the game clock. At the 3:17 mark he hit another one, this time hobbling down the court, hands raised in the air as the crowd screamed, "Reg-gie, Reg-gie, Reg-gie."

But Miller, praised after the game by ESPN basketball analyst Jack Ramsey for "hitting the big shots when they counted," wasn't through. With 2:32 remaining, seconds before Dennis Rodman left the floor with six fouls to the tune of "Hit the Road Jack," Miller faked number 91 into the air and hit a critical two-pointer from the top of the key. That provided an eight-point lead. Indiana tried to squander their advantage with the clock winding down due to three inexcusable turnovers, but Miller iced the game with two cool-as-can-be free throws with just 10.6 seconds remaining. Chicago couldn't recover, and the result was a 107–105 Pacers victory that left a deadpanned, ashen-faced Larry Bird so exhausted it looked as if he was the losing coach at the postgame news conference.

Miller's heroics reminded fans of a similar performance by Larry Legend in Game Five of the 1991 playoffs against Indiana. During the game, Bird dived for a loose ball and fractured his cheekbone. Earlier in Game Five of the Celtics-Detroit series, Celtics fans saw a premonition of things to come when a pigeon flew down from the rafters and landed in the paint under the Celtics' basket. Fans started screaming, "Lar-ry, Lar-ry, Lar-ry," and suddenly there was the Birdman running on court, where he proceeded to annihilate the Pacers with superb play.

Though Miller was clearly the hero in Game Three, Bird shared center stage. Unwilling to hurt the feelings of certain players, especially Jackson and Mullin, whom the coach dearly loved, Bird was hesitant to bench them even when their play was below average. "Bird has a strong sense of loyalty," Pulitzer Prize–winning author David Halberstam, covering the game as part of research for a book on Michael Jordan, said. "He realizes the matchups for this series are tough, but out of loyalty, he's reluctant to make changes.

It's hard for him to get away from the ballplayers who got him here, but with Jackson for instance, the Bulls have been eating him up. Today, Larry played Best and Rose, and they came through."

Bird played down the changes, but it was clear that when the game was on the line, Jackson and Mullin were on the bench. And so was Rik Smits. When the Pacers made their run toward victory, Best and Rose joined Derrick McKey, Antonio Davis, and Reggie Miller on the court. That matchup caused the Bulls fits, and it was a tribute to Bird that he stayed with the lineup.

Another key to the win was the physical play of the Pacers. As the game entered the final minutes, Indiana's big men banged bodies inside. If one of the Bulls, especially Michael Jordan, tried to dart down the lane for a lay-in, he was hammered. Toni Kukoc and Steve Kerr got so tired of being knocked around, the two superb shooters missed critical free throws. "We've got to be physical and stay physical," Antonio Davis said after the game. "It's easy to get caught up in the Bulls mystique, and we can't do that."

Trailing the Bulls two games to one—a better fate than had befallen the Lakers, who had lost the first three games to Utah—Indiana took to the court on Memorial Day with confidence. Bird's first playoff coaching win against Chicago had dissolved all aura of invincibility the five-time world champions had, and the Pacers were bent on tying the series before traveling back to the United Center. Michael Jordan played down Indiana's chances, proclaiming that the Game Three loss was "just a bump in the road." The *Chicago Tribune*'s headline agreed, stating simply, "Bulls Hit a Pit Stop."

Dennis Rodman believed Indiana was a team on its last legs. During Game Three, he was more interested in bantering back and forth with Pacers fan Kathy Harrison than watching action on the floor. "He said my rings were cubic zirconia and that he had more money than I did," Kathy said. "But we had fun."

Rodman wasn't as upset with Harrison's remarks as he was with the officiating. Apparently Bird's nasty remarks regarding the men with the whistles (Phil Jackson remarked, "Now that Larry is complaining, we know he's a coach."), had paid off, for in Game Three Indiana got its fair share of the calls. Scottie Pippen, whose second-quarter collision with Antonio Davis midcourt could be heard on the straightaway at the nearby Indianapolis Motor Speedway, was neutralized by early fouls, and Rodman, who seemed mesmerized by a pretty redheaded Dutch reporter after the game, believed he was singled out as well, saying, "My new name is the Phantom. All these f...... referees."

With "the Phantom" absent from the starting lineup for Game Four, played the day after veteran driver Eddie Cheever won the Indy 500 and Utah polished off the Lakers to complete a shocking four-game sweep, Indiana and Chicago played a memorable game that left fans around the world delirious. For three and a half quarters, a fever pitch surrounded the combatants, and then they decided to step it *up* a notch as time wound down to the final minute. That's when the play of Scottie Pippen, Derrick McKey, Reggie Miller, and Michael Jordan decided the outcome, which would either push the Bulls toward the brink of victory in the series or permit Indiana to tie Chicago at two wins apiece.

With the score standing at 94–93 Bulls and 4.7 seconds remaining, reliable Scottie Pippen stood at the line with two shots. If he made them, or even just one, Larry Bird could in all likelihood start packing his golf clubs for Florida. After wiping the sweat from his brow, Pippen cradled the Spalding ball in his hands, and then a miracle occurred—he missed both, causing Reggie Miller to later say, "Pressure can get to anybody. At that point in time, it got a hold of Scottie."

As Pippen's second attempt fell to the floor, Derrick McKey and Michael Jordan, who had spent the off-day between games shooting 84 at a nearby golf course, scrambled for the ball, which scooted out of bounds. After officials huddled, the ball was awarded to Indiana with 2.9 seconds on the clock and the Pacers season hanging in the balance.

When the battle resumed, McKey stood near center court poised to inbound. According to a new play Rick Carlisle created two days before, Reggie Miller was positioned under the basket. A split-second after McKey was handed the ball, Miller, a noticeable hobble in his gait, shuffled his way toward a double-pick set on the left perimeter by Smits (who played a superb game totaling 28 points) and Antonio Davis. Reggie's defender, Ron Harper, got lost in the shuffle—but when Miller emerged into McKey's view, an arm-waving Michael Jordan confronted him.

As the five-second time limit for getting the ball inbounds wound down, McKey was as cool as an iced lemonade on a hot summer day. While 16,560 fans roared louder than a DC-10, McKey waited until Miller shoved Jordan out of his way and positioned himself just to the left of the letter *s* in "Indianapolis" emblazoned on the wooden court.

McKey's pass was perfect, and Miller was so open he could have taken a month to shoot. In fact, he didn't feel rushed, he said, because of what Bird had told him during the timeout. "It's funny," Miller said later, ". . . when it was 2.9 seconds left and [we were] drawing up the play, no one else but him would say, 'There's really like 3 seconds.' Only someone of that caliber would really know that. I think the mortal men and the mortal player would think, 'You have to get the shot off even quicker.' "

Armed with Bird's wisdom, Reggie whirled his body around toward the basket, squared up, leaped into the air, and with perfect form, arched the ball toward the 18″-diameter rim. As the clock ticked to the .7-second mark, the biggest shot of the Pacers' NBA season nestled into the net, giving them a 96–94 lead. Miller limped downcourt, arms raised, spinning and hopping as if he had just won the $175 million lottery awarded the previous week. In comparison, Larry Legend, his face devoid of any emotion, stood on the sidelines looking like he'd just found out his laundry was back from the cleaners a day early. Phil Jackson later viewed the tape of Bird and said, "I thought he was catatonic."

Miller's shot had ripped the heart out of the Bulls, but it was still beating. Tex Winter diagrammed his own play; and when Chicago returned to court, Toni Kukoc assumed Derrick McKey's role. Kukoc performed admirably, finding Michael Jordan on the left perimeter. With Pacers fans gasping for breath, the Great One took the pass, wheeled into the air, double-pumped under the long arms of Derrick McKey, stuck his tongue out, and spiraled a three-pointer toward the hoop.

While Miller's ball had dipped into the net, Jordan's had little arch and banged aggressively against the backboard. The ball ricocheted off the glass, dived into the cylinder, rolled around the inside of the rim, and then popped out of the basket as if it was a popped kernel of corn. Jordan, whose butterfly bandage over his right eye made him look like a wounded prizefighter, lowered his head and walked off the court. Reggie Miller leaped into the air with joy as Bird heaved a sigh of relief over what seemed to him a ho-hum, yes-we-expected-to-win victory.

Later, Reggie Miller summed up Jordan's effort. "You've got to remember [Jordan's] shot went in and out, a double-clutch bank shot in and out," Miller said. "There's probably no other human being—including myself—who would have gotten it to the rim. So I'll still stick with those odds. I'll still take him [Jordan] in Vegas."

MICHAEL'S MAGIC

*"Michael is on another level. Karl Malone is awesome. . . .
Reggie can be that way, but on a team you also need role
players . . . But Michael, well, he's something else."*
LARRY BIRD

The Chicago Bulls postgame show after Game Four was a beauty. Phil Jackson, who said every time Reggie Miller was touched it "looked like he had been hit by electric shock," blamed the officials. "That was an unbelievable finish," the bearded one complained. "The players felt like it was Munich '72 revisited," a reference to the U.S.–Soviet Union debacle at the Olympics when the Russians were given several chances to win the gold-medal game. Later, Jackson, whose outrage cost him a $10,000 fine, added, "I call it eight men on defense. Man, they were killing us out there."

Michael Jordan was even more antagonistic, saying, "It's us against the world, even the referees." Dennis Rodman decided to attack NBA commissioner David Stern and other league officials, saying, "I wish I could put a diaper on all of them and burp them because I think they all have indigestion when it comes to the Chicago Bulls." *Chicago Tribune* writer Terry Armour didn't care for the bellyaching, using the headline "The Gripes of Wrath," to banner his column.

On the winning side, Jalen Rose provided the best quip. Asked about Miller's winning shot, Jalen grinned and said, "If someone leaves Reggie open, that's like brushing his teeth in the morning." Larry Bird, whose rapid-fire speech pattern at the postgame news conference caused him to mangle the English language with "I seen that one," preferred to credit the crowd and his players' attitude toward the Bulls. "The fans wouldn't let us quit," the Birdman said. "And we took the ball to them. We were the aggressor."

So much so that too much aggression on the part of Jalen Rose caused him to be suspended for Game Five. Leaving his seat to investigate why Reggie was pulled into the Chicago bench during a melee in the final minute of Game Four had brought the wrath of league officials. Bird, who chastised NBC for repeatedly airing retakes of the incident, was disappointed, saying that Rose was merely reporting to the scorer's table to replace Miller. "Sure it bothers me that they didn't believe me," Bird said. "But there's nothing I can do about it."

Despite Rose's overzealous blunder, Bird hoped the Pacers' aggressive mind-set carried over into Game Five, played on May 27th at the spacious United Center in Chicago, which one reporter labeled a "mausoleum." At the eye of the storm was Michael Jordan, determined to pull his Bulls through. Reggie knew His Airness would be ready, saying, "As you know, as long as the other side's got that black cat out there, we need everything we got to stay in this series." The Bulls' Steve Kerr knew Jordan was ready, saying, "He didn't say a word for two days. When he's upset, he doesn't say anything, but he gets a look about him that means somebody's in trouble." What Miller didn't count on was a lackadaisical effort by him and his teammates that produced one of the team's worst showings of the year. Larry Legend also had a hand in the disaster.

If Pacers fans had known that Bird was going to wave the white flag and surrender as the second quarter began, they could have watched a rerun of Seinfeld. Shorthanded due to the absence of Rose, Bird decided to throw in the towel when the Pacers fell behind 29–16 at the end of the first quarter after the Bulls made a run similar to the annual "Running of the Bulls" in Pamplona, Spain. Michael Jordan, whose 29 points moved him past the 35,000 mark for his career, posted up Reggie Miller for easy baskets; Scottie Pippen raced around the court like a man trying to forget a bad dream, which his performance in Game Four had been for him; and Toni Kukoc displayed once again that Dale Davis had no prayer guarding him.

Trailing by 13, Bird could have revved up his starters by reminding them, "Hey, fellows, forget Game Four, this is Game Five and you need to get your butts in gear." But true to his low-key personality, Larry sat the veterans on the bench and put a makeshift lineup on the court that couldn't have beaten the Nuggets, let alone a championship team out for revenge looking for a "two-peat three-peat."

The unlikely five were Fred Hoiberg, who hadn't played for a month; rookie Mark Pope, a season removed from playing in Turkey; Travis Best; Chris Mullin, who had been socked in the head by Rik Smits early in the game; and Antonio Davis. They were overwhelmed for six straight Bulls points in two minutes and seventeen seconds, which stretched the Bulls lead to 19. Bird finally reacted by substituting Reggie Miller and Rik Smits—realizing that having Pope and Hoiberg instead of Rose, who watched the game from his hotel room, and McKey play with the reserve unit was a disaster. Meanwhile, Chicago sped along, and by halftime they dug the hole deeper by opening up a 25-point lead.

Even when the Bulls led by 33 in the second half as television viewers retired to bed, Bird kept his calm demeanor (the *New York Times* said, "Bird's words are as soothing to his team as a warm bath."), nervously pecking away at his cheekbone, puckering his lips, tugging at this shirtsleeves, and clasping his left knee in his hands as he leaned back in a cushioned chair. At halftime, the Pacers coach reminded his troops that they had to chip away at the Bulls lead "one point at a time," but Larry's words fell on deaf ears to a team that might have been better challenged by a screamer like Larry Brown.

The final 24 minutes looked like an exhibition game, or a Bulls practice session—for Indiana, though they fought hard, never recovered. The Bulls played like the Harlem Globetrotters, especially on a play where Toni Kukoc recoiled a behind-the-back whiz of a pass to Michael Jordan, whose dunk cemented the five-time NBA champions' stamp of superiority.

When the curtain finally fell, Chicago owned a 106–87 win in a city that worshipped the bronzed statue of Michael outside the United Center like it was a religious shrine and featured ads for his favorite cologne on bus billboards. While the Bulls celebrated (Michael Jordan said, "Tonight was unexpected dominance"), the Pacers locker room was a morgue. "I have a headache," Chris Mullin said, aware that his team had missed 18 shots in a row and gone three straight minutes without scoring. "But not from the hit in the head. They dominated us in every category, every area."

Bird, clearly irritated, discussed his favorite subject, being physical. "Chicago comes out strong all the time," the coach explained. "That's why they are the world champs. We didn't hit anybody. We had an opportunity to nail a couple of their guys. If we lay a couple out on the floor, they don't come in so easily the next time."

Dour faces among the Pacers were in order, since nearly everyone had contributed to the debacle. Unlike games throughout the season, where one player came through when another faltered, no one was able to come to the rescue when the highlight for the Pacers faithful who had trekked up to Chicago for the I-65 series had been legendary jazz pianist Ramsey Lewis's resounding rendition of the Star-Spangled Banner. Miller seemed more fluid with his movement, but his shot selection was horrendous. Smits appeared fatigued, and he was overwhelmed by Longley, the Melbourne, Australia, native who had scolded his teammates for complaining so vocally about the officiating. Chris Mullin never got his bearings after being elbowed in the head by Rik Smits seconds after the game began; Jackson and Best showed little spark and looked confused; and the Davises played like diaper dandies instead of beasts on the backboards.

Plain and simple, Bird's boys were blown out, prompting Skip Bayless of the *Chicago Tribune* to write, "The Pacers laid the biggest egg any Indiana farmer has ever seen." The lopsided verdict marked only the second time that had occurred in 96 games. Perhaps the two whirlwind, miracle victories in Indianapolis had taken their toll, especially against a Bulls team that had their game faces on from the second they hit the court for the pregame warm-ups. "Our concentration level was awful," Bird said. "I can't believe we didn't show up to play."

With the Pacers trailing three games to two, Bird knew he needed to motivate his team like never before. In order to make certain they learned from their mistakes, he made them watch a horror show, the first half of Game Five, in slow motion. Smits couldn't believe his eyes, saying, "It was worse than I thought."

Bird's words prior to Game Six, scheduled during a week when India and Pakistan shocked the world with nuclear testing, had to be strong, decisive, and guaranteed to inspire. He knew firsthand what an embarrassing loss in the playoffs was like, having been a part of the 33-point loss by his Celtics to the Lakers in 1984. Reggie believed more might be needed. "We want to go to where he's been," Miller said of his coach. "He's been to the mountain top and back and talked to Moses and the rest of them." Asked what Moses may have said to Bird, Miller replied, "[He told] him, 'We've still got your number 33 jersey, and if you really want to suit up, they could use you.' He's right, we could use him down in the post."

Bird didn't suit up for Game Six, but he was determined to find the right combination of players who would go out and fight Chicago with intensity like he provided in the old days with the Celtics. Fortunately, he was dealing with a Pacers team that understood the concept of team play. After Game Four, Skip Bayless of the *Chicago Tribune* had been most impressed with the Indiana coach's ability to shuffle his players. "He truly is Larry Legend," Bayless said. "Who else could bench their starting point guard and their All-Star center in the fourth quarter without having a mutiny?"

Their backs to the wall, the Pacers' facial expressions made it appear that they were posing for a mug shot prior to the opening tipoff for Game Six. Friendly smiles were gone, replaced with intense expressions that meant business. Rick Carlisle's pregame workout with the Pacers big men was a free-for-all, sparked by shoving matches not often seen in championship wrestling. Dale

Davis's demeanor made it appear he had just been released from prison and was about to confront his accuser.

Indiana hit the court with the ferociousness of stormtroopers. Early on, Mullin set the tone by bashing Jordan's head as he sped down the lane. Away from the ball, A.D. smacked Pippen with a right cross that caved his ear in. Every shot the Bulls attempted was contested, especially Jordan's, like the 10-footer jumper from the key that was blocked by two Pacers.

Unfortunately, Reggie couldn't find any spring in tired legs, and suffered a dismal outing, scoring 8 points on 2 of 13 shooting— but the offensive slack was picked up by the big fella, Rik Smits, who played a near-perfect game, hitting 11 of 12 field goals and 3 of 4 from the line to total 25 points. Mark Jackson, whose three three-pointers highlighted his superb performance in the first half, and Dale Davis, who mystified the Bulls with 19 unexpected points, his turnaround jumpers a thing of beauty, also contributed.

Bird coached his finest game of the season. Rotating his multiple-use players like a chess master, he outfoxed Jackson, who seemed more concerned with griping about the officials than keeping focus on Bird's substitution pattern. Bird's best strategy was to bench Mark Jackson and Chris Mullin for most of the second half and replace them with Best and McKey or Rose, who took turns shutting down Jordan after he had blistered the Pacers for 23 points in the first three quarters.

Of the trio, it was Travis Best, the transplanted native of Springfield, Massachusetts, who shone brightest. Playing with confidence, the Georgia Tech Yellow Jacket became Indiana's most potent weapon as the game wound down toward the three-minute mark. Living up to the faith Bird placed in him, Best utilized his speed and quickness to break free of the Bulls, who were determined to prevent him from accelerating down the lane and either throwing up a jumper or dishing off to a teammate.

After a Pacers timeout with 3:07 remaining, Best directed Indiana's offense, buzzing around the court, a fatigued Jordan in tow. With 1:27 showing on the clock, Best stepped up his game, becoming instrumental in a sequence of plays that decided the game.

Operating on the left perimeter, he passed the ball around and between his legs while he looked for Rik Smits at the post. Pressing to cut off the passing lanes, the Bulls bunched up around Best enough that an illegal defense violation, their second of the game, was called by official Hue Hollins—much to the chagrin of Jackson, who labeled the call "bullshit" after the game. Regardless, Reggie Miller hit the resulting free-throw and the game was dead even at 87 apiece.

At the 1:09 mark in the final stanza, Travis Best tried once again to make something happen. He barreled down the lane, but despite the fact that he was knocked on the floor, no foul was called. Travis protested, but the officials ignored him in a "take-no-prisoners" nailbiting game that featured 20 lead changes.

While Best guarded Steve Kerr, Jordan peeled off a pick and was open for a 15-footer, one he could normally make with his eyes closed. But surprisingly, Air Jordan couldn't knock it down, much to the disappointment of Jackson, who called it the "most important miss of the game."

Off the rebound, Travis Best controlled for Indiana, and he worked his way to the right perimeter where he hoped to find Reggie, who had posted up Michael. But Jordan's defense was airtight, and Miller waved the play off. Best took a look at the shot clock, realized the situation was grave, and made a break toward the baseline. "I knew a shot had to go up," Best said later. "We couldn't afford any passes at that point . . . I knew I had to beat Steve [Kerr] and get a shot."

The options for Best were to pull up for the jumper or head into the land of the giants, where Luc Longley and Dennis Rodman were ready to bat any shot away. Travis opted for the latter, and though the big men stretched their arms toward the ceiling, Best exhibited an acrobatic move worthy of a trapeze artist and lofted the ball off the backboard. Serendipity continued shadowing the Pacers season, when with precisely 33.3 seconds remaining, the brown ball ticked off the rim and nestled into the nylon net.

After a timeout, a sing-song to a Billy Idol tune by the capacity crowd of 16,566, and two free throws from M.J. that knotted the score at 89, Bird and his assistants had a decision to make. They could call a timeout and set a play, which the Bulls expected, or take possession and continue the action.

Bird opted for the latter, and when Travis Best headed down the court, the Bulls were a step slow getting back. "We didn't call a timeout after the free throws, didn't want to let Chicago get set up," Bird said later.

Travis Best took advantage. He rifled down the lane and was poised to score when a fatigued Michael Jordan, who had been chasing Reggie around all evening, fouled him from behind.

While the improvement of Jalen, Dale, and Antonio were Bird's greatest accomplishments during his miracle coaching season, the transformation of Travis Best from a tentative player whose confidence level ebbed and flowed like he was a raw rookie to an aggressive, can-do player who wasn't intimidated by Michael Jordan, warmed the coach's heart. True to that renewed spirit, Best stepped to the free-throw line, bounced the ball once, hesitated, and then bounced it four more times before launching two perfect free throws that provided the upstart, underdog, who-are-these-guys Pacers with a 91–89 lead with 8.5 seconds to go.

Phil Jackson remained confident, and why not? In the huddle, he and the Bulls assistants diagrammed a play that was guaranteed to work. Off a pick, Michael Jordan would glide into the left front court, take the out-of-bounds pass, fake McKey into the second row, and then cut toward the basket.

True to form, Michael executed the play perfectly, cuddled the pass bounced to him, and then headed for the Promised Land— realizing he could score while being fouled, toss in the free throw, and send the pesky Pacers on their way to summer vacation. Just when it appeared that such a Hollywood ending might occur, the impossible happened. Michael stumbled to the floor, apparently tripping either on his own feet (most observers' analysis), or one of Derrick McKey's size 16½ basketball shoes (Phil Jackson's and Jordan's supposition).

As Jordan braced himself for the fall, the ball squirted out of his hands and into McKey's. He was fouled, and when he made the first and intentionally missed the second, letting the clock run out, the crowd at Market Square Arena went bonkers and television audiences around the world were treated to a rare occurrence—a Larry Bird grin.

Prevailing 92–89 in a heart-pounding, hold-your-breath, check-your-hearing-the-next-day basketball game, Indiana had shocked a Bulls team that had been packing for Salt Lake City for the last week. "This should have been over long ago," Dennis Rodman, who was a nonfactor for the fourth straight game, said. "How can we lose to these guys?"

The Worm should have talked to Larry Bird. He knew why: his players had been aggressive, "taken it to the Bulls," as he liked to put it. They had been the aggressor, never backed down, never given an inch. Their poise under pressure, and the ability to produce under pressure, had been the difference. Chicago was the tentative one in Game Six, not Indiana.

Was Larry Legend, who nearly peeled the skin off his upper lip by scratching it throughout the final three minutes, satisfied? Asked if his team had played physical enough for him, he answered, "No, and they never will." Questioned about whether the Pacers had come to play, however, he heaped praise on his team, saying, "Wednesday they quit on me. . . . When it was time to suck it up [tonight], they did it." Regarding the officiating, Bird quipped, "If I see David Falk [Jordan's agent] refereeing, I know we're in trouble."

Jordan's unlikely stumble with the game on the line was the latest in a series of oddball plays that caused one to suspect angels were surely perched on Larry Bird's shoulders. Time and time again (Milwaukee's Michael Curry missed a wide-open jumper to win, Toni Kukoc missed three straight free throws, Scottie Pippen missed two, refs called an illegal defense at an unlikely time, the Great One simply fell down, and so on), Indiana was blessed with just the right miracle at just the right time. Bird was living the charmed life, leading his spiritual team to the brink of ending the Chicago Bulls dynasty.

To do so, Bird the motivator had to create a mind-set in the Pacers for Game Seven that reproduced the efforts in Games Three, Four, and Six. That meant being aggressive, knocking somebody down, and taking the action to the Bulls so that by the fourth quarter the weariness of their ages might catch up with them. Bird knew if his team could be even or within a few points at the three-minute mark, they could win and head west to Utah. "I told them it would be a two-possession game at the end," Bird said later. "And that if that happened, we could win."

Bird's words to his players before the game were true to his nature—low-key, but the intensity of the message was there. Earlier, Dale Davis had described his coach's demeanor, telling reporters, "He's incredibly calm. I can look at his eyes and see the concentration. That's why he was a great player. He's like a silent killer."

Coach Bird, who believed that players were the stars of the game and not the coaches, had another perspective. "The one thing that I've got to show my team is that I've got poise. They're watching me. They need someone to lean on, not a cheerleader whooping and hollering. I don't want guys to get too high or too low. . . . What I try to do is stay even-keel and show them I have a lot of confidence in them."

Bird's magic had gotten to Michael Jordan, whose superstitious nature caused him to always be the sixth man in line, just ahead of Dennis Rodman, as the Bulls bounded on the court. In fact, he reportedly listened to religious music for the first time as he drove to the United Center before Game Five. He and his teammates couldn't believe Indiana had challenged them the way they had, since they saw the Pacers as *Tribune* writer Skip Bayless described them in his column before Game Seven: "To the Bulls," Bayless wrote, "Reggie is a spindly shooter who isn't tough enough to be a Michael . . . Rik Smits—or 'Schmitts,' as Phil Jackson condescendingly pronounces it—is basically a lead-footed geek . . . Mark Jackson is a slow, unathletic point guard with an ugly-looking push shot . . . Chris Mullin now plays like a bald guy at the Y . . . Jalen Rose is an undisciplined streetball player prone to pouting . . . Travis Best is an out-of-control turnover waiting to happen."

Bulls' observations aside, Indiana considered themselves Chicago's equal, having split 10 games. Now Game Seven was high noon at the O.K. Corral, a battle for supremacy in what could be the last game for Michael Jordan in a Bulls uniform.

The pace for the winner-take-all game was frantic from the opening tip as more than 55 million watched on television worldwide. The keys were for Indiana to control the boards and impede the Bulls' famed triangle offense, which Zenmaster Phil Jackson (whose Indian name was "Swift Eagle") had described as "a five-man tai chi—the basic idea being to orchestrate the flow of movement in order to lure the defense off-balance and create a myriad of openings on the floor."

The first three quarters resembled a heavyweight championship fight, and then the action really picked up. The upstart challenger (Indiana) came out swinging, and at the 5:25 mark of the first quarter, built up a 20–8 lead. Every Pacer was operating at full throttle, especially Reggie Miller, whose high-arching jumpers were filling the hoop.

Meanwhile, the champ seemed to be gasping for air. Michael Jordan and his compatriots appeared sluggish—and, more importantly, their slow start kept the sellout United Center crowd, whipped into a frenzy by 21 scantily dressed "Luv-a-Bulls" cheerleaders and armed with signs that read, "Bye Bye Birdie" and "M.J. Will Make the Bird Sing," out of the game.

Ever the wily fox, Phil Jackson called a timeout, gave his players hell for lackadaisical play, and sent them back to make certain that Jordan's pregame "guarantee" of a win wasn't going to be a lie. At the other end of the court, Bird, whose Celtics had won six of eight Game Sevens while he wore number 33, praised his team for their effort. He knew the Bulls were on the ropes, and susceptible to a knockout punch that could end the Chicago dynasty before the cocky, swaggering Bulls could climb off the canvas and fight back.

While more than 43 minutes remained, two key plays occurred that dashed Bird's hopes. First Smits and then Miller, who had told NBC's Bob Costas that if the Pacers won they would end up on the covers of *Time* and *Newsweek* and as the answer to a Jeopardy question, lost the ball when the Pacers had a chance to stretch their lead. Smits's miscue was deadly, for it allowed Scottie Pippen to take a perfect pass from Jordan and break away for a slamming dunk that brought the Bulls faithful back into the game.

Unable to pad his team's lead, Bird, who had brought the team to the United Center "basketball ready" by ordering them to don their uniforms in their hotel rooms, watched the 12-point lead become 8 by quarter's end. "We had a chance for the kill," Bird lamented later. "But we haven't been able to hold a lead all year long."

A sign of things to come for Bird occurred at the 8:36 mark of the second quarter. While Michael Jordan would score 13 points in the stanza to pass Kareem Abdul-Jabbar as the greatest playoff scorer in NBA history with 5,764 points, diminutive Steve Kerr—who looked more like a college freshman than a professional ballplayer—swished a long-range three-pointer that cut the Pacers lead to two. Kerr's contribution (he hit another three with 4:53 remaining in the half to give the Bulls a four-point lead), and that of seldom-used Jud Buechler, who pulled down four rebounds, served notice that the Bulls bench had come to play.

By halftime, Chicago's edge was three points, but Bird was having indigestion over another statistic: Indiana had been outrebounded 33–21. All season long, the Pacers coach had griped about the team's Achilles' heel: their inability to block out, hit the boards with vengeance, and snatch loose balls triggered by errant shots. Bird, the master of such things during his Celtics days, realized that unless his Pacers, who seemed to be playing in a mechanical mode instead of letting things flow, attacked the Bulls and wore them down, they were doomed.

In the third quarter, Chicago kept pressure on Indiana as Bird searched for the right on-court combination. Miller added 7 points to the 15 he totaled in the first half; but it was another sharpshooter, this one from across the Atlantic, who proved that Larry Legend hadn't learned from a disastrous experience earlier in the season when Indiana played Chicago. Simply put, Bird didn't get it, still didn't understand that Dale Davis couldn't guard Toni Kukoc, whose rapid-release long-range jumpers were already in the air before the slow-footed Clemson alum could react.

Bird's mistake cost the Pacers dearly, for the Croatian swished three rainbow threes on his way to 14 third-quarter points. His power surge caused Bird to say later, "Kukoc hit some great shots tonight—some with hands in his face," but Larry had missed the point, having failed to bring a quicker defender in to guard the left-hander.

Others contributed to the Pacers' ineffectiveness. Holding a three-point lead with 6:55 left in the third quarter, Indiana had a chance to extend its margin when Derrick McKey's sticky fingers batted the ball away from Jordan. Rik Smits tied him up, with the clear advantage to the Dunking Dutchman, who towered over M.J. by nearly a foot. Inexplicably, Smits controlled the tip, but swatted the ball directly into the hands of a startled Scottie Pippen. When Steve Kerr buried a three to tie the score, Indiana had lost a great chance to take a five- or six-point lead over the Bulls, whose icy demeanor and glassy eyes revealed their fear of the upset-minded Pacers.

As the fourth quarter began, Phil Jackson gambled and won. Foul trouble—and a pouting session from Dennis Rodman, upset over being replaced in the starting lineup by Kukoc—forced the coach to play a makeshift lineup that included Kerr, Dickey Simpkins, Jud Buechler, Luc Longley, and Scottie Pippen. Realizing that Michael Jordan, inspired by the presence of his cancer-stricken father figure Gus Lett, was exhausted, Ron Harper was stricken with back pain, and Kukoc needed a rest, Jackson rolled the dice with an unlikely fivesome, hoping Indiana wouldn't break into a huge lead. They didn't, though it wasn't the fault of a revitalized Smits, who kept Indiana in the game after having virtually disappeared for the first three quarters.

The challenger and the champion, cheered on by superfan Bill Murray, whose hat with Bulls horns made him look like an undernourished Viking, traded blows as the clock wound down to 6:08—when Steve Kerr hit a three to tie the score at 77. Then two pressure-packed plays dictated the outcome of the biggest game in Indiana's NBA playoff history.

Larry Bird's team trailed by just two with 2:02 remaining when

Pippen, ever the graceful warrior, hit a baseline beauty and was fouled by Antonio Davis. True to the Pacers' good fortune, serendipity appeared ready to take over when Pippen missed his free throw. Those who felt that the Pacers were truly a team of destiny had reason to hope that they could score and be within one or two with a minute and change remaining.

But Indiana's luck ran out when Michael Jordan, positioned between two Pacers, wasn't blocked, wiggled his way into the air, and gobbled up the rebound. On the Pacers bench, Larry Bird nearly poked his tongue through his left cheek and clasped his hands so tight it appeared blood might drip out.

Jordan's key rebound provided the Bulls with a fresh 24-second clock—and even though they failed to score when Pippen rushed a three-point attempt, they were primed for victory. With Indiana trailing by four, that outcome was assured when Mark Jackson, entrusted by Bird to finish the game instead of Travis Best, who had been inconsistent, committed the most critical turnover of the Pacers season by attempting to softly lob the ball over Ron Harper's outstretched hands to Rik Smits in the post. The Bulls' number 9 intercepted; Jackson's face bore a "Why'd I do that?" expression, and Indiana's chances were extinguished.

Bulls fans and the Chicago bench began to celebrate, realizing that their beleaguered team was set for a date with Karl Malone and the Utah Jazz in the NBA Finals. Indiana's mercurial season ended with Smits tossing up a desperation, rushed three-pointer with less than 10 seconds remaining. Dale Davis recorded the final Pacers shot with an attempted tip-in, but the ball fell into Luc Longley's hands. He passed to M.J., who cradled the ball in his left hand (he later gave it to Gus Lett) while he pumped his right fist into the air in ecstasy.

Across the court, number 31, Reggie Miller, stood transfixed, his hands on his hips, frustrated, watching Jordan. Though Miller led the Pacers in scoring with 22 points, Michael held him to one shot and no points in the fourth quarter. Jordan, who had lectured his teammates during halftime by basically saying, "Shut up and play," was off to compete in his sixth conference finals in the 1990s and put an end to the suggestion that the season was the

Bulls' "last dance." Reggie headed for an off-season filled with thoughts of what might have been after the excruciating 88–83 loss.

Despite a gallant effort (Chicago newspapers spouted headlines such as, "Whew, the Agony of Victory," and "Never a Doubt, Right?"), Miller and his band of warriors had fallen short. Offensive rebounding stats told the story—Chicago 22, Indiana 4. Despite 38 percent shooting from the floor, and 58 percent from the foul line, the Bulls had done what championship teams do— they found a way to win. Indiana, which suffered just its 30th loss against 68 wins in the near-miracle season, would have four months to lick their wounds before rejoining their Hall-of-Fame-to-be coach for training camp.

Predictably, the Pacers locker room was gloom and doom. Soft voices filled with disappointment answered reporters' questions. Moist eyes and long faces prevailed, for despite their coach's calm demeanor, the Pacers were a very emotional team. "This really hurts," Reggie Miller admitted, his lip quivering, the words catching in his throat.

During his postgame press conference, a tie-less Larry Bird was polite, but agitated. Like superior athletes such as Jack Nicklaus, Cal Ripken, or Joe Montana and others who believed anything other than winning a championship meant failure, Larry Legend was in shock, his brain unable to comprehend why his team had gone down to defeat. "We had them right where we wanted them," he said. "We wanted to stay close and have a chance to win . . . I thought we had a good enough team to win, but they made the plays and we didn't."

Perhaps Bird made a mistake by not showing his players a copy of the videotape *Larry Bird: A Legend*, before the game. Filled with highlights of Bird's wondrous career, it spelled out how number 33 had destroyed playoff opponents by performing with all-out intensity and a will to win like few others in sport. Those Pacers who had let their coach down with subpar efforts in Game Seven with the Bulls needed to study the tape in the off-season.

In closing out his press conference, Bird's poignant Birdisms included, "A couple of those offensive rebounds ripped our hearts out," "A lot of little things beat us today," and "Chicago was quicker to the ball . . . we were outmatched." Responding to a question comparing losing as a coach to that of losing as a player, Bird said, "It feels about the same." Asked if he thought the long series might make the Bulls vulnerable in the next round, Bird looked at the reporter like he was crazy and said, "Personally, I don't care about the Bulls."

Regarding the Pacers' progress during the season, Bird said, "I saw them grow. We want them to play hard, move the ball around, and not worry about who scores. . . . But I didn't get the team to where I wanted them to be." Persuaded to assess Michael Jordan, who told reporters, "This game was about heart, you saw a lot of heart [from the Bulls] out there," Bird said, "He's the best player in the league, probably the best player ever."

Glancing out of the corner of his eye, looking for an NBA media official to end his misery after the customary 10 minutes, Larry Legend ended the press conference with humor. Complimented by a reporter who called him "a breath of fresh air," Bird grinned and said, "Thanks, but the officials still stink."

After 98 games, the rookie coaching year for Larry Bird had ended. Though the Pacers lost the Eastern Conference championship to the Bulls, it was truly a season to remember—filled with dazzling highlights, miracle finishes, and true grit, all triggered by the exceptional performance of Coach Bird and his players.

For rookies Mark Pope, Austin Croshere, and Etdrick Bohannon, it had been a fantasy experience. Playing for Larry Bird had not only improved their games, but permitted them to rub elbows on a daily basis with the living legend. "My life will never be the same," Bohannon said.

Fred Hoiberg and Mark West had mixed memories. Hoiberg knew Bird appreciated his feistiness and work ethic, but was disappointed in his inability to provide instant offense off the bench. West had been crippled with his leg injury—but even if healthy, his playing time would have been restricted since Rik Smits was healthy for most of the season.

Travis Best learned that Bird trusted him at crunch time, and came through with inspired play in the playoffs. A free agent, Best had to decide whether to share point guard duties with Mark Jackson for the next season or sign with another team for big bucks where the job was his. Regardless, Best had improved under the tutelage of Larry Bird, calling him "Someone who really believed in me."

Bird's influence on Jalen Rose was clearly seen, for the Birdman had saved his career. Rose realized more of his potential under the Pacers' first-year coach, who didn't chastise him every time he made a silly error. Heading into the new season (Jalen was under contract, though his agent believed him to be a free agent), Rose would be expected to step up his play, and become an even greater factor.

Forwards Dale Davis, Derrick McKey, Antonio Davis, and Chris Mullin had been a blessing for the Pacers, though Bird was highly disappointed in their rebounding skills. McKey still didn't play as hard as Bird expected; Double D seemed unable to learn how to properly block out; A.D. was inconsistent on the offensive boards; and Mullin, though providing offensive punch and leadership, had trouble with matchups in the playoffs.

On the positive side, McKey had been a factor on defense while providing scoring, Dale had improved his offensive game so that the opposition actually had to guard him when he posted up for five-foot jumpers, Antonio had learned to utilize his quickness inside against bigger defenders, and Mullin still shot the lights out on occasion. All would be welcomed back to training camp, where Bird would seek to improve their rebounding skills.

Rik Smits had been a welcome surprise to Bird, especially since his tender feet held up for most of the year. Except for a few mental lapses, especially in the playoff series against the Bulls, Smits was a bulwark in the middle. His shooting touch was astounding for a man 7'4", and soft hands permitted him to be a fine passer, especially on the break. When he returned for the new season,

Bird would work on rebounding position and expect even more consistency from the free agent whom Donnie Walsh had every intention of signing.

Mark Jackson was a favorite of Bird's, for his gritty attitude and enthusiasm for the game of basketball paralleled Larry's. If the Pacers had a most valuable player, it had to be Jackson, for his leadership and inspirational manner set the tone for what had been a truly blessed season. Bird knew his point guard was the glue that held the team together, the one player whose ego never stood in the way of team play.

For Reggie Miller, the season had been a winner. Despite setbacks, Sir Reginald kept attacking, and his ability to be the player to go to in the final seconds of the game gave confidence to his teammates that any game was winnable. Reggie had started the season with something to prove, and he had—that in the annals of NBA history there were few who overshadowed him when it came to clutch shooting. Coach Bird had said it all when he commented, "He's even better than I thought he was." Miller, in turn, worshipped Larry Legend, saying in retrospect, "This has been like a dream for me, to play for Larry."

Those sentiments prevailed as Reggie cleaned out his locker at Market Square Arena, ready to cash his $40,000 share of the Pacers' $579,250 playoff pool earnings. Wearing a striped golf shirt, shorts, blue sneakers, and a baseball hat turned backward, Miller said he'd told Bird, "When I finish my contract (in 2000), then you can go home. Until then, you're going to be on the sidelines."

Assistant coaches Dick Harter and Rick Carlisle had enjoyed an experience unlike any before. From day one, Bird had made them specialists, giving them free reign over the defensive and offensive strategies for the team, respectively. Harter molded a slower-than-slow team into a cohesive unit that attacked the opposition like piranhas. Carlisle, the tireless worker who challenged the Pacers players to step up their games even in pregame warm-ups, provided an innovative plan that permitted Indiana to take advantage of its offensive skills.

Besides the interaction with Harter and Carlisle, Larry Bird had enjoyed the camaraderie in the locker room, the friendships with his coaches and players, and the flow of adrenaline when game time approached. He also had fond memories of the practices, watching the improvements in the rookies and veterans alike; and the taste of victory, something he had sorely missed while being away from basketball.

What Bird had not experienced were many of the rigors of coaching others encountered. During the Pacers' near-miracle season, Bird had not had to deal with pouting players upset over playing time or tiffs with teammates, lengthy losing streaks that drove coaches to drink, media constantly questioning his coaching methods, or criticism from a disgruntled general manager or owner. In effect, Bird had skated through an almost-too-good-to-be-true, fantasy season mostly filled with laughter and joy. How the Pacers coach dealt with true adversity remained to be seen.

If one believed the Bird droppings scattered along press row all season, there was a question as to whether Larry would return to coach the Pacers. If the truth be known, Bird, though uncomfortable with the press, had had the time of his life and would be the man in charge when the new season rolled around. He had simply used the indecision as to whether he would coach again as a motivational ploy, one designed to make his team play that much harder.

"I've got a three-year contract," Bird said at midseason. "That might be enough." After the Pacers' final game against the Bulls in the regular season, Bird said, "It has been more managing players than coaching. But I'll make improvements if I come back next year and go from there. I'll sit down with the players after the season, talk to them, and see how they react to everything we've done. If they like it, I'll go from there." Later, he added, "This is a players' league. If they want to look in a different direction, I can understand that."

Just prior to the playoffs, Bird expanded on his statements, saying, "This is the right job for me because it's a small market. . . . But I'm not going to do it for very long because I'm not cut out to do this. Sometimes I stand there and think, why am I doing this?"

At his final press conference of the season, the Birdman reiterated his thoughts about coaching, saying, "I'll talk to my players and see if they like what we're trying to do. If they come to me, and tell me they want somebody else to lead them, that's fine with me." Then he added, "So whatever they decide, you know, my golf game's a little rusty, hell I can pick that back up."

Donnie Walsh just smiled when he heard Bird's words. "He's got that kind of integrity," Walsh said. ". . . If he sensed he wasn't the right guy here, he's the kind of guy who wouldn't want to be here." Dale Davis knew what Bird was doing, adding, "That just shows his commitment to us. He doesn't want to sell us short."

Yes, Larry Bird would return to coach, more than anything because of the three-year commitment to do so. The Bird word was as good as gold, the one characteristic that his coaches and players respected more than anything. "When Coach Bird says something," Mark Jackson had proclaimed, "it's like it's right out of the Bible."

Jackson's compliment summed up what had truly been a remarkable entrance into coaching for Larry Bird. Here was a man who had never coached basketball in his life, who took on a bunch of alleged underachievers and not only became the Coach of the Year in the NBA, but led his team within a few baskets of the finals. As the 1998–99 season approached, many believed he would lead his players to a world championship, adding yet another chapter to the saga of Larry Legend.

POSTSCRIPT

Larry Bird: myth, legend, or real-life human being? That's the question that remains—and it isn't easy to answer. If anything, Bird's first year of coaching in the NBA only added to the Walter Mitty story, for once again he produced when others believed he didn't have a ghost of a chance.

While the Pacers fell short of their goal of an NBA championship, the team won more games than any other in the history of the franchise. And they advanced to the finals of the Eastern Conference championship before falling to the redoubtable Chicago Bulls, who achieved their repeat three-peat goal to beat the half-a-step slow Utah Jazz in an NBA championship series that saw Michael Jordan pick up his sixth NBA Finals MVP award. Scottie Pippen aided Jordan's cause with superb play, but it was Dennis Rodman who garnered most of the headlines when he missed a Bulls practice to join Hulk Hogan on a telecast of World Wrestling Tonight, where the two slammed a chair over the head of an unsuspecting foe.

There are several paths to connect to the Bird legend. His autobiography *Drive* provided insight, as did an enlightening instructional publication entitled *Bird on Basketball*, which he wrote with author John Bischoff in 1986.

Birdwatchers could also check out Larry's website located at www.larrybird.com, where assorted items were available such as: Larry Bird/Magic Johnson photographs ($89), 12″ × 12″ pieces of Bird's high school floor ($139), Bird "Fading into the Boston Garden Floor" lithograph ($129), Boston Connection hotel items such as a Bird's Nest Lounge tall barstool ($250), "Larry's the King" playing cards ($7), Bird wristwatch ($65), Springs Valley High School basketball teammates uniforms (warm-ups $675), Larry Bird ISU College Salvino Statue ($285), and Bob Cousy autographed white 1994–95 Celtics jersey ($450), among many others. Private autograph signings could also be set up, though Scott Smith, apparent proprietor of the website, warned in April, "This is the last scheduled signing we have before Larry gets elected into the Basketball Hall of Fame. I have a very strong indication that Larry will raise his prices *after* this scheduled signing session."

The word on Bird could be garnered with trips to Martinsville, Indiana, where Larry Bird Ford flourished along State Road 37; or Terre Haute, where a visit to his Boston Connection hotel, restaurant, and convention center provided enough "Larrobilia" for a lifetime. Sandwiches in that restaurant's Boston Garden (where they had an "early Bird special") included the Johnny Most (chicken or tuna salad sandwich), Record Book Ribeye, the K.C. Cod, the Three-Pointer ("our huge famous hand-breaded tenderloin"), and the Springs Valley Special (Indiana ham and American cheese). Also available were Georgia Bird's Famous Sticky Rolls. Nearby was the Bird's Nest Lounge, which served Boston Beer and a "tea party" drink. Visitors to the Boston Connection complex could also walk around and view such Bird mementos as his three Maurice Podoloff NBA Most Valuable Player trophies; his Naismith Trophy from college; numerous uniforms from his playing days with the Celtics (green 33), Indiana State (light blue 33), and the Olympics (white 7); his Olympic medal; and the ball used to score his 20,000th point in the NBA against Washington on November 30, 1990. Also on display was an unforgettable photo of Larry lying prone on a massage chair playing with his adopted daughter Mariah, whose tiny head was nestled against his knees.

More Birdwatching could take place in French Lick and West Baden, the home of mineral baths and plush casinos in the early part of the 20th century, where there was a good Bird story on every corner. In the Valley, Larry Legend was still known as a good ol' boy. Bird didn't spend as much time there as before, but townsfolk knew he'd be around during summertime. That meant Birdwatchers could flock to Butchie's, owned by Bird's friends Butchie and Diana Terwiske, in nearby Dubois, where the south wall was filled with Larry Bird posters (one had him wearing three white letter sweaters emblazoned with *M*, *V*, and *P*), a Wheaties cereal box with Larry's picture on the front, and an old pair of worn-out Bird sneakers. When he was in the area, Bird would saunter in and down a cold one while gulping down a dressed bacon cheeseburger (a one-third pound burger with lettuce, tomato, pickles, onions, and mayonnaise).

Regardless of the pursuit, figuring out who Larry Bird really was remained difficult. Only his wife Dinah saw his private side, for most of the others who worked with him or knew him were scared to offend the superstar. His agent, Jill Leone, continually walked on eggshells, as did others who dealt with "Larry's orders" on a day-to-day basis. Keeping Bird happy was the key—and he didn't want for much, but there was the constant reminder, especially in the Pacers organization, that it was Bird as well as Donnie Walsh who was the boss. "I'd never want to cross Larry," a Pacers official said. "Donnie, he can forgive and forget—Larry, never."

If there was a mystery to Bird's life, it dealt with his relationship with his daughter Corrie, born when Larry was a student at Indiana State. In the May 4, 1998, edition of *Sports Illustrated*, Bird was embarrassed to be mentioned with NBA stars Patrick Ewing, Juwan Howard, Larry Johnson, and Shawn Kemp in an article entitled "Where's Daddy?" Journalists Grant Wahl and L. Jon Wertheim detailed the lives of children born out of wedlock to sports superstars, and though Bird declined to be interviewed for the article, Corrie Bird discussed her puzzling relationship with her famous father.

Besides initially denying that Corrie was his child, and refusing through the years to visit her or answer certified letters or acknowledge report cards and photos sent to him, Bird completely ignored his daughter after he was named coach in Indianapolis, just an hour away from Terre Haute. Hope that a reconciliation between the two was possible was heightened when Larry and Corrie met before the Pacers' final home game in April. "Dad seemed interested in what I had to say," Corrie told *Sports Illustrated*. "He walked me to the car, and he hugged me. I hope I can see more of him now."

But in late May, Corrie, whose facial features and deep-set blue eyes bore a great resemblance to Bird, may have lessened the chances of bonding with her father by appearing on Oprah Winfrey's television program. Asked whether she ever saw Larry when she was young, Corrie, a sophomore at Indiana State, answered, "No, I never saw him. Never spent a Christmas or Thanksgiving with him. . . . And he never came to see me play basketball or graduate from high school." Queried as to why she thought her father behaved that way, and continued to not see her, Corrie, who had worn her father's number 33 while playing high school basketball, and kept a roomful of Bird memorabilia that included pictures with her dad when she was a baby, said, "He's shy and backward, and I think he's ashamed of how he handled things. But I'm not bitter, not angry . . . I just hope we can see each other in the future."

Bird's inability to deal with Corrie didn't appear to diminish the enormous respect there was for him both in and out of sports. He was a winner, the epitome of the American sports hero, one who had led his small-town high school team to victories, taken a rag-tag Indiana State Sycamores team to within one win of an NCAA championship, led the Boston Celtics to three world championships while winning the MVP as many times, and then retired before he made a fool of himself on the hardwood. In his rookie season with the Pacers, Bird proved he could be successful again, taking a group of self-doubters and molding them into contenders. Following the season, he was elected into the Naismith Memorial Basketball Hall of Fame, capping a playing career that seemed more fiction than fact.

Through it all, Bird had acted like a gentleman, maintaining his composure and trying to lead by example. That had been the case during his entire sports career, and he had influenced those around him—players and coaches alike—in a positive way. In a day and age when many athletes and coaches acted like prima donnas, the camera-shy, ever humble Bird was the exception to the rule.

Armed with the memories of his rookie coaching season, Larry Bird could now take his boat out in the Gulf of Mexico and think about what lay ahead. Or play a few rounds of golf, and recall special moments that had made the year so rewarding. Once again, Larry Legend, NBA Coach of the Year, had come out a winner. Was anyone really surprised?

BIBLIOGRAPHY

Bird, Larry, with John Bischoff. *Bird on Basketball*. Reading, MA: Addison-Wesley, 1986.

Bird, Larry, with Bob Ryan. *Drive*. New York: Bantam/Doubleday, 1989.

Indiana Pacers Media Guide, 1997–98.

Jackson, Phil, with Hugh Delehanty. *Sacred Hoops*. New York: Hyperion, 1995.

Johnson, Earvin "Magic," with William Novak. *My Life*. New York: Random House, 1992.

Larry Bird: A Basketball Legend. 40 min. Los Angeles: CBS/Fox Video, 1991.

Levine, Lee Daniel. *Bird: The Making of an American Sports Legend*. New York: McGraw-Hill, 1988.

Lipofsky, Steve, and Roland Lazenby. *Bird: Portrait of a Competitor*. Kansas City, MO: Addax Publishing Group, 1998.

May, Peter. *The Big Three*. New York: Simon and Schuster, 1994.

May, Peter. *The Last Banner*. New York: Simon and Schuster, 1996.

NBA.com website. http://www.nba.com/

Ryan, Bob. *The Four Seasons*. Indianapolis: Masters Press, 1997.

Shaughnessy, Dan. *Seeing Red: The Red Auerbach Story.* New York: Crown, 1994.

Smith, L. Virginia. *Larry Bird: From Valley Hick to Boston Celtic.* French Lick, IN: Self-published, 1982.

In addition to the above sources, the author consulted Associated Press wire stories, *Basketball Weekly*, *Charlotte Observer*, *Chicago Sun-Times*, *Chicago Tribune*, *Esquire*, *Indianapolis Magazine*, *Indianapolis Monthly*, *Indianapolis Star*, *Los Angeles Times*, *New York Post*, *New York Times*, *Pacers Weekly*, *Sport Magazine*, *The Sporting News*, *Sports Illustrated*, *TV Guide*, and USA *Today.*